YOUR HOUR

YOUR HOUR

BY REV. M. RAYMOND, O.C.S.O.

THE BRUCE PUBLISHING COMPANY

Milwaukee

Library of Congress Catalog Card Number: 62–20237

© 1962 The Bruce Publishing Company
MADE IN THE UNITED STATES OF AMERICA

•

Lovingly Dedicated
to
Mother of Us All
MARY IMMACULATE
Who so lived His Hour — and Hers — as to
Participate in Christ's Wondrous Work of Redemption
and
to Her Loving Daughter
DARME
For the way she is awaiting the HOUR
which will be
HERS

•

OTHER WORKS
by
Rev. M. Raymond, O.C.S.O.

The Man Who Got Even With God

God Goes to Murderer's Row

Trappists, the Reds, and You

A New Way of the Cross

The Family That Overtook Christ

These Women Walked With God

Three Religious Rebels

Burnt Out Incense

God, a Woman, and the Way

Love Does Such Things

This Is Your Tomorrow . . . and Today

You

Now!

The Less Traveled Road

BOOKLETS

Is Your Home Like This?

Life Is Someone

The God-Man's Double

Father, You Are Leading a Dangerous Life

Doubling for the Mother of God

Whispers From the Wings

Running Off With God

Are You?

Life is a Divine Romance

You Can Set the World on Fire!

Say FIAT and Remake Your World

What Are You Doing to Jesus Christ?

Do You Want Love and Life?

Have You Met God?

What's Wrong?

Help God Be a Success

A Trappist Does a Startling Thing for You

Facts About Reason, Revelation, and Religion

For Your Own Defense

Message From Those Killed in Action

To Mothers Whose Sons Are in the Service

All the above obtainable from
Abbey of Gethsemani, Inc.
Trappist P.O., Ky.

CONTENTS

YOUR HOUR

I

PURPOSE AND PLAN

Rejoice and be glad!

Enter into the joy of God *now!* Why wait? He made you to be happy not only in the hereafter, but very especially in the here and now. So why not go along with God? Doing so will give you something quite different from that pedestrian thing called "peace of mind." It will give you a joy of spirit, called "inebriation" by some, and a happiness of heart that most assuredly is blessedness and very near to being bliss. That is God's purpose for you right now. And His plan? That centers around "your hour." For, from before Time was, God had decreed that you were to have a specific experience that was to mean much to Him — and everything to you; an experience which, following the plan drawn up for His Christ, can very legitimately be called "your hour."

"And oh, thank God for God," cried Joyce Kilmer in the last line of a poem composed when black difficulties broke round him like surges of an angry sea. Echo him. For if your difficulties loom more large, your gratitude should be more great. Thank God for God the Father. Thank God for God the Son. Thank God for God the Holy Spirit. Thank this three-personed God for having so related you to Him who is Creator, to Him who is Redeemer, and to Him who is Sanctifier that your every breath and heartbeat has meaning for each of Them and Their eternal glory. But none are so laden with meaning as those that will fill "your hour." You are important to God — very important. Be glad, then, and rejoice!

That is the purpose of this book — to make you happy. Its plan is to have you base that happiness on God's own truth as given us in the Gospels. Any other base would be unworthy of God and too weak for you. For yours is a tumultuous and a tottering world; made so by men who love the darkness rather than the light. Stability is

1

to be found only in the unmoved Mover of this restless universe
and in His Christ who is "the same, yesterday, today, and forever"
(Hebr. 13:8).

Fear stalks your land. Crippling anxieties and neurotic unrests
swarm round about you. But that is only because the highly publi-
cized gospels of Expediency and Efficiency have had too many followers who have been altogether too faithful, while the only true
Gospel, and the only Gospel of Truth, has been too hesitantly trusted
and too listlessly tried.

The evangelists of Efficiency and Expediency promised happiness
for human beings who would follow their gospels and achieve material progress and temporal success. That progress has been made.
That success attained. But where is the human happiness? No matter
where you turn in your tumultuous world you trip over heaps of
broken promises and stumble amid writhing miseries. These evangelists were false prophets and their gospels tissues of lies. But in the
only Gospel of Truth you find promise of a happiness that is complete and of a joy that can never be lost; and those promises will be
kept. For they are made by Him who can never deceive — the God
who has decreed that you are to have "your hour."

That fact should fill your world with a brilliance very similar to
that which broke about Bethlehem's shepherds the first Christmas
night, and should have you hearing in your heart that message of
the Angel which ran: "Fear not; for, behold, I bring you good tidings
of great joy . . ." (Lk. 2:10). If your contemporaries are not free
from fear it is only because they have not listened to the "good
tidings." If they are not throbbing with joy it is only because they
have failed to do what those shepherds of long ago so wisely and
willingly did; they have not "gone over to Bethlehem to find out the
truth about this thing the Lord had made known to them" (Lk. 2:15).

You know that those shepherds found the Lamb of God who one
day identified Himself as "the Way, the Truth and the Life" (Jn.
14:6). If modern man has lost his way, is fumbling for truth, and
knows not real life or living, the reason is obvious: he has not
"sought out Mary and Joseph, and the infant cradled in a manger"
(Lk. 2:16). If he is angry at life because it appears one huge frustration; if he is soured and depressed because his horizons are all dark;

is it not because he has refused to see the Light of the World of whom
St. John speaks so movingly saying:

> When time began, the Word was there,
>   and the Word was face to face with God,
>   and the Word was God.
>
> .   .   .
>
> All things came into being through him,
>   and without him there came to be
>   not one thing that has come to be.
>
> .   .   .
>
> In him was life,
>   and the life was the light of men.
> The light shines in the darkness,
>   . . . the true light
> which illumines every man.
>   . . . to as many as welcomed him
> he gave the power to become children of God —
>
> .   .   .
>
> And of his fullness
>   we have all received a share —
> yes, grace succeeding grace;
>   . . . grace and truth have come
> through Jesus Christ (Jn. 1:1–17).

Grace and truth and light are still coming through Jesus Christ,
but, as of old, for too many "the Light shines in the darkness, and
the darkness does not lay hold of it." But you are among those who
have "welcomed Him," and you have been "born not of blood, or
of carnal desire, or of man's will; no, you have been born of God."
And it can be said with truth that you have been born *for* God; for
each of the Three Persons, who are the one and only living God.
For God the Father depends upon you to carry out some part of
His Providence and carry on some phase of His Creation; God the
Son is looking to you to complete His wondrous work of Redemption
by turning it into salvation for yourself and others as you, like St.
Paul, "fill up in your flesh what is lacking of the sufferings of Christ"
(cf. Col. 1:24); God the Holy Spirit needs you and your cooperation
so that He can fulfill the mission given Him by the Father and the
Son: that of the sanctification of the world. Yours is the heart-thrill-

ing, all-but-incredible call to be helper to the omnipotent God who has willed to need your assistance.

Is it any wonder that you are commanded to rejoice and be glad? Creation is completed. Yet God the Father, to whom that wondrous work is attributed, requires your aid to carry on that completed work by the continuing process that is called "concreation." Redemption has been accomplished. Yet God the Son, who achieved that marvel of mercy superabundantly, needs your help to make that accomplishment the triumph that is named salvation. The sanctification of man is a work that can be wrought only by God; for He alone is holy. Yet God the Holy Spirit needs your cooperation not only for the sanctification of your own soul, but for the success of the mission given Him by Father and Son. He has been sent to take all things in our disjointed universe and link them to the one and only Center — Christ. His is the mission to lay hold on everything that has been established and reestablish each in Christ; to reach out to all creation and re-create it through, with, and in Christ Jesus, the Lord. And you, by birth, baptism, and your present breath are called to help Him succeed. You can help Him with every beat of your heart, but never so effectively as the way you make that heart of yours beat in that hour which you can call your own.

In a world where the individual human is made to feel less and less important, where machines are being multiplied daily to do not only the manual work formerly done by man, but now even the mental work; in a world where almost every advance in technology seems to minimize the significance of men; it is healthy and wholesome to grasp the theological truth about the temporal, eternal, and the almost infinite weight and value — to God and the world — of the least of us mortals. That truth, of course, is the title of this book. You, whoever you are, no matter what your social, economic, political significance or insignificance, are to have an hour on which the very glory of God, the everlasting bliss of your own being, and the eternal happiness of others will hinge.

Pressures are mounting on all sides. They tend not only to fragmentize, but even to atomize human existence. What will integrate your life and living more completely than the truth which served Cardinal Newman so well; the truth which tells you that an all-wise

God has created you to do Him some definite service; that He has called you into being, and keeps you in being to do some one work that can be done by no other in all the universe; that He has given you a mission which is as specifically yours as is your own name, and as inalienably yours as your own ontological personality?

That conviction gladdened Newman's whole life. It can gladden yours. For with the saintly Cardinal you can say: "I will trust Him. Whatever, wherever I am, I can never be thrown away. If I am in sickness, my sickness may serve Him; in perplexity, my perplexity may serve Him; if I am in sorrow, my sorrow may serve Him. He does nothing in vain. He knows what He is about." Indeed He does! That is why He has called you to have "your hour."

God's purpose is clear. He has written it in every book of the Bible. He has written it in every work of His creation. He has written it in your own conscience and consciousness. He is to be glorified and you are to be made glad.

His plan is almost equally as clear. It lies in that "hour" each intelligent creature can call his own. Lucifer had "his hour." So did Michael, Gabriel, and Raphael. Not all lived them in the same way. Adam had an "hour." On it depended all the hours of man. He fell in that "hour" — and all men fell with him. But a merciful God decreed there would be a Second Adam who would have one "hour" specifically His own — and on it would hinge the hourless eternities of every man. In that "hour" this Second Adam fell, and fell, and fell again, but rose and went on to lift His "thorn-wreathed head and smile from the Cross upon a conquered world." Christ's "hour" was one of the cross and one of conquest. Since that "hour" it would seem that our omnipotent God, infinite though He be in ingenuity, has but one shape for every human soul. He used it for His only Son. He will use it for His every son. It is the cruciform. But that does not mean mere suffering; it means suffering that is made sacrificial. It does not signify tragedy, but that testing which when passed "in, with, and through Christ" spells joyous triumph and triumphant joy. It tells you that all life is not only serious, but sacred; yet no part of it is as sacred or serious as that "hour" which you can call your own. That is the "hour" which, when lived through properly, brings you not only to gladness that can never be tainted, glory that can never be tarnished, but to God who is Life, Love, Beauty, Truth, and Being. That being so, who would not grow avid for its coming?

But because all this requires Faith, and because someone has ignorantly said that "Faith can stagger on the mystery of pain," the plan of this book will be to introduce you to individuals whose "hours" were filled with that mystery of pain, but whose Faith, far from staggering, grew strong enough to leap with joy.

What they have done, you can do. So, rejoice and be glad!

II

IT WAS GLORIOUS FOR FATHER CARL

Have you ever looked into a man's eyes and seen in them more than human radiance? Have you ever been allowed to view therein something of the splendor of God, that rare luminosity that can only be a reflection of divine glory? That experience would have been yours any day in late December of 1948 and early January of the following year, had you stepped into room 143 of St. Joseph Infirmary, Louisville, Kentucky, and been introduced to Father Carl Miller, S.J.

Here was a man who had been flown to the United States only two months earlier from deep in India where for twenty-two years he had lived and labored among a tribe of aborigines called Santals.

There was nothing impressive about him physically. He was of ordinary height. And while sickness had now drawn the skin taut over his face, you could see that there never had been anything truly distinctive about any of his features. The sallow, leathery skin told of almost constant exposure to wind and sun. The partially bald head, with its fringe of somewhat untidy hair, testified to a total lack of fastidiousness. He seemed most ordinary until he looked you in the eye, smiled, and spoke a word or two. Then you sensed the intangible yet compelling power of a rare spiritual personality.

Ask Father Carl anything about himself and his state of health and you will receive polite replies, but replies that tell you next to nothing. But question him about India or his Santals and you will be enchanted by an enthusiastic, witty, truly fluent account of that far-off land and those practically unknown people. As that account flows on, you will not have to be any expert psychologist to realize that you are listening to the eloquence that comes from love.

But right there your puzzlement will begin. That a Jesuit priest, and a foreign missioner at that, should be polite but noncommittal about himself and his sickness would not too greatly surprise you. But what would very nearly startle you is the energy displayed by

7

this man who appears to be little more than skin and bones. But it is the light that sparkles in those deep-set eyes that fascinates. Father Carl Miller becomes alive with something more than mere human life when talking about these aborigines he so fondly calls "my good and simple people." As the clear, well-modulated, pleasant-sounding voice goes on, you will find yourself asking silent questions about this man that can be answered only by those who have intimate knowledge of his background. As the refinement and culture become more and more manifest with every passing moment, you may find yourself asking more silent questions about the methods and the mentality of those Jesuit superiors who have wasted this man on such a mission as that to Santals.

But if you stay long enough, and listen closely, you will learn that Father Carl was not sent to India; he had volunteered to go there. What is more, you will gradually come to realize that there is a very satisfying explanation not only to what the Jesuit superiors allowed, but to what Father Carl had so avidly sought. He had crossed the world, leaving behind him all that makes for luxurious living in America, to dwell in a house of mud that he had built next to a church of mud, that he might lift thousands of aborigines out of the mud of ignorance, superstition, and moral degradation. "Love does such things." And Carl Miller was a man of love.

He had been born on a farm outside Toledo, Ohio, just as the nineteenth century entered those so-called "gay nineties." But before the twentieth century was born, Carl Miller found himself more than curious about such things as steam, electricity, and telegraphy. Before he was deep in his teens, he was earning a man's salary in the locomotive shop in Toledo. But before he was out of his teens, he was vowing his life to Jesus Christ in the Society that bore Christ's name.

He followed the usual course for all young Jesuits, but he followed it in no usual manner. After his years with the arts, he plunged into the study of philosophy, but soon found himself giving all his spare time to those things that had so aroused his curiosity when a mere boy. The course in physics drew Carl Miller as any powerful magnet draws steel. He passed all his philosophy examinations with success, but it was his triumph in physics that made the Provincial of the

Missouri Province assign this young man to St. Louis University just before America entered World War I.

Radio in any useful form was still years off, yet young Carl Miller paved the way for that pioneer radio station known as WEW when, at the height of World War I, he designed and installed the wireless telephone at St. Louis University. In early 1918 the Government was snatching up everything that could be used as war matériel, so the faculty at St. Louis University was very happy to have the enterprising, inventive, and ever practical mind of Carl Miller at their disposal. Thanks to his ingenuity, the University's laboratory was able to boast of a variable voltage battery system when such systems were not easily come by. A few years later, when the Jesuits decided to build a new high school in that city, they entrusted the plans for the science department to Carl Miller, and were not surprised when the completed work was hailed as the most up to date in the state.

In those days it was customary for the Society of Jesus to give their young scholastics five full years at teaching in their high schools or colleges before allowing them to enter the course in theology. Carl Miller spent his five years at St. Louis University except for one brief interlude during which he traveled to the Missouri Province's mission in British Honduras. Most scholastics would have taken this period as a time for looking over the colony and studying natives and native ways. Not so Carl Miller. He spent his time installing an electrical plant at St. John's College, an installation that rendered the entire mission an invaluable service.

It was inevitable that the name of this restless mind should become known outside the Society of Jesus and even outside the educational world. Colonel George Fabyan, of the Geneva Research Laboratory, at Geneva, Illinois, heard of Carl Miller and, after delicate negotiations with his Jesuit superiors, succeeded in being able to commission the energetic scholastic to design the first instruments for measuring sound that were ever used in that laboratory.

You would wonder how one young man could accomplish so much in the little time allowed him outside his regular teaching hours. But your wonder grows to very real amazement when you learn that on top of all these scientific achievements he accomplished much in the field of literature and of organization. Thanks to his energy the

Jesuit Science Association was founded, and thanks to his literary ability it actually flourished. For he not only took on the duties of secretary for the physics section of that Association, but initiated and edited the lively and always-looked-for Bulletin called *High Voltage*.

What is the explanation for such accomplishments? Is it the natural energy usually found in the scientific genius? Is it the assured result of a true dedication? Not in Carl Miller's case. The only satisfactory explanation is the one already given: Love does such things. As a Jesuit novice he had learned from his master, St. Ignatius, that love is shown more in deeds than in words. Carl Miller would express his love for Christ his Leader by accomplishments . . . or, at least, in manly efforts toward accomplishments. For that was another lesson he had learned in his novitiate from the same master: it is not the effects produced that count so much with God as the efforts put into the task; for these are eloquent of love.

Naturally you would expect the Jesuit superiors to channel all this evident ability along the lines it was already running; and more than likely your natural expectations were being fulfilled by those superiors. But the actual course for young men in the Order is to devote themselves almost unreservedly to the study of theology for four full years after their regency as scholastics. Each is allowed to follow his bent to some extent, and Carl Miller unquestionably was alive to all that was going on in the world of science during his years of immediate preparation for ordination to the priesthood. But it was formal theology and the wonder of that sacrament of orders that held the center of his attention until June 27, 1923 when he was ordained a priest.

The long course of studies was not yet over. Carl Miller had been made a priest of God, but St. Ignatius would make him — and every other son in his Society — a zealous priest of God. And Ignatius had the root meaning of that word in mind when he determined his goal. The priests of the Society of Jesus would be aflame with love for Jesus Christ if Ignatius could have his way. And he resolved to have his way as far as that was possible; so he decided that at the end of the already long course of training another year of special training should be added, that of tertianship — or a year in the *Schola Affectus* . . . the School of Love.

Carl Miller spent this last year at Paray le Monial, France, where over three hundred years earlier Christ had appeared to Margaret Mary and pleaded for love from His members. Here Blessed Claude de la Columbiere of the Society of Jesus had listened to Margaret Mary tell of her apparitions of the Sacred Heart. In such an atmosphere Carl Miller went through the Spiritual Exercises of St. Ignatius for thirty days just as he had done at the beginning of his life as a Jesuit eighteen years earlier. How differently the Exercises spoke to him during his tertianship than they had during his novitiate! Now he understood that first and most important Exercise called "The Foundation and Principle" as he could never have understood it when he was still a boy of eighteen. That he had been created by God to know Him, love Him, and serve Him on earth, and to be happy with Him forever in heaven, was a truth that pulsed for the young priest in a manner it had never done before; for he now realized with St. Paul that Christ was his life; that the Father's glory was his life's work; and that everything else in creation had been brought into being to be used "*tantum quantum*" — just in as much as — they aided him in the prosecution of this work. What is called "detachment" was recognized by the Tertian Father as a misnomer if it is taken to mean only something negative — a "detachment" from all selfish or self-made desires for success, long life, health, fame, and the like. He saw it now as a positive attitude of mind and will, a warm and loving attachment to the will of God. He "made himself indifferent," as St. Ignatius directs, to all things, seeking *only* that which more surely enables a man the better to achieve the end for which God had created him.

Ignatius not only rested the religious and priestly life on this Foundation, he made of it a Principle as well. In this one Exercise he would have his men learn not only whence they came, why they were, and where they were going, but also learn the source or fountainhead whence all their actions should flow. He would have them desire and choose "*only* that which would better lead them to the end for which they had been created." For that word *only* he used an absolute word, a decisive word — *unice*. This soldier-saint demanded much of his followers, more perhaps than any other Founder of a Religious Order. He would have his men develop a soldier's hardihood and a soldier's flexibility in adjusting himself to any and every condition of living and battling. That is why he laid such heavy stress on the fact that they "must make themselves *indifferent.*" For he would have them ready for any and every assignment; free, as only free-lancers are free, to go, at a moment's notice, wherever they were called upon to go, and be ready to do whatever they were asked to do. With one of those rare insights which mark the spiritual genius, this man from Loyola saw that this spirit of detachment or indifference could never be overemphasized in the spiritual life of any man. On it depended every real advance a man would make in the life of the spirit; and every failure in this same life could be traced ultimately to a lack of this detachment or indifference. The logic of it was inescapable. He who desires the end, must also desire the means to that end; and what could be more reasonable than to "desire and choose *only* that which would better" lead one to that end?

As a Tertian, Father Carl Miller reflected long on this Foundation and Principle; and made a very thorough examination of conscience. He asked himself if, all through his life as a Jesuit, he had desired and chosen *only* that which would better lead him to his end. It is a searching question; one that frequently brings about a total change of life. But Carl had little reason to give negative answers to that question. Yet he did not stop with an examination of the past. Ignatius never meant any man to do so. Carl looked ahead and asked how he could apply this Principle to the years that were before him. In what field of endeavor could he more surely promote the glory of God and attain the highest personal sanctity? In the field of science he had already accomplished much, and he humbly hoped he had accomplished it all for the greater glory of God. Unquestionably God had endowed him with real talent for the sciences. Yet he knew in his heart that the science of all sciences and the art of all arts was the sanctification and salvation of souls. Hence the question: Could I do more for God by working more immediately with souls? It was a trying question for Carl Miller, just as it is a trying question for every priest in any Order or Congregation devoted to intellectual pursuits and education. Carl would "make himself indifferent"; yet Ignatius had also said that "insofar as it is left to the liberty of our free will we should desire and choose only those things which better lead to accomplishment of our end." Did Carl Miller have any liberty in the matter?

Unquestionably it was during this long retreat of his tertianship that Father Miller looked long at the Patna Mission in India, which, only five years earlier, had become the responsibility of the Missouri Province. He saw there over thirty million people, many of whom had not even heard the name of Christ. He saw there fewer than twenty Jesuit priests. He felt he had some liberty in the matter. He could not demand that he be sent, but he could freely offer his services; he could volunteer, and then "make himself indifferent" as to what his superiors would do with his free-will offering.

But it is not at this point in the Spiritual Exercises that Ignatius would have any retreatant make his "election." Here he is only laying the Foundation and setting forth the Principle. But from here on to the time when the "election" is to be made, each new meditation has as one essential function the perfecting of this spirit of detachment and indifference. Ignatius knew human nature as few men have known it. He also knew much of God's ways and God's plans for men. So, after setting forth truths in what is called the "First Week" of the Exercises, truths that of themselves seem excellently well calculated to enable any man of intelligence and moderate good will to attain his end as a creature of God, he goes on in the "Second Week" to give each retreatant Him whom God has given to every man: The Light of the World, Jesus Christ, who said of Himself: "I am the Way."

Ignatius realized that God had given us Jesus Christ first of all to redeem us; then, to reveal to us the beauty and lovableness of God in a manner we humans can understand; and finally, to show us what a true son of God is like, so that we might learn from this Man among men the way to our true life. Jesus Christ in the final norm of all that is right in the life of any child of God; for He is the perfect expression of filial holiness. The only way to God for us humans is through the knowledge, love, and imitation of this only Son of God made Man. Hence, Ignatius strives to awaken in the soul a generous enthusiasm for the person and the cause of Christ, and a strong, personal love for Him as Leader. That is why he has his men and all his retreatants make the meditations on the Kingdom of Christ, the Call of Christ, the Two Standards, the Three Degrees of Humility, and the Three Classes of Men in this Second Week of the Exercises. The most sluggish will be stirred by these considerations, the generous will be impatient to offer their all for Christ's cause, and deem it an honor to follow such a Leader.

The man from Loyola was not only a soldier, he was a chivalrous soldier. He would have his men filled with like chivalry. They were not to be satisfied with merely following Christ, merely sharing in His labors and fatigues; they were to be men who would "signalize themselves in every form of service." There is the ideal of the real Jesuit. He will be what is called an *insignis* — a man who is eager to go "beyond the call of duty." Ignatius would have a Company of heroes.

At Paray le Monial Carl Miller once again heard the call of Christ, and once again resolved to be an *insignis*. That is why his provincial back in the States received his offer to go to the Patna Mission.

There have been those who questioned whether Ignatius of Loyola ever developed contemplatives. The answer to that question is Loyola himself first, then the countless men like Carl Miller who ever kept their gaze fixed on Jesus Christ, and who have loved Him with all their manly hearts just because of what He was. If contemplation can be described as a "looking and a loving," Ignatius of Loyola developed nothing but contemplatives. Another answer lies in the final Exercise of the Spiritual Exercises called the *Contemplatio ad Amorem* — the "Contemplation for Obtaining Love." It is not only the climax of the Exercises, it is their compendium. Francis Suarez has called it a preparation for divine contemplation itself. In this Exercise one finds God Himself — through Jesus Christ. Unquestionably such a finding is the end of every human soul's quest, the climax of all spiritual striving.

Perhaps those who question whether Ignatius ever developed contemplatives have been thrown off by this mighty man's spiritual "pragmatism." If ever there was a practical man of the spirit, Ignatius of Loyola was that man. He offered this contemplation at the end of his Exercises to foster in the soul of the retreatant a living, practical, and ever progressing love of God. And if that be not the end of all true contemplation, one may well ask: What is? Ignatius' "pragmatism" is shown in the two memoranda he sets forth at the very opening of this contemplation. He reminds us that "love is proved *by deeds*." How well one poet has put that truth when he says:

> "Bramble and briar will soon discover
> Who is the liar, and who the lover."

Ignatius' second reminder is perhaps even more pragmatic — and much more profound. He tells us that "love consists in a mutual interchange of gifts," so that every genuine lover shares with the beloved all that he has; yes, and all that he is. Self-giving is the final authentic deed which proves love. Was Ignatius borrowing from St. Paul? The Apostle to the Gentiles once said of Christ: "He loved me, and gave Himself up for me" (Gal. 2:20).

At any rate, Carl Miller made this Exercise in the town where Christ had manifested Himself as the Sacred Heart, and held out that human Heart of His as symbol of His human and divine love for us men. Carl asked for an "interior knowledge of the many and great benefits he had received from God" so that this knowledge would lead him on to "true gratitude and a resolve to love and serve His Divine Majesty in all things." Then he made a lover's study of all the gifts God had lavished on him through "Creation, Redemption, and personal endowments." It was an almost endless list, yet Carl realized that he could sum all up in the truth that God had given him Himself. Ignatius then asks: "what, with great reason and justice, I ought to offer and give His Divine Majesty in return?" The answer is obvious. One should give not only all that he has, but all that he is. That is why Ignatius suggests the form of the grateful return in his famous prayer *Sume et Suscipe*: "Take and receive, O Lord, my liberty, my mind, my memory, and all my will. Whatever I have or hold, Thou hast given me; I restore it all to Thee, and surrender it wholly to be governed by Thy Will. Give me only Thy love and Thy grace, and I am rich enough, and ask for nothing more."

Carl Miller said that prayer with new seriousness and newer sincerity. But he was not yet through with his Contemplation for Obtaining Love. There was one further consideration: A turning

from a contemplation of God's gifts to the contemplation of God
Himself. He looked long and lovingly at God's greatness, His goodness, His splendor and beauty, and finally, at His love. This was no
contemplation of abstractions. The visible things of this world led
him on to a vision of the Invisible. The physical beauty of the
universe gave him insight into the beauty of the Maker of this universe. The intellectual beauty and perfections in saints and angels
gave him some idea of the uncreated intellect of God. The moral
beauty in Mary the Immaculate One set him adoring the infinite
beauty of God who made her, and filled her with grace, filled her
with Himself. Finally there was Jesus Christ, the image of the
invisible God, the "Splendor of the Father's Glory." The lovableness
of Christ set his heart pounding; for God, as David sang, is "the God
of my heart." It has been said that when a human soul withdraws
itself from created things in order to contemplate Christ, it bursts
into flame. Now if the contemplation of the beautiful face of Christ
makes one's heart burst into flame here on earth, what will happen
to the soul when Faith is replaced by vision? "God is Love," says St.
John. And "God is my portion forever" is what David sings. When
Carl Miller asked himself at the end of this contemplation: *"Quid
retribuam Domino pro omnibus quae retribuit mihi* — What return
to God shall I make for all that He has given to me?" what answer
could he give but that *Sume et Suscipe* — and offer himself for India?
     That background is necessary if you are to understand this man
with the light of God in his eyes.
     He went to India in 1926. For the next twenty-two years he lived
as only a lover of Christ could live. Gajhi was his headquarters. But
he was not in his headquarters often, for the Patna Mission covered
over thirty-five thousand square miles wherein over thirty million
people dwelt, but not twenty thousand Catholics. Yet Father Carl
realized that each and every one of the more than thirty million had
been made by and for God; that for each of them the Word had
been made flesh, had lived and died that they might live forever;
that each had an immortal soul that was to live with God or without
God forever. His was the privilege to tell these people the truth
about God and themselves. How could he stay put in one place?
He must be about telling them.

But there was the first difficulty. How could he tell them when he did not speak their language? Hindi was the most common language of the land, but who could count the dialects? Then there was the caste system. How could an American ever cope with that? Finally there were the religions: the Moslem and the Hindu.

Father Carl learned Hindi and many a dialect. He also learned how to cope with the caste system. But the religions proved the real battleground. The fledgling missioner needed all the love for Christ that Ignatius had generated by his Exercises and his long years of training; for the very atmosphere of the place was enough to stifle any Christian soul. The Hindu could name more gods and goddesses than Father Carl could count with any ease. The mighty Ganges that flowed through the Patna Mission was to these people a mighty goddess to whom they offered sacrifice, even human sacrifice. This young Jesuit priest, newly arrived after a year in the atmosphere of Paray le Monial and all its memories of the Sacred Heart and His love for men, had to stand on the banks of the Ganges and see Hindu priests tie up goats and throw them far out into the river. Such idolatry would be enough to sicken his soul, but when he saw devout Hindus plunge in after them hoping to save a sacred victim and so bring upon himself the blessing of the goddess, he knew even a physical nausea. When he saw many of these swimmers perish in the struggle and then learned that they were considered fortunate to have lost their lives in this manner, for then they had died on the bosom of the great goddess, he knew that Ignatius' meditation on the Two Standards was no work of imagination. Father Carl was face to face with its reality. Christ and anti-Christ met in India — and Father Carl was following His Leader. Carl realized that he had to stay very close to his Leader, for he was not long in India when he saw certain things that could be accounted for only by remembering that there is a devil and that he never takes a holiday.

The move was on to convert the Santals, the aborigines who, more than likely, are the real natives of the land. But these poor people lived in villages no mean distance from one another. So, with Father James Creane, Father Carl plunged into that energy-consuming program of visiting as many villages as possible every day to pick up every stray bit of information that might be shaped into material to bring to these people the good news shepherds once heard outside Bethlehem. Father Creane became known as "The Santal Tramp" and the hero of these people who represent one of the oldest of civilizations and as yet one of the least developed. Father Carl went deeper into what is called "the bush," and dealt with villages less responsive; but that only made the former scientist the more determined.

He built himself a mud hut at Gajhi after he had constructed a church of mud. From there he set out on bicycle to visit village after village. You can imagine the roads deep in India. You can imagine the heat of the day and the heat of the night in that land which lies only twenty degrees above the equator. Yet this man drove his bicycle over those roads and in that heat thirty and thirty-five miles a day to meet with incredulity when he was not met with indifference or insult. . . . And that for twenty-two years.

He was one hundred and fifty miles away from Patna, the Mission's center. So he seldom saw his fellow missionaries once he had set up what he called his headquarters, that mud hut, at Gajhi. His villages held the poorest of the poor. It was not long before Father Carl was not richer than any of his parishioners; for his kind heart gave away money to this one to buy oxen to plow a field, to that one to get bricks to wall in a well, to that widow to help feed her children, to this young mother to clothe her child.

While on tour, and he was almost always on tour, Father Carl carried along a dozen or so rubbery pancakes and a pound of tea. When at home he would cook over a wood fire and add a tin of beans or some prunes as a delicacy. On one of his last tours his tires all but fell off his bicycle. Before he could buy new ones he had to approach a railway man, who was a Catholic, and beg the money for them. This good fellow chuckled as he handed over the needed cash but stopped when his eyes fell upon the disreputable canvas sneakers Father Carl was wearing. He took the priest into the nearby station and forced a pair of shoes on him. It was Father Carl's turn to chuckle, for this was no new happening; time and time again during the two decades of years he had pedaled his way among the Santals someone had to awaken him to the fact that he was neither fully fed nor properly clothed. The truth is that Carl was living his *Sume et Suscipe;* that he had become a Santal that he might bring the Santals to Christ, and Christ to the Santals. To him the whole thing was a divine romance — rugged though it was.

Whenever possible he would light his oil lamp at night and tap away at his portable typewriter turning out articles for magazines or letters for friends that would set many a reader chuckling at his wit even as they set them blinking in unbelief at some of his stories about his aborigines. He might be living among the uncultured but that was no reason for him to allow his wit to dim or his intellectual interests to flag. Confreres in the States, mindful of his scientific bent, sent him journals of science. Carl would page through these whenever he could, and peruse some of the more interesting articles. What he was actually looking for in such journals were ways and means to help his Santals. He had taught them how to build mud houses, how to wall in wells, how to be more hygienic, and even how to farm more scientifically. But he was never done with looking for newer ways for doing things better. These practical approaches to everyday works gave him opportunity to tell the Santals about the things of eternity.

After twenty-two years of this lonely life Father Carl could number only two thousand Catholics in the scattered villages that were his mission. Only those who know nothing about the difficulty of converting Hindus and Moslems will consider that a meager harvest. Only those who know little of God's ways will fail to marvel at what God accomplished through this small man who seemed to be made of iron.

But then one day in October of 1948 this little man of iron had to remind himself of St. Ignatius' insistence that each member of the Society take ordinary care of his health. There is not much room for hypochondriacs in a Company of free-lancers such as Ignatius wanted his Society to be. But then again there is no room for the foolhardy and imprudent either. Loyola would have a "sound mind in a sound body" in all his men. So he wrote into his Rule that they should take "ordinary care of their health" simply that they might thus be enabled to promote the greater glory of God. But he also wrote into that Rule the fact that sickness is no less a gift and blessing from God than health. So Father Carl was being a true Jesuit when he mounted his bike one October day and pedaled his way over thirty-

five miles of dusty road to catch a train that would bring him into
Patna where he would admit that he had not been feeling well for
some time; that he suffered a chronic pain in the back, and had lost
his appetite.

Soon after that report he was in the Holy Family Hospital and
was being closely examined by one Sister Elise, a nun-doctor. She
said little to Father Carl, but his superior at Patna was told that it
was highly advisable that Father Miller be flown back to the United
States and placed under expert medical and surgical care. The superior hated to do it, but he was wise enough to follow the nun-
doctor's advice. Father Carl took the command to return as he took
everything else in life — puzzled a bit, but unquestioning in his
obedience.

He flew back by Pan-American. It had taken him close to two
months to reach the Mission back in 1926. Now, twenty-two years
later, he did not need two full days to span the Pacific and be rushed
on to Chicago. From Chicago he was hurried to Louisville — and
there the diagnosis made by Sister Elise was confirmed: Carl Miller
had cancer of the pancreas. An exploratory operation showed that it
had spread too far to be checked by any surgery.

During November he was given deep x-ray therapy. By the end
of the month Father Carl learned the prognosis of the experts: Six
months at most to live, most probably much less. Did he believe it?
Does anyone believe it when he is told he is going to die? With
his mind, of course. That, after all, was the only thing he was living
for — the hour of his death. But the mind can be so detached from
the living person! Does anyone accept with his whole heart, body,
and being, the announcement that he is soon to die? It can be
doubted. Father Carl took it all quietly enough. He noted the gradual
loss of weight and of energy. But he was not giving up. He was not
yielding the field to the cancer. He would fight on — for his Santals.
India was still calling. There were millions on millions who knew
not Christ. How could he give in to a little disease?

He was at his typewriter far into the night every night during
that November. No articles for magazines. He had typed his last
magazine article on the plane as he flew over the Pacific. He had
airmailed it from San Francisco as he changed planes. Now he was

typing out an appeal for prayers. He was calling on the hundreds of priests and nuns whom he had come to know by mail, and asking them to storm heaven for a miracle. It was not that he was afraid to die, but that he feared many in India would never know real life. This miracle was not sought for himself; it was wanted for his aborigines.

On the morning of December 8 he offered the Mass of the Immaculate Conception. During it he told our Lord and our Lady that he was perfectly "indifferent"; that he wanted only the will of God; but that since part of that will was that we should ask, he was asking. He repeated the request heaven had heard a hundred times and more a day since his return to the States, but this time he added with a bit more fervor than usual, "yet not my will but Thine be done, O God." It was the last Mass Carl Miller ever offered. He was so weak after it that he literally staggered back to his room.

As Christmas approached, he would get out of bed, stand at the bureau, and strive to stay upright as he offered what is called a "dry Mass." He would endeavor to say all the prayers of the Missal without, of course, any real Consecration. Steel though his will was, it was not strong enough to hold up the sagging body.

He had to assist at Mass in a wheelchair that holy night. Mass from such a position for any priest is real sacrifice. Who knows but such a Mass is more efficacious before God than when the priest is able to pronounce those sacred words of Consecration in the name of and with the power of Jesus Himself? True though that may be, it is still something of real agony for any priest to be held away from the altar. But such agony brings the true priest closer to the New Law's Only Priest — and Carl Miller was a true priest if ever there was one.

It was on his return from Christmas Masses that he made the remark he was to repeat more than once in the ensuing fortnight: "My best work for India began when I arrived at St. Joseph Infirmary." That is a mysterious remark, and the remark of a real mystic. Cancer might be eating away the body of this missioner, but not his soul. That was battening on the experience. That was seeing ever more clearly just what life is all about, and what we mortals mean to God. If we are to do anything worthwhile for the omnipotent One, we must do it "through Christ, with Christ, and in Christ." Actually, it is He who does all things that are of worth in and through us. Father Carl was hearing the words of Christ, spoken at the Last Supper, with hearing that was much more acute than it had ever been. "I am the real vine, and my Father is the vinedresser. He . . . cleans any branch that does bear fruit, that it may bear yet more abundant fruit. . . . I am the vine, you are the branches. One bears abundant fruit only when he and I are mutually united. . . . This is what glorifies my Father — your bearing abundant fruit . . ." (Jn. 15:1–8).

The doctrines of the Mystical Body and the Communion of Saints were taking on more vital and much more personal meaning for this man whose heart was in India and whose soul burned with love for his Santals. Thousands of miles of land and thousands of leagues of sea might separate them physically, but neither land nor sea could keep him from touching them spiritually and ministering to them with all the might and mercy of God. This little man of iron was awakening to the value of suffering as he had never been awake before. That is why he could make that daring statement: "My best work for India began when I arrived at St. Joseph Infirmary," despite his twenty-two years of heroic, utterly unselfish and totally dedicated service to the Santals.

Let us eavesdrop on Father Carl and hear what is churning in his soul as the cancer gnaws away on that body of his.

Sister James Marion, the supervisor of the floor, comes to his room and asks if there is anything she can do for him.

"Yes, Sister," comes the sprightly reply. "If you can find time, I wish you would write a few more letters for me. . . ."

"Asking for that miracle, I suppose," says Sister.

"Exactly. While there is life, there is hope; and I am still very much alive."

The young but very wise nun looks at him a moment then quietly asks: "And is your hope as vigorous as your life, Father Carl?"

"Much more, Sister. Very much more. Oh, I am not closing my eyes to reality. I know how weak I am. I cannot hold a pen, Sister. I would not ask you to write for me were I able to so much as tap out a few lines on a typewriter. I can hear all the doctors do not say.

I can read their minds. They give me very little time to live. But, Sister, I know something they do not know. I know how much Mother Mary loves India. She can fool the best of doctors. I am hoping she will — and soon."

"But, Father Carl, she loves you, too," says the nun. "Who knows but that it is she who is calling you in from the streets of the world. You have been out a long time. . . ."

"Hush! Hush, Sister! I am only a boy. I have done nothing for her Son as yet. I know now that when I go back to India I will have a better method for making converts. I will pray more. I will suffer more. I see now that I only worked while out there. . . ."

"And I see that you will be a good boy for me right now and get into bed. I'll take the dictation later, Father dear."

The worldly-wise, those who call themselves "realists," would call such talk "folly." But they know nothing of the "folly of love"; they know not what it is to aim at being an *insignis*; they know nothing about living out a *Sume et Suscipe*. Father Carl was being more realistic than the greatest realist; he was living under the gaze of God. More, he was living with the very breath of God. He knew what God had done in him by baptism, confirmation, and holy orders. He had stamped him indelibly, three separate times, with that character which is a share in the priesthood of Christ. With the great St. Paul he could say: ". . . for me to live means Christ and to die means gain." And he could go on and speak to his Santals as Paul spoke to his Philippians and say: "Suppose I continue to live in the flesh? Well, that means for me fruitful labor. And yet I do not know which to choose. In fact I am hard pressed from both sides, desiring to depart and be with Christ, a lot far the better, yet to stay on in the flesh is more necessary for your sake" (Phil. 1:21, 24). Of course he wanted "to depart and be with Christ," but, haunted as he was by the thought of those millions who knew not Christ, he prayed not so much as Christ had prayed in Gethsemani but as Mary had prayed at Cana — a prayer that brought forth Christ's first miracle. What she said of the wedding guests, he could say of his Santals: "They have no wine." No, they had not the real wine of life: the truth about Jesus Christ. So Father Carl was willing "to stay on in the flesh" — but only on condition that such was the will of God in his regard. He was asking for a miracle, and asking it through that Mother who had won the first miracle, but he was asking it for the sake of his Santals and not for his own sake.

That Mary and Cana were very much in his mind was evidenced when some Jesuit confreres came to visit him from West Baden. Among them was Father Henry Milet who had spent a quarter of a century in parish work in the larger towns of Patna. He greeted his old missionary pal with the Scriptural phrase: "Well, Father Carl, it seems that your hour has come. You can say confidently what Jesus said when His hour had come: 'Glorify your son.'"

Father Carl smiled as he replied: "Not so fast, Father Henry. You are already in the Cenacle. I feel that I am only at Cana. Did not Christ say there: 'My hour has not yet come'?"

Whereupon a younger Jesuit, a Scriptural scholar, spoke up and said: "You two must have been listening to Fulton Sheen lately. He makes much of the relation between Cana and Calvary precisely on the point you two have just touched: Christ's words to His Mother, especially as they refer to His hour."

When Father Carl broke in with "So?" the young man went on to detail how Bishop Sheen was fond of preaching on the Third Word from the cross: "Woman, behold thy Son" by taking his hearers back to that hour at Cana when Christ had first addressed His Mother as "Woman." He told how Bishop Sheen claimed that Jesus always used the word "Hour" in reference to His Passion, death, and resurrection. Hence, when He spoke of it at Cana, He was equivalently saying in our language: "Mother dear, do you realize that you are asking Me to proclaim My Divinity — to appear before the world as the Son of God, and to prove My Divinity by a miracle? The moment I do that, I begin the royal road to the cross. When I am no longer known among men as the son of the carpenter, but as the Son of God, that will be My first step toward Calvary. My Hour is not yet come. Would you have Me anticipate it?"

That precipitated a lively discussion which brought out, thanks to the young Scriptural scholar, relations not only between Cana and Calvary, but relations between these two and Paradise. For God had used the word *woman* in the Garden after the original sin. Speaking to Satan, God had said: "I will put enmities between thee and the woman, and thy seed and her seed: she shall crush thy head." The woman was Mary. Her seed was Christ. The crushing of the head took place on Calvary. So, even in Paradise, as God speaks to the Tempter, the careful Scriptural scholar hears both the hammer blows that will nail Christ to the cross and the first syllables of that Third Word: "Woman, behold thy Son."

When one of the group asked about the title "Woman," the young scholar told that it was a title of dignity in the ancient world and in the ancient languages, but then went on to point out that it held overtones of deep dogma when used by Christ both at Cana and on Calvary; for it told of Mary's universal Motherhood, her role as Second Eve, her function as Coredemptrix and Mother of the Mystical Body of Christ.

Father Carl was very quiet during the exposition but the light in his eyes told that his intellect and heart were functioning at lightninglike speed. He had told Sister James Marion that he had no time for anyone who would not talk to him about Jesus and Mary. Now he was getting his fill of the subject that was life to him. When a lull came in the conversation he sat up in bed with vigor and said: "Does not all this explain that mysterious passage in the Gospel which tells how Mary placed her 'firstborn' in the manger? So many have mistakenly believed that that word implies that she was to have other children. We know she was to have millions on millions, but not according to the flesh; only in the spirit. Jesus was her only Son in one sense, but all men are her children in the other."

"Exactly," said the young scholar. "In one of his encyclicals, Pius X told how Mary, carrying Jesus in her womb, was carrying each of us spiritually; for in carrying the Head of the Mystical Body physically, she was carrying the whole Mystical Body spiritually. In fact it can be said in carrying the Second Adam, the Head of redeemed mankind, she was spiritually carrying all men who were redeemed by Jesus — and that means every man."

"But to get back to Cana," said Father Carl. "Jesus did anticipate His Hour, did He not? He worked a miracle, showed His Divinity, and His disciples believed in Him. I, too, believe in Him and Mary. Won't you men pray to Mary, asking her to tell her Son that my Santals have no wine, and add that I will willingly carry it to them."

"You're incorrigible," said Father Milet with a laugh. "We will pray, Father Carl. But in the meantime you are not to forget that Cana and Calvary are closely related, your hour may not be one of pouring out wine that is made from water, but of pouring out blood and water. Yet, if that be your hour, remember that it is your greatest hour, for in it you will be saying your Mass as Christ said His."

Late that evening, when Sister James Marion came for the dictation she had promised to take, she found a pensive Father Carl awaiting her. Before he began his dictation he asked her if she thought every man had "his hour" just as Christ had had His. The nun was nonplused. Seeing it, the priest gave a résumé of the discussion that had taken place in his room that afternoon, and ended with the quiet question: "Do you think my hour has come?"

"Father," she replied, "I have charge of the Cancer Clinic here. All I can say about that disease is that it is absolutely unpredictable. I have seen people, whom I thought would be dead in a few months, go on for years. I have seen others, whom the doctors thought of as cured, suffer a recurrence that took them off in no time. You know what your doctors think. You know how your strength has failed. . . ."

"I know. I know," said Father Carl hurriedly, "but I still trust Mother Mary. Let's get on with those letters."

On New Year's Day Father Carl again assisted at Mass in his wheelchair. He was noticeably weaker, but whoever talked with him could only conclude that while he was a very sick man in body, his mind and soul were not even ill. He conversed fluently and even cheerfully. Somehow he always managed to bring the conversation around to India, the power of Mary Immaculate, and the possibilities of miracles being wrought through prayer. On Epiphany he talked animatedly about the Wise Men and how they had come out of the "East" — maybe even from India. He dwelt on their wisdom in following the star and the reward that was theirs for that wisdom: they found Him who is Wisdom! But on the Sunday following the Epiphany, a Trappist who was across the hall heard Father Carl trying to persuade the nurses to wheel him to Mass. They finally had to summon Sister James Marion, who simply said: "Father Miller, what is it that you ask everyone to pray that you do?"

"That I give God, cheerfully, promptly, and without reserve, whatsoever the good God asks of me."

"Precisely! Everyone on this floor has heard you say that many times, Father. Now give God this desire of yours to assist at Mass. He is asking it through your doctors, and they are asking it through us."

There was silence for a moment. Then the clear voice of the priest came across the quiet corridor: "*Dominus est.*"

The Trappist smiled when he heard it. What memories it stirred! How often he had heard that expression on the lips of the Jesuits! Every retreat they had given him resounded with the phrase. It seemed like a summation of their lives. He well knew whence it came. It is taken from the gospel story of our Lord's appearance to His Apostles in the early dawn by the Lake after they had been fishing all night and had caught nothing. John and Peter, obviously, are at the back of the boat by the tiller. When the Stranger on the shore tells them to cast the net to the right and they obey only to find that they were then "not strong enough to haul it up into the boat because of the great number of fish in it," young John recognizes the Stranger and says to Peter: "It is the Lord" — or, as the Latin has it: "*Dominus est*" (cf. Jn. 21:1–7). Jesuits are taught, and try to teach all others, to recognize Christ in every event of their lives and say with John: "*Dominus est.*"

When Sister James Marion came to the Trappist's room and asked him if he wouldn't visit Father Carl and console him for loss of Mass this Sunday morning, the monk was only too glad to grant her request. He went over and was surprised to find the Jesuit sitting up in bed and seemingly as alert as any man in perfect health. The introduction was hardly over when Father Carl was asking the monk what had taken him to the Trappists.

"I wanted to be a good Jesuit and live always in the Society of Jesus. I could think of no better place to do that than behind the cloistering walls of Gethsemani in the Trappist regime. It is ever so much easier to live in His society there than where you have been. . . ."

"Capital!" exclaimed Father Carl, and the monk was almost startled by the light in the sick man's eyes. He had seen such a light a few times before. Once was the very day he had detrained at Gethsemani and had been met by an aged lay brother who offered to drive him to the Monastery in an ancient one-horse carriage. He had looked into that lay brother's eyes, the first Trappist he had ever seen, and knew that he was looking into lights that had not been kindled by any fire of earth. He had thought to himself that morning that he was looking into gleams that came from heaven. Later he fondly described them as "the light of God's glory." He moved closer to the bed. Father Carl had clasped his hands in enthusiasm and repeated his exclamation: "Capital! I believe I know exactly what you mean. In that sense my Santals should be Jesuits. So should every human being. Wait until I see some of my Dominican friends and tell them that they, and everyone who gets to heaven, will be Jesuits, and will remain such for all eternity! We will all live in the society of Jesus then, won't we, Father? But tell me, how do you manage it? Is it simply a matter of the practice of the presence of God? Is that what you mean?"

"Well, yes, and no, Father Carl. For others I suppose it could be that. But for me it is simply a matter of remembering who I am. It was a Jesuit who taught me. Do you know Father Dan Lord?"

"Indeed I do. He belongs to my Province. Or perhaps I should say I belong to his."

"Well, Father Dan saved my life." When the Jesuit stirred in bed and showed keen interest, the monk went on: "I was floundering around a bit when I first joined the Trappists, wondering just what it was all about — especially for a fellow like me. Oh I saw clearly enough the penance, the wholesale dedication, the headlong plunge into following Christ, else I would never have entered. But there were times in that first year that thoughts of the active ministry came to me, work for souls, work with souls. I can see now it was nothing but a temptation. But at the time it was one that so strongly appealed that I was ready to yield to it. Then I found Father Lord's little book on *Our Part In The Mystical Body*. That settled everything for me. I know my vocation now. It is to be His member. That means living in the society of Jesus in a very special manner."

Again that light flashed in Father Carl's eyes.

"Oh, Father, you are a godsend to me. For days on days I have been thinking on ways and means of getting closer to Christ and His mother. This idea of yours of living in the society of Jesus, as you put it, strikes me as superb. The initials after my name will mean ever so much more to me now. What is more, I've had one dominant desire since returning to the States — you know I am back only a few months after twenty-two years in India among simple souls, but souls who have been loved by Christ and who, once converted, love Christ with all their being. Since returning I have been begging God and Mother Mary to enable me so to live that everyone who meets me meets Christ. Your idea about being His member gives me great consolation. It even gives me hope that maybe my prayer has been answered. Now if I only live like His member. . . ."

"I wouldn't worry too much about that, Father Carl. Not after your twenty-two years in India. . . ."

"But there, Father, is the worry. What kind of a missioner have I been? Oh, I've worked hard. But did I do that work for Christ or for Carl? That question haunts me these days. We are so selfish — and selfishness can be so subtle. . . ."

The Trappist chuckled before saying: "St. Francis de Sales had something to say on that point, Father. It was his conviction that self-love, or selfishness, would die some fifteen or twenty minutes after we did. And I have heard of one of your own good lay brothers who, when asked as he was dying, 'Are you suffering, Brother?' turned to the wall as he groaned: 'Terribly — and from that incurable ailment called self-love.' So I wouldn't worry too much about your work in India. . . ."

"But I do, Father. Christ was never selfish. And I'm supposed to be Christ."

"What translation of the New Testament have you been reading?" asked the monk with a smile. "And what kind of a course in dogma did you take? You are not *supposed* to be Christ; you *are* Christ. Made so by baptism, more so by confirmation, and most so by ordination. That is the ontological and theological fact, Father. We *are* His members."

"But there's the rub, Father. What we are ontologically and theologically, as you put it, we fail to be psychologically and morally, if I can put it that way. We did not hear too much about the Mystical Body when we were studying theology. Your reference to it today, and your insistence that we are His members, only makes it the more shameful that we fail to be who and what we are. But come now and tell me how to be a mystic, a real contemplative. . . ."

"Whoa!" cried the monk as he stepped back from the bed. "Now you're asking too much. Only a true mystic and a real contemplative could tell anyone else how to become a mystic and contemplative; and I doubt that he would, even if he could. As for myself . . ."

"But you are a contemplative. Every Trappist is."

"We live the contemplative life, Father Carl. But that is something distinctly different from contemplative prayer."

Just then Sister James Marion came in. Father Carl turned to her and said: "This man will not let me in on his secrets, Sister. Speak to him and make him obey."

"He's asking the impossible, Sister. He wants to know how to become a mystic."

"Well, who doesn't? Tell me, too, Father."

The Trappist laughed lightly. "I'll see you two later," he said, and bowed himself out of the room. Once back in his own room he shook his head. How often he had been stirred by this same question. Letters had come to him from obviously earnest souls hinting at, if not actually asking, what Father Carl and Sister James Marion had just requested. To find the Holy Spirit blowing over the world and inspiring so many souls with longing for greater intimacy with Christ thrilled him. But to find so many confusing what he thought should never be confused filled him with a sense of frustration. He had read much on the matter, and finally concluded that Dom Lehodey, O.C.S.O., and Jacques Maritain had arrived at the truth when they distinguished clearly between mystical life and mystical prayer. He was convinced that the same distinction held between the contemplative life and contemplative prayer. To keep many from feeling discouraged he longed to show them that without ever being blessed by God with the great gift of "infused contemplation" they could live a life that was truly "contemplative" and be very real "mystics," but he had wondered often just how he could convince them.

As he was thus pondering, the Sister came to his room with the question: "Why didn't you tell Father Miller how to become a mystic? He's puzzled by your withdrawal."

"Did I tire him?"

"No. You inspired him. You should have heard him talk after you left. And you should have seen the light in his eyes."

"That light — isn't it thrilling, Sister? I call it the gleam from the glory of God."

"Father Miller is a very holy man, Father. I've had him on this corridor for two months now. But why didn't you tell him?"

"A wise man never carries coals to Newcastle, Sister, nor salt water to the sea. Father Miller is telling me more about mysticism than I could ever tell him. For that matter, so are you."

"I — Why, Father, I can't even say my Rosary right; nor stay awake during meditation."

"What's your idea of a mystic, Sister?"

The little nun straightened some books on the bureau, rearranged the flowers in the single vase, then flicked some imaginary dust off the mirror before she began with: "Well, I suppose he is a person very close to God. . . ."

The monk saw she was laboring, so he broke in with: "I read a very descriptive word recently that, at first, startles you, but on reflection you see that it does describe. The writer spoke of souls being 'God-intoxicated.' As I say, that term startles. Yet one can read much about spiritual inebriation if one delves into the literature on mysticism. Of course every comparison limps — and this one has its distinctive limp. Yet it also has its distinctive point. There is an analogy between carnal or physical intoxication and that spiritual inebriation the older writers spoke about. A mystic is one who is filled with God; one who can be called 'drunk' with God. What wine or whiskey can do to a man, God does to his mystics. A person who is 'under the influence' as we say, is often very happy, carefree, good-natured, generous, and even amorous. Yes, he loves everybody. Haven't you ever seen a man in this condition, Sister?" When she smiled and nodded, the monk went on: "Apply that analogy to Father Carl. Is he a happy soul, a generous soul, a carefree soul?" The nun's large blue eyes lit up. The monk went on: "Is there anyone who would dare deny that he is a most loving soul? That man is 'drunk' with God, Sister. Who but a 'drunken' man would want to go back to those aborigines in India; back to the dirt of their abodes; back to the heart-crushing loneliness of a foreign land, among a foreign people, who speak a foreign tongue, and think thoughts that are utterly alien to your own? Believe me a man has to be filled with God, filled to the point of inebriation, to be like Father Carl is this moment. So you see why I did not dare attempt to tell him how to be what he already is."

"But —" began the nun.

"No 'buts' about it, Sister. There is a mysticism of action, a mysticism of prayer, and a mysticism of suffering. The first is for the many, the second is for the very few, the last, I suspect, is for all of us. Father Carl, I sincerely believe, has lived, and is now living, all three. Dom Lehodey, a wonderful Trappist, defined a mystic very exactly; that is to say, he defined the mystical life by saying 'it is a life lived under the habitual direction of the gifts of the Holy Spirit in what St. Thomas called the superhuman mode.' Don't let those big words scare you, Sister. You were given the seven gifts at baptism. They have been operative, never doubt it. Jacques Maritain agrees with Dom Lehodey, and never did he make a wiser or a more practical remark than when he said: 'The precise moment when the mystical life begins cannot be ascertained in practice, but every Christian who makes progress in grace, and tends toward perfection will, if he or she lives long enough, enter into the mystical life.' "

"If she lives long enough. I wonder how long I'd have to live before — "

"Now, now, Sister, don't fall into the all too prevalent error of confusing mystical prayer and mystical life. You can be a mystic without ever knowing the ecstasy of mystical prayer. There are seven gifts of the Holy Spirit, only two of which stand out in the lives of mystics of prayer: wisdom and understanding. But in the lives of those very real mystics of action, counsel, piety, fear of the Lord, or even knowledge will dominate. In the case of the mystics of suffering, fortitude will be most manifest, with piety, most likely playing a very close second. Have you not discerned very real piety in the life of Father Carl? Have you not noted his filial attitude toward God? He talks as if he were but a child living under the gaze of his Father. As for fortitude — Look at how he has taken this cancer of the pancreas, and see how anxious he is to get back to India."

"But he is always asking about prayer. He has even asked me — "

"That is natural, Sister. For what are we but a gnawing hunger for God, a veritable desert thirst to know Him and love Him better and better. Of course he asks about prayer. But prayer and perfection are not synonyms, Sister. I have read many an experienced director of souls who insist that contemplation — even the kind that can be rightly called 'infused' — is not the prayer of the perfect alone. Many very imperfect souls have been graced by God with such a gift, at least for a time; while, on the other hand, many truly perfect souls have never known this great boon. I'll wager you yourself have met people further advanced in prayer than they were in virtue, and vice versa. I believe that many a religious ought to take to himself those words: 'Had thou but known the gift of God?' We do not dwell often enough on what God has made us by His sacraments and His grace. By baptism we were made Christ, Sister. If we only realized that, we would see that Christ not only lives in us and we live in Christ, but, in very truth, Christ is our life. Have you never been alerted to the fact that you are living the Mysteries of Christ, Sister? Not only the Joyful and the Sorrowful ones, but the Glorious ones as well, and even most especially. You are living the Resurrection right now; for it is by the vivifying Christ that we live, Sister; and only the risen Christ is Vivifier. 'We are alive to God in Christ Jesus' St. Paul teaches. I need not tell you that it is in the risen Christ that we so live to God. We all need to ponder Paul's words to the Ephesians: 'God made us live with the life of Christ. . . . Together with Christ Jesus and in Him, He has raised us up . . .' (Eph. 2:6). Indeed we live the Glorious Mysteries. If you will take the one word 'Christ-consciousness' for your meditation tomorrow morning, and try to ascertain all it means to you personally, I'll wager you won't have any difficulty staying awake."

"I shouldn't have told you my difficulty!" exclaimed the little nun. "But I want to thank you for some very good ideas — and some very encouraging ones. You make the religious life sound so simple."

"Exact word, Sister. Not easy, but simple. Yes, it is that. It was meant to be that by our good God, who is the *Ens Simplicissimum* — the most simple of all beings. It is tragic the way we so often complicate it."

A single gong sounded softly. Sister James Marion started. "That's my bell. I'll see you later, Father."

Late that same Sunday afternoon the Trappist heard Father Carl calling earnestly: "Rita! Rita!" Before the young nurses' aide could answer, the monk went over and found Father Miller sitting on the side of his bed, his face an ashen gray, and a peculiar glint in his eyes.

"Oh, Father," gasped the sick man. "I tried to get up to care for myself. . . . I hate to bother these good people around here. . . . But . . . I guess I'm weaker than I thought. . . . My head seemed about to snap off my shoulders."

The monk helped the priest back to his pillow. Father Carl breathed heavily for a little while, then he began to speak of how good God had been to him all his life. The Trappist listened with a joy that was tinged with holy envy. He knew he was listening to a holy heart being articulate. As the sick man went on, the monk could not but think that he was assisting at part of this good missioner's "Mass"; for he had the conviction that we all should make the Mass our life, and our lives a veritable "Mass." He likened what he was listening to, to the Preface; for it is therein that it is said: "it is meet and just — truly meet and just that we always and everywhere give thanks to God."

When the Jesuit paused, then began to speak again of the Patna Mission, and even say that he had hope of serving God there once again, the Trappist bent over and quietly said: "Father Carl, let's be realistic. What hopes have you of recovery?"

"None. None whatsoever, humanly speaking. I have faced facts, Father, since before I boarded the plane in India. I have believed my doctors. I know how I feel physically. I know I am a dying man, almost a dead man. But I also know Mother Mary's power — and her love for India. I would not be a bit surprised if she stepped in any minute now."

"Are you expecting her to?"

The Jesuit turned his eyes full on the Trappist. Again the monk was moved by that brilliant light in those depths. Again the words came to his mind: "the glory of God." "Father," said the sick man slowly. "I have prayed with fullest Faith. I have prayed earnestly. I have had many others praying, too. But always I have prayed, and told God to hear those others praying, with the full force of the 'Fiat' Mary spoke at Nazareth, and Christ spoke in the Garden. I believe I am completely 'indifferent,' Father. If God wants to cure me, I'll go back to India gladly. If He does not want to cure me, I'll go to Him perhaps more gladly. My realest prayer has been that I give God cheerfully, promptly, and without reserve whatsoever He asks of me."

"Father Carl," said the Trappist softly, "you are saying your Mass. You are near the Communion and even the Post Communion. . . ."

"You mean my 'dry Mass'? I say that often each day. . . ."

"No, Father Carl, that is not what I am referring to. I am speaking of your life. You have made it a veritable 'Mass.' Your 'Offertory' was made at your entrance into Religion, or at your vow taking, or perhaps at your volunteering to go to India. Undoubtedly, it was made on all three occasions. The 'Canon' has been long. Twenty-two years in India. Now you are at your real 'Consecration' and about to enter into your real 'Communion.' This sickbed is your 'Paten,' Father Carl. On it you have held out yourself. These linens can be looked upon as your 'Corporal' — You have laid your body out on them. Now you can say, and I'm sure you have said in your heart, if not with your lips: 'This is Your Body, Jesus. This, Your Blood.' You can say that with rigorous truth, Father Carl; for you are His member."

The Jesuit reached out and squeezed the Trappist's hand. "Thank you, Father," he said softly and with great emotion. "Thank you. You make living and dying glorious!" The lights in the sick man's eyes were brighter than they had been. The Trappist was almost mesmerized by them. But then the Jesuit stirred and in more intense tones said: "Father Milet, a fellow Jesuit and a fellow missioner in India, was here the other day. He told me 'my hour' had come. I believe you are saying the same thing in different words. Let me tell you what I did not tell him. Every hour has been my hour and His —

the Christ. But this last hour has been the most glorious of all. He has been closer to me since my return to the States than He ever seemed before. It has not been hard to suffer this cancer, Father. Not when He has been so real to me. If Father Milet was right in using that term about 'my hour'; if it is true that we all have 'our hour' just as Jesus had His, then tell everyone that it is the most glorious hour of their lives. All they have to do is go along with God, yield themselves to Christ, offer every breath and heartbeat. . . ."

The two priests sat in silence a moment, then Father Carl again said softly: "Yes, it has been glorious. I feel I have done more for my Santals here in Louisville than I ever did for them in India. Suffering is a great teacher, Father. It shows you how to say what you call your 'Mass.' It shows you how to join yourself to Jesus. It shows you how to be a missioner."

"It shows you how to be a real member of the Mystical Body," added the Trappist. "And cheer up, Father Carl, you'll be able to do even more for your Santals when you reach heaven. Never forget what the Little Flower said about spending her heaven on earth. . . ."

A newer light leapt into the Jesuit's eyes. "I never thought of that," he said enthusiastically. "That makes this 'hour' even more glorious. But I am not going to give up hope until Mary closes my eyes. Since they are still wide open tell me, Father, how to become a contemplative. When I go back to India I want to work as hard, yet give more time to prayer."

"If you are to go back, Father Carl, you had better rest now. You are tired."

"Never too tired to talk of God and His Santals. Tell me, Father —"

"Not now, Father Carl. You need rest. I must go. I will offer my Compline for you and your Santals."

"That's very kind of you, Father. But early tomorrow . . ."

"Yes, early tomorrow."

Very early the next morning the Trappist, as he started toward the chapel to offer Mass, noticed Father Carl's door open and his small light on. He entered, placed his hand on the priest's leg — for he had kicked off all the covers — and thinking that Father Miller was in semislumber, said softly: "I'll give you a special memento in Mass this morning, Father Carl."

A faint "Thank you, Father," was all the monk heard as he turned and hurried away. When he returned after a somewhat prolonged Thanksgiving, he found Father Miller's door closed and a "Do Not Disturb" sign hanging from its knob. He went to his own room and read more Office before breakfast was served. When the maids came to clean his room the Trappist took his Breviary to the sun porch to offer his prayer for the hour of Prime. He had just completed his petition that "his words, thoughts and actions be directed to the doing of God's will that day" when Sister James Marion approached. Her large blue eyes were shimmering in tears. She came close to the monk, placed her hand on his, and somewhat shakily said: "He's gone to God. . . ."

"Oh, Sister, why didn't you call me?"

"I was expecting you to pop in after your Mass, as you have been doing. I thought you would join us in the Prayers for the Dying. . . ."

"But I saw him just before my Mass. He seemed to be resting. . . ."

"He was then in his agony — if you can call it such. Actually, he just slipped off quietly. He answered the prayers for some time, then just stopped breathing." She reached for her handkerchief.

"Rejoice, Sister! Don't cry. Father Carl has caught up with his Captain, Christ. He is now enjoying what you and I have to wait for. Now he can contemplate to his heart's desire. Now he can be that mystic he wanted to be."

Before the monk could offer any more consolation, an attendant called Sister away. The Trappist was left with his Breviary and the awe-filling silence of the closed door marked 143. He slowly went to his room and after praying that God be Father Carl's "Reward exceeding great," he began to ponder on the lessons of this holy priest's life. The word that haunted him most was "glorious." He could hear the way Father Carl said "Yes, it has been glorious." Then he began to reflect on the thought presented by Father Milet: each one of us is to have "his hour." . . . Could it be? Is there some portion of time, some experience we are to live through, which God has set apart from all eternity as "our hour," that time in which we are

to show Him most especially that we are His children and that He
is our God?

Before he answered that he thought of Father Carl's words about
"every breath and heartbeat." Of course each belonged to God. There
was no hour in any man's life that was not "his hour" and God's
hour. Yet Christ had spoken often about "His hour." What did He,
Truth Incarnate, mean? The first reference was at Cana, at that
Wedding Feast, when Mary had said: "They have no wine." But
His more insistent references had come during the Last Supper in
the Cenacle. St. John gives at least seven sentences in which Christ
speaks of "His hour." There the reference is clear. He is speaking of
His Passion and Death. But if that was "His hour" what are we to
think of the long years of the hidden life and the laborious years of
the public life?

The monk pondered the matter for some time before he recalled
what Trent had said about the Passion and Death. The Council had
used the word *"principaliter."* That could only mean that His every
hour had redeeming value, but that His last "hour," that of His
Passion and Death, held the *principal* actions that redeemed us. That
clarified the situation for him. Every action, and every "hour" of
Christ's life, was redemptive, but most especially those actions and
that "hour" which He had called "His own" — those last hours.
So with humans: every hour is to be given to God, but most especially those last ones, such as Father Carl had lived through since
coming to Louisville. It is in these that we are called upon to show
our faith and our love. It is in these that we are to live as Christ
lived in His.

When Sister James Marion came with his bedtime "feeding," and
began with: "I'm missing Father Miller already," the monk broke in
with: "I'm not. He's been more present to me this whole day than he
ever was while alive; and he has been teaching me more. What a
lesson for life he teaches by insisting that we are to have "our hour" —
you, yours; I, mine." When a tiny frown appeared on the nun's
forehead, the Trappist said: "Sister, we were redeemed by Christ's
birth as well as by His death; by His hidden life as well as by His
public life; by His activities as well as by His Passion. But it was
principally by what He did in what He called 'His Hour' that heaven

was opened for us. We are His members. We must follow Him and, while glorifying God with our every moment, be prepared to glorify Him most by what is 'our hour.' That is to be our most glorious experience of life. It was for Father Carl. He told me so himself. It can be for any of us. It is meant to be that for all of us."

"Oh, Father, if we could only get everyone to understand that. But when suffering sets in — "

"Suffering is an evil, Sister, and something no one of us who is normal will ever welcome for its own sake. But we are wise when we remember that it is only a relative evil. Sin is the only absolute evil, Sister. Hence, we know that from this relative evil we call suffering, the all-wise God, and the intelligent man, should derive good, and even great good. Philosophy will take us that far, and when thus oriented, I believe unwholesome suffering and unnecessary pain is avoided. But when we look at it theologically, what vistas open up! We 'fill up in our flesh those things that are wanting to the Passion of Christ, for His Body which is the Church.' That is what Paul taught his Colossians. That is what the Holy Spirit teaches us. It is that truth which makes 'our hour' so glorious, Sister. We can glorify God and help Christ save the world by doing nothing."

"Nothing?"

The monk chuckled. "That was my reaction when I first read the line: 'The world is saved by those who do nothing.' But the writer then went on to show that Christ did nothing while on the Cross — but suffer. What did Father Carl do while here in Louisville compared to what he had done during those twenty-two years in India? Nothing. Nothing at all — save to suffer. But as he himself claimed, and as you and I can well believe: 'his best work for India was done here in St. Joseph Infirmary.' Yes, and perhaps his best work for God and himself. Do you realize that, most likely, right now that he is actually living in the society of Jesus, and enjoying to the full that Contemplation of Love which ever increases love. Life is wonderful, Sister, but death can be glorious! I feel sure it was for Father Carl. In fact, Sister, cannot we say with theological truth that he did not die today, but that he knew a resurrection, an ascension, and a throning at the Father's right hand? Life is not only a romance, Sister; it is a divine romance."

"You make it sound so, Father. But how many of us find it that way?"

"Well, it is not the fault of our divine Lover, Sister. Many of us insist on going through life in a state of semianesthesia just because we refuse to think theologically and live our Faith really and realistically. This hospital is teaching me much about God and myself. Did you ever know that St. Thomas has claimed that we follow the Law of Gravity and the Law of Falling Bodies in the Spiritual Life?"

"No!"

"Sister, drop a stone from the roof of this infirmary, and, the closer it comes to the earth, the faster it will fall. So in our Divine Romance: the closer we come to our Beloved, the faster we fall in love! That is what you witnessed in the case of Father Miller. The longer he lived 'his hour,' the brighter grew his flame of love. You could see it in his eyes. That was love light, Sister, that made them glow with what I have called 'God's Glory.' Not a bad name when you realize that God is Love."

As he rose to take the cocoa Sister had brought, the monk concluded: "Take that for your meditation tomorrow, Sister, and you'll stay wide awake again."

"I shall try both!" exclaimed Sister as she made for the door.

"Here's to God — your Divine Romance — and 'your hour,' Sister," the monk said, as he drank the now cold cocoa.

III

"NO SAD SONGS"
FOR JOAN

Father Carl's realism bares for us the two poles between which our attitude toward suffering should ever flow. He asked to be relieved of it; and with soul-deep earnestness. He even begged for a miracle. That is truly Christian; for it is typically Christlike. To realize this all we need do is ponder the reply Jesus gave those messengers from John the Baptist who came asking if He were the Messias or no. "Go and bring word to John about what you hear and see: the blind recover sight and the lame walk; lepers are made clean and the deaf hear; dead men rise again and the humble have the Good News preached to them" (Mt. 11:4, 5). It was a very direct reply. It was a very positive "Yes, I am He"; for when John heard that report he heard again the Prophet Isaias making those magnificent promises about the One who was to come, the true Messias: "Say to the faint-hearted: Take courage and fear not. . . . God himself will come and save you. Then shall the eyes of the blind be opened, and the ears of the deaf shall be unstopped. Then shall the lame man leap as the hart, and the tongue of the dumb shall be free" (Isa. 35:4–6). And again: "Thy dead men shall live, my slain shall rise again" (Isa. 26:19). Finally, "The spirit of the Lord is upon me, because the Lord hath anointed me: he hath sent me to preach to the meek, to heal the contrite of heart" (Isa. 61:1).

Now note well that the signs of authentic Messiasship were relief from suffering and even release for the dead. In other words, the work of salvation which was to be accomplished by Christ was the liberation of the entire man, both body and soul. How evident this is from the commands given by Christ as He sent His Twelve out on their first mission: "As you go along, preach on this text: 'The kingdom of heaven is close at hand,' attend to the sick; raise the dead; make lepers clean; drive out demons" (Mt. 10:7, 8). The

41

Man-God was keenly conscious of suffering and the crying need to relieve it. So is His Church. For what is His Church but "the continuation of the Incarnation"? Hence, if we can say that one of the purposes of Christ's miracles was to anticipate the integral salvation of man: body and soul, we can also say that the role of the Church is to introduce us to the mystery of the same salvation, with the hope of its perfect realization at the "last day." That is why she has such respect and reverence for the human body. She knows it is an essential element of the human being. She knows it is to rise and be glorified. Hence, she knows that one of her functions is to repel all attacks on it. That is why she blesses such everyday things as bread, butter, oil, wine, water, cheese, lard — every food and every medicine. She does this that through them we may retain or recover health of soul and body, that sin and sickness may be avoided, that the power of Satan may be driven off, and we may possess real joy.

Hear her pray: "Grant to thy servants, we beseech Thee, O Lord, the grace to enjoy continual health of body and soul. . . ." Listen to every priest as he bows over the sacramental Body of Christ before receiving Him in Holy Communion: "May this partaking of Thy Body, O Lord Jesus Christ . . . be profitable to the safety and health both of soul and body." Almost incessantly in the Holy Sacrifice of the Mass the Church will lift her voice in pleas for our health, bodily as well as spiritual.

That is one pole. We are to recognize sickness, suffering, and death for what they are: they are evil. But that is not the only pole, and Father Carl showed us that. He recognized sickness and suffering as something that could be sublimated into sacrifice; something that could have worth, inestimable worth, for God, and self, and souls. That is why he was glad and even gloried in his sufferings. He saw them as invaluable for his Santals.

But that attitude of soul was nothing new. Father Carl's entire attitude was but a repetition of what St. Paul taught in season and out of season. In fact, we can find a whole theology of suffering in the writings of this Apostle to the Gentiles; and from it learn how to make life what it was meant to be by God — all joy.

Paul suffered — more perhaps than any of us will ever be asked to endure. He begged to be relieved of it — just as we may ask. But the answer he received is the one we need to hear — and hear clearly. "My grace is sufficient for thee" (2 Cor. 12:9). And the addendum is something we especially need to learn: "for my power is made perfectly evident in your weakness." Once we realize that, then we will cry out as Paul did: "Gladly, therefore, will I boast of my infirmities, that the power of Christ may spread a sheltering cover over me. For this reason I take delight, for Christ's sake, in infirmities . . . for when I am weak, then I am strong" (2 Cor. 12:9, 10).

Whence came his strength? From "the power of Christ." Now that is the fact that gives every Christian reason to pause and examine himself. Too willingly, perhaps, we tell of "our operation" — after it is over, and we have regained our health. But how often have we "gladly boasted of our infirmities" before that "operation of ours"? How Christian are we? Surely we cannot bury our heads like ostriches and refuse to look at that thing which has our world writhing: sickness, suffering, and death. Each is almost as universal as the air we breathe, and each is to come to everyone of us who does breathe in air. For, as St. Paul told his Romans, they are "the wages of sin" (Rom. 6:3). And they are wages each of us will earn; for we are all children of the original sinner. So the very personal question we each must answer is: How shall we spend that wage? Will it be like St. Paul and Father Carl: gladly and even gloriously? Or will it be like those who find in these wages only a curse?

The real lesson to learn from Father Carl is what has rightly been called "the Christian mystery." It is that taught so pointedly by St. Paul to his Philippians: "I would know Christ and what his resurrection can do. I would also share in his sufferings, in the hope that, if I resemble him in death, I may somehow attain to the resurrection from the dead" (Phil. 3:11). We entered that "mystery" at baptism. "Do you not know," asks St. Paul, "that all of us who have been baptised into union with Christ Jesus have been baptised into union with his death? Yes, we were buried in death with him by means of Baptism, in order that, just as Christ was raised from the dead by the glorious power of the Father, so we also may conduct ourselves by a new principle of life" (Rom. 6:3, 4).

How have we been using that "principle"?

There is sound sense in our common saying: "Like father, like son." But what we Christians should realize is that this common saying can have resonances in the realm above mere nature. By baptism we were "born of God." He, therefore, is our Father, and we are His children. Consequently, ours is the responsibility of so living that others may be able to recognize our Father, who is God, in us, His children. That is no light responsibility. So grave is it that one man has very justly said: "The greatest proof of God's existence, of the truth of the Christian Religion, and of the Divinity of the Catholic Church, is not to be found in the order in the universe, nor in the history of the Passion and Death of Jesus Christ, nor in the marvelous organization of the Vatican, but in the lives of holy Catholics. God-like living by humans is irrefutable testimony to the Divine."

"But," you may ask, "what is Godlike living?" The answer is: *Jesus Christ*. For Godlike living consists in deliberately striving every day and in every way to be Christlike. That, of course, sounds trite. But its triteness does not diminish its trueness. Rather, it emphasizes it. The call, and even the command, to be Christlike is as old as Christianity, and it will be sounded so long as Christianity endures — and that is until Time's end. Paul issued it to his Romans: ". . . put on the Lord Jesus Christ . . ." (Rom. 13:14). Pius XII issued it again in that epoch-making Encyclical, *Mystici Corporis*. "Let those, then, who glory in the name of Christian, all look to our Divine Saviour as the most exalted and most perfect exemplar of all virtues; but then let them also, by careful avoidance of sin and assiduous practice of virtue, bear witness by their conduct to His teaching and His life, so that when God appears they may be like unto Him and see Him as He is" (No. 58 America Press trans.).

Nowhere, perhaps, will this command prove more difficult than in the day we are paid "the wages of sin" — suffering and death. But all we have to realize is that Jesus Christ, by suffering and dying, has conquered both suffering and death. He did so not by doing away with them, but by transforming them. That is the actuality which enables members of Christ to find joy in sickness and glory in suffering; for, with St. Paul, we realize that "what is lacking to the sufferings of Christ I supply in my flesh for the benefit of his body, which is the Church" (Col. 1:24). How the "wages of sin" have been transformed: they can now buy salvation. That is what Father Carl Miller realized. That is why he found his gnawing cancer a source of glory.

But, you may object, all that is understandable in a man like Father Miller who was a religious for four decades of years and a priest of the great high God for a quarter of a century; but for us ordinary humans. . . . That objection is answered by a girl like Joan Gasser.

Here was a young woman standing on the threshold of life. Twenty years of age, in her senior year at Nazareth School of Nursing, endowed with just about everything a young woman craves: looks, sanguine temperament, and a personality that assured her of wide popularity, she was standing on tiptoes with eager expectation. Then, one day, just four months before graduation, she noticed a slight swelling in one of her lymph glands. Just some allergy, she thought. She would have one of the interns look at it to see if there was not some way it could be reduced quickly.

She smiled to herself when the intern examined it with real care. But, a few days later, when a resident doctor called her and took a look at the same swelling, her smile faded a bit. "It's nothing, Doctor. I'm sorry the intern consulted you." But the resident examined it with even more care than had the intern. Then he stepped back and put questions to Joan which showed that he was probing with his mind even more carefully than he had with his fingers. On leaving, he tossed back over his shoulder the advice that Joan was not to "run herself ragged, racing all over the hospital."

"He's nice," thought Joan as she adjusted her starched cap, fluffed out her luxuriant dark hair, and started for her station. But when a laboratory technician came to her that same afternoon to take some blood specimens, Joan began to wonder if that resident was as nice as she first thought him. With a touch of asperity she said: "Oh, let's stop this nonsense, Martha. It's nothing. Just some allergy. I consulted an intern just to see if I could get some salve or something to make it disappear."

"Orders are orders, Joan. I only work around here. I've got to go back to lab with some of your blood, or someone up there is liable to take some of mine. It's a hard life, Gal. So, come now and let me have some of that Kentucky blue blood of yours."

Joan submitted gracefully enough, but her large eyes still held glints of resentment toward that "nice" resident. He had given her no hint that this was coming. Yet, the call of a patient on the floor, followed soon by tray time, dissipated even that resentment. So it was the usual lively, seemingly carefree Joan who went back to Lourdes Hall that evening for a change of uniform.

The next morning, even before she had half finished the bed making, she was summoned to the linen room. There stood a member of the staff. "Miss Gasser, I believe."

"Yes, Doctor."

"How has your appetite been of late?"

"Ravenous, as usual, Doctor."

"Good. And your energy — notice any letdown?"

"We student nurses are always tired, Doctor. Some say we were born that way, but I claim I got this way since coming into training."

The doctor hardly seemed to be listening, for his eyes were filled with thought as he studied the smiling girl before him. "Hmmm," was all he allowed himself until he cleared his throat and said, "The next question could embarrass some students, Miss Gasser, but I don't think it will bother you. Have you lost any weight lately?"

"Wish I could, Doctor!"

"Good. Any soreness accompany that swelling?"

"None at all. Just by accident I discovered it one day as I was washing up. It's nothing."

"Hope you are right, Miss Gasser. Probably you are. But we'll see what x-ray and lab have to say. I'll see you tomorrow or the next day. In the meanwhile don't work too hard."

"Thank you, Doctor. That's the best prescription I've ever heard."

Two days later she was filled with ideas about the coming Valentine Dance; for, as Prefect of the Sodality, under whose auspices the dance was being conducted, it was her task to make the auditorium look less like a gymnasium with a basketball court, and more like a ballroom with a shining dance floor. She had discussed it with some classmates, and finally decided to set up a statue of our Lady as Queen of Hearts, floodlight it with mellow-glow lamps, then surround it with gold streamers punctuated with small red hearts trimmed with silver. She was studying a rather large statue of our Lady at the end of one of the corridors of the hospital, wondering how it would look in the auditorium, when a classmate came up with the word that she was wanted in Sister Mary Benigna's office right away.

"What have I done now?" asked Joan.

"That's your worry, Gal," replied the classmate, "but if I were you, I'd hurry. Sister sounded most serious."

Fifteen minutes later Joan was back on corridor, but plans for the coming Valentine Dance were not crowding her mind as they had been for days. Instead, she was trying to recall all she had ever heard or read about Hodgkin's disease. What she could recall was not very much. So that night saw her looking it up in the medical dictionary, and then paging through her pathology book. What she found in those books was none too heartening. What she now remembered about a patient or two who had had the disease, sobered her greatly; for Sister Mary Benigna had told her that the doctors were fairly well agreed that her lab tests showed she had Hodgkin's.

In the dark of that night her roommate heard her crying. "Joan," she called. No answer — but the crying ceased. "Joan, are you awake?" Still no answer. The roommate settled deeper under the covers, telling herself that, most likely, Joan had been dreaming. But Joan Gasser was doing anything but dreaming. She was facing the fact that just six months before her twenty-first birthday, and just under four months before graduation, she was found to have a disease that was fatal.

How the word got around, Joan never knew. But, within a week, everyone in Lourdes Hall had offered sympathy and made suggestions; and it seemed to Joan that almost everyone among the almost thousand workers in the huge hospital had been informed. So many were showing sympathy and sorrow in their eyes and embarrassed smiles, that Joan herself was growing embarrassed. But then she resolved to accept the reality for what it was within herself, but show a lightheartedness concerning it to all others. When one of the nursing Sisters asked her what she planned to do about it, Joan laughingly replied: "Forget it as far as I can, Sister. Go along as if nothing had happened. I'll graduate and even take State Boards. God will take care of me."

That she meant those brave words was evident the night of Valentine's Day when Joan appeared at the dance wearing the very latest in evening gowns, and was really the life and the belle of the ball.

The months slipped by and Joan's resolve crystallized. She went along just as if she had never heard that diagnosis. That is how it appeared on the surface. But down in her soul something quite different was going on as Sister James Marion learned in May.

The first Saturday of this month is Derby Day in Louisville, and it seems that everyone is talking horses. In 1949 there was a large field entered for the Derby. That set some oldsters predicting that there would be an upset; for whenever the barrier is lifted before more than a dozen thoroughbreds, there is such a crowding for the rail that many a favorite gets pocketed and the horse who was hardly given an outside chance to win, runs home ahead of the field and is wreathed in the roses. That is what happened in 1949. Hence, the name "Ponder" was on countless tongues as the evening shadows crept across the land. But Joan Gasser, though she had watched the race on television, was talking to Sister James Marion about realities which race crowds seemingly never think of. Joan had sought out Sister for a final consultation concerning the May Procession and the Crowning of Our Lady that was to take place that same evening. As Prefect of the Sodality, Joan was to have the privilege of crowning our Lady that year. Once Sister had answered her query, she asked Joan how she was feeling.

"As if I were just coming alive, Sister."

That puzzled the nun. She knew what Hodgkin's was and what it meant. How could this youngster think she were coming alive when a fatal disease was running in her blood? Joan saw the puzzlement in Sister's eyes, and smiled. "Sounds queer, doesn't it, Sister? But the truth is that only now am I realizing what every child of Mary should know from the beginning. She is our Mother, Sister; yes, our Mother. She has helped me come to life these last few months. I know not how brave a front I have put on, but I will tell you that I was anything but brave for weeks and weeks after I learned what I have. It just did not seem possible! I read all I could in the books, Sister. I know what Hodgkin's is, and what it means. But slowly . . . no, not so slowly! Rather suddenly I awoke to the fact that I am a child of Mary and a child of God. That awakening has changed everything. It really seems that I have just come to life."

Just then an orderly broke in and called Sister away. It was a very awed nun who followed the orderly. She felt that she had seen into a soul; that she had heard words from the depth of another's being. It was a simple statement the girl had made, yet the tone of voice gave the words an aura of something Sister James Marion could not name, but which she felt was so different from what usually comes with human speech that she felt awed.

Later that same evening Sister sought out Joan. Both were very happy, for the rain, which had threatened all day, had held off and allowed them to have their May Procession and the Crowning of Our Lady in the Grotto of Lourdes at the back of the hospital. They had reason to feel happy, for the procession had been magnificent. The entire student body had participated, dressed in full uniform, even to the colorful cape; for it was chilly enough to allow for them. Each student nurse had carried a lighted candle as she walked along singing the favorite hymns to our Lady. The nuns had followed them, a few of the orderlies, interns, and residents, then the chaplain and a few priests, and finally Joan with her assistants all dressed out like a bridal party. One youngster carried a satin pillow on which rested a splendid crown. As the procession ended in the Grotto, with nurses, nuns, medical staff, and clergy arranged in colorful fashion before the Shrine, Joan and her escorts approached the statue, then with dignity and a little shyness, Joan took the crown from its pillow and placed it on our Lady's head. More than one in that candle-lighted group thought that soon Mary might be crowning the girl who had just crowned her. Yet, the most unconcerned person in the entire assembly seemed to be Joan Gasser. When Sister managed to get her alone afterward, she congratulated her on a magnificent piece of work.

"Oh, Sister," replied Joan, "you are too kind! Let's be honest. That was your work, not mine. I have the name of being Prefect, but you are the real force behind the Sodality."

Sister said, "Child, you are generous. Let me say, Joan dear, that you looked lovely this evening."

Whereupon the girl extended her arms, pivoted slowly, displaying the beauty of her gown. "All I need now, Sister," she said, "is the groom."

Sister let her pivot once again, then took her by the hand and led her into a nearby parlor. "Joan, I want to know your secret. How do you do it? Aren't you at all scared?"

Joan Gasser sobered immediately. She gave a quick glance over her shoulder to assure herself that no one was near, then said: "Sister, I wouldn't tell anyone else in the world what I am going to tell you. I know you will keep it to yourself. I was more than scared when I first heard what I have. I cried that first night, Sister; for I just could not believe it. I had looked up the books about Hodgkin's and just could not bring myself to believe that I had such a deadly thing. I hoped the lab had made a mistake. I guess I prayed that the doctors were all wrong. But then, gradually, as I told you this afternoon, I came to life. I can't say when it all began; maybe it was at Mass or after Communion; maybe it was while preparing that Valentine's Dance, or getting ready for some meeting of the Sodality. But somehow or other, the truth has become clear to me that a Child of Mary is just that — a child of Mary. Why don't we learn this the moment we join the Sodality, Sister? Oh, we use the words. But what do they mean to us? Not as much as being a student nurse or a member of St. Joe's Staff." Joan saw Sister's eyes widen. "Oh, it is not your fault, Sister. You tell us just what it means to be a Sodalist. But we are dumb, or foolish, or something. The truth just does not register."

"What truth, Joan?"

"That we are to be like our Mother. Oh, Sister, it's all right to say that we should dress modestly, conduct ourselves with decorum, watch our speech and actions, be representative Sodalists. But there is ever so much more to it than that. Those things are mostly external. To be like Mary internally . . ."

Joan stopped. Sister did not know whether the girl was looking for words or felt embarrassed by having said so much. "Internally?" she said after a short pause.

"Yes, Sister, internally! A Child of Mary must be all I said about modest, dignified, pure in mind, heart, body, and soul. But that is nothing to what I see what it means now. We are to do what Mary did, Sister. We children of Mary are somehow or other to bear Christ."

The phrase seemed to startle the girl. Her eyes opened wide, a tiny frown appeared between her eyes, then she smiled. "Yes, that is it. We are supposed to bear Christ — not physically as did our Lady, of course, but really just the same. When I came back from the Communion rail this morning wasn't I like Mother Mary? Did I not have Christ in me really? And all day today and every day, so long as I am in the state of grace, am I not like Mary? Do I not carry the living Christ? Not sacramentally all day, of course, but just the same I have Him, haven't I, Sister?"

"Of course," said Sister softly.

"Well, that is what I mean by coming to life. I'm beginning to realize now what it means to be a Sodalist. I, like Mother Mary, am to carry Christ about in me all the day through. When I first knew what I had, I thought of our Lady, Sister, but I thought of her as Comforter of the Afflicted, as Help of Christians; yes, even as Mother of Sorrows. For I would not be honest if I did not admit I felt quite sorry for myself for some time. But now, Sister, I think of her almost always as Cause of our Joy. I'm coming alive, Sister."

"Indeed you are, child. You are even teaching me, your Moderator, truths about the Sodality I had only half caught. Keep up the grand work, Joan. Our Lady will bless you."

"Oh, she's taking care of me right now, Sister. Now let me thank you for allowing me to crown her today. It was a glorious thrill."

They parted then. But Sister went back to her floor thinking on how wonderful are the ways of God. Either He had given this girl a very special insight into her relation to Mother Mary by some singular grace, or He had awakened in her all she had heard and read about the Sodality. For only the year before Pius XII had published his *Bis Saeculari*, an Apostolic Constitution, which the

Pope, who was himself a Sodalist, called the *Magna Carta* for all Sodalists. In that Constitution His Holiness had named four characteristics as essential for every real member of the Sodality: a consecrated devotion to Mary, a deep and intense interior life, which would naturally flow over into a dynamic apostolic life, and all these worked out under the leadership of Christ in His Church.

Anyone who doubts that physical sickness is often given by God to awaken one to newer spiritual life has but to watch this young girl live out her resolve to be another Mary.

At the end of May in 1949 Joan was graduated with her class. By early fall she was registered in Kentucky, having passed all the State Board exams; hence, she was fully qualified now to serve as a graduate nurse. Contrary to many expectations, she did not return to her Alma Mater, St. Joseph Infirmary in Louisville, but signed on as assistant supervisor at Our Lady of Mercy Hospital in Owensboro, her hometown. One may well wonder if the very name of the hospital did not have as much to do with Joan's choice as the fact that she would be nearer home; for the insight granted her in the spring of 1949 appeared as a dominant motif in the subsequent living of Joan Gasser.

In no time this new member of the staff of the hospital was known as one of the most affable, likeable, and capable nurses in Our Lady of Mercy. Joan herself admitted that she felt freer in Owensboro than she had at St. Joseph Infirmary in Louisville; for very few in the town, let alone in the hospital, knew of her condition. This relieved her of the always embarrassing task of accepting well-meant sympathy, and of the necessity of answering direct questions as to the progress of the disease. To watch her at work gave rise to the always important question: Does the human soul grow? Substantially, of course, it cannot. But accidentally? Can it grow stronger and, as it were, larger? Joan answered that question daily; for a newer serenity was noticeable, a self-possession, and sureness in all her attitudes told of an inner security that could come only from her soul. Of course the soul grows! Each new grace received and used adds to the soul's vigor. That is why Joan Gasser could give herself to her duties every new day with a readier smile and an almost tangible greater assurance. Hodgkin's disease may be silently gnawing away at her body, but her soul knew increase of strength daily as she advanced in what Monsignor Guardini has called "the art of dying." Joan would have called it rather "the art of really living." For that art actually consists in giving each day, and every hour of each day, a definite direction. For any day without direction is not a day; it is but a fragment of time, and a torn fragment, at that. Joan realized this; that is why she pointed herself, all she did, and all she was, straight at God. She had learned this lesson from Mary; for what did our Lady do from earliest childhood, and especially after her *Fiat?*

Cancer of the blood, for that is what Hodgkin's disease really is, had set the truth of all truths coursing in Joan Gasser's blood; for now she knew that, by baptism, she had been made a Christopher — a bearer of Christ — hence another Mary.

Before Christmas, Joan paid a visit to her alma mater. Some thought she looked pale, drawn, and, despite her ever ready smile, somewhat haggard. When Sister James Marion questioned her it became evident that her soul's color was anything but pale; for the young girl thrilled the nun, and gave her a refreshing look at her own vocation, when Joan told of the joy she knew within her as she went about her work carrying Christ.

"Sister, haven't you often envied priests the privilege that is theirs to carry Christ in a golden pyx hung about their necks as they go on a sick call?" asked Joan.

The nun paused a moment before replying: "Joan, I have often been jealous because I was not born a man so that I might be a priest. Yes, I have envied them. Why do you ask?"

"The thought often struck me, as I watched the chaplains going about in the early hours of the morning bringing Communion to the patients, that they are singularly blessed to have such a mission in life. Like you, I guess I, too, resented the fact that only the male of the species could do such a thing. I suppose I said something like 'It's a man's world, all right.' But only a few weeks ago I was talking to a priest when suddenly he quoted something he said came from St. Paul. It was something about our bodies being temples of the Holy Spirit. But he ended by saying something that made me wonder if he were reading my mind. He said: 'Glorify the God in your body.'" It startled me at first. It sometimes frightens me to realize that God is so near. But that one sentence sums up life for me now. I know we were made to glorify God. But I never had thought of glorifying Him in our bodies. You know we always seem to think of going to Church to visit Him in the Blessed Sacrament, or of kneeling down and saying some prayers in a quiet corner of your own room. But this idea of carrying Him about in my body, and glorifying Him there, is something new for me, and it makes life so wonderful and changes nursing into something very like the priesthood. Look, Sister, the chaplain comes to the sick in the early morning with Christ in the sacrament. Then he may visit once again during the day. But we nurses are in and out many, many times a day. Now if I have God in my body, don't I bring Him to those sick?"

"Of course. But not in the sacrament."

"No, we may never do it that way, but we do bring Him really, don't we? We carry Him . . . how shall I put it – ?"

"Spiritually?"

"That's not the word I was looking for. He is in me by grace. That is a spiritual thing. Yet there is another word I have heard or read. It wasn't 'spiritually.' "

"You're not thinking of 'mystically' are you, Joan?"

"That's the word, Sister. The Mystical Body is a reality, isn't it? I'm a member. Now where a member of a body goes, the person who owns that body goes, doesn't she? If my foot or my hand comes in this room, I come in. Can I say the same thing about the Mystical Body? I'm Christ's member. Where I go, doesn't Christ go?"

The nun thought for a moment, then hesitantly replied. "I really don't know, Joan. But of this I am sure, you have the Three Persons within you when you are in grace. Hence, you not only bring Christ, you bring the Three Persons into every room with you. That's enough for me. You can ask some priest about the Mystical Body. I'm not too sure. But your example seems to point that way. I'll have to study the doctrine more myself."

Many a theologian would have paused as had Sister James Marion; for Pius XII, in his magnificent encyclical, had warned against those who "out of their fancy draw some deformed kind of unity. They want the Divine Redeemer and the members of the Church to coalesce into one physical person." So, if Joan thought for a moment that she and Jesus formed one physical person she was most wrong. But the Pope also taught that the union effected between the Head and the members "is something sublime, mysterious and divine . . . and that the unbroken tradition of the Fathers from the earliest times teaches that the Divine Redeemer and the society which is His Body form but one mystical person, that is to say, to quote Augustine, the whole Christ. Our Saviour Himself, in His high-priestly prayer, has gone so far as to liken this union with that marvelous oneness by which the Son is in the Father and the Father in the Son" (No. 82 *ibid.*). So, if that is what the young nurse meant, she was anything but wrong; and her insistence on the word *mystically* in place of the one offered by Sister, "spiritually," seems to indicate that she did grasp this wondrous truth correctly, and wanted to live it out in an apostolate to the sick.

It was no delusion that Joan was living. The chaplain might bring Christ into a patient's room under the veils of a consecrated Host for Communion once a day, but Joan, under the veils of her disease-ridden body, brought Him there many times a day; for Christ was in her just as He was in the Host — only the manner of His presence differing. That is theological fact. So Christ radiated out from this cheerful young nurse just as truly as He did from the weightless wafer of wheat after Consecration; one manner being sacramental, the other mystical — both, however, real with the reality of God. And the thrill that Joan knew was that she, by duty, had to go into many a room to which the chaplain would never be called. She hoped, prayed, and believed that, in such cases, Christ "communicated" with these sick people in His own wondrous way, and with great efficaciousness.

A year passed. Then another. Joan kept cheerful and busy. But twice in this second year she had to take a few days off to allow the medical men to do what they could for her ever worsening condition. She was faithful to her resolve to take all the therapies God offered through His medical science, but more faithful far to the determination to stay always in His hands and to keep Him in her heart.

At the hospital, patients and supervisors were calling her "an extraordinary nurse" — but little did they know just how extraordinary she was; for few in Owensboro knew of her real condition. Other girls of her age and her acquaintance could plan ahead to higher steps in their career, look to marriage, a home and a family of their very own. But Joan could not. She knew her future was brief, but she was not letting anyone else know it; for pity was one thing she did not want, and self-pity one thing she would not indulge in. She joined a social sorority and a Catholic Women's charity group. To both of these organizations she gave what she gave at the hospital: a warm heart, all the energy she could summon, a pair of capable and very willing hands, and an active and ever agile mind. She knew she was going to die soon; and she actually willed it simply because God, who was her Father, had so willed it. But she would waste no time simply waiting for death to come. She would go out, as it were, to meet it; for she knew it was not death she was to meet, but the ever-living God — and the God of everlasting Life.

That is why she could so insistently tell Sister James Marion and a few other intimates that she was "coming to life." It was true! For this girl realized what so few Catholics realize: that Christianity is not only a Creed, a Code, and a Cult; not only a philosophy and a way of life, but actually a life in itself. As time went on she came to ever clearer realization that the Christian mysteries of the past are mysteries of the present time; that she was actually living the very mysteries she commemorated on her Rosary. It was to her former sodality moderator that she one day explained how, at first, she dwelt long on the Sorrowful Mysteries, thinking that from Christ's Passion and Death she would draw all her strength for living with this thing that meant death to her. But suddenly she felt such joy in her being that she came to view the diagnosis of the doctors as a kind of an "Annunciation" — and then went on to live the Joyful Mysteries of Christ and Mary's Life. Every day there was a "Visitation" as she carried Christ within her and went into patients' rooms like another Mary going to Elizabeth. As for the Nativity, this young girl realized that "He came and He comes." Her query which required no answer was: "Does He not take birth in our hearts at every Holy Communion?"

It was statements such as this that showed this Sodalist was truly "coming alive" with true Christian life. She knew that while she could separate the Fifteen Mysteries into three separate categories for her Rosary, yet in real life there was almost always an intermingling of all three kinds. She had her sorrows, but she also had her joys, and knew her real glory. Unquestionably the Holy Spirit was working with His Gifts in this young nurse, for she was seeing into the realities revealed by St. Paul but so seldom realized by Christians. Her freedom of spirit came from truth. How well Christ had said: "the truth shall make you free" (Jn. 8:32). Joan Gasser was free from all those foolish fears, stupid angers, crippling and even soul-shriveling resentments that seize so many who are found with cancer. The truth she had grasped, and which had gripped her, was the one spoken of by St. Paul when he said ". . . if we have died with Christ, we believe we shall also live with him . . . we are alive to God in Christ Jesus" (Rom. 6:7–11). She came to know what baptism had done to her: set her alive with the life of the risen and ascended Christ. She never said it, but she recognized the fact that it is in the glorified Christ that we Christians "live and move and have our being" (Acts 17:28).

Leo the Great had reason to cry: "Christ's Ascension is *our* exaltation." For he realized that St. Paul was speaking of fact when he said: "together with Christ and in him, he has raised us up in the heavenly realm" (Eph. 2:6). Joan realized she was one with Christ even here on earth, and did not have to wait for union with Him in any future life. Thanks to what is called sanctifying grace she could speak boldly, as boldly as did St. Paul, about living "in Christ Jesus" and tell of Jesus Christ living in her. It was this truth that simplified life for her and made living a very real loving.

Let no one suppose that it was easy. It is never easy to become like Jesus Christ. But it is simple. He has given everyone the means. His Church is there with His seven sacraments, and each of these give the Christ-life — or, as it is called, grace.

Joan Gasser suffered. She suffered in body, in mind, in emotions, in will, in her entire being. That is beyond question. But she knew how to suffer — as Christ's member; and that made all the difference!

Just about the time this Owensboro girl was radiating Christ to all about her, there appeared a motion picture called "Claudia" which is worth recalling just because of the way it highlights Joan Gasser's wisdom. The leading role in the motion picture, that of Claudia, depicted what seems so common today: a young wife whose life is that of a moth or butterfly — just a continual flitting about from one sweet gaiety to another, dipping in and out of all the bright lights in town, sucking what she could out of this sweet pleasure and that. But Claudia did have one redeeming trait: her genuine fondness for her mother. When Claudia learns that her mother is soon to die, all light and gaiety go out of her world. She is filled with pain at the thought of losing her mother. Then David, her husband, bends over the stricken girl and whispers the sentimental lines: "Make friends with pain, Claudia — make friends with pain; and it will stop hurting."

That, as anyone who has suffered knows, is arrant nonsense. So long as pain is pain, it will hurt — and no normal person will ever "make friends with it." But there is a way to make pain bearable. Joan Gasser had found it. It lies in making friends with God — and seeing His purpose in pain.

We make friends with God by being what He wants us to be. He wants us to be Christ's mystical members; and it is that membership which gives highest possible purpose to pain. For once we are His members we can use all pain, no matter what its nature, trifling and passing as well as gripping and excruciating, to "fill up what is wanting to Christ's Passion, for His Body, which is the Church" (Col. 1:24). That is what Joan Gasser did. Thus she became a savior with a small "s," as Bishop Fulton Sheen has so often said, just as Christ became Savior with a capital "S." Suffering can be sublimated into sacrifice. When it is, then the victim is truly Christ-like, and knows how to "glory in his or her infirmities" (2 Cor. 12:9), as did the great St. Paul. That, and that alone, explains Joan Gasser, the dying girl who always said she was always "coming alive."

For three and a half years the dual process went on: the disease gnawing away at her body, while her soul grew. Many, who thought they had known Joan quite well, were forced to confess that it was only toward the end that they saw her real personality in fullest bloom. They marveled at this fact, but had they known the deepest truth about personality they would have ceased wondering. Martin D'Arcy, S.J., has said that "one cannot be a person without being a relation." That statement startles anyone who has been brought up on scholastic philosophy; for it is there one learns that a person is alone, unique, seemingly completely isolated, and is utterly incommunicable. Yet, here is an outstanding Catholic philosopher asserting what sounds diametrically opposed to this view. Yet he proves his point quite convincingly when he says that "as a living and loving relation, the person looks to the term of the relation of which he is a part. Hence, we are really ourselves only when we look to God, not so much to *possess* Him as to *belong* to Him." He goes on to say that "the principal aim of a person is not to *have* God; not to *enjoy* God; but to live *by* Him and *for* Him." That is what Joan Gasser aimed at doing, and that is why her real personality became more and more manifest.

Pere Philippe, a Carmelite, explains Joan and her striking personality, perhaps a bit more fully, when he says: "The person is absolute, yes; but it is also relative. That is not a contradiction; that is only a mystery — the mystery of love which will not be satisfied with the intellectual likeness of the object, but desires to live as it is in itself and to live with a life that is at the same time the life of one and the life of the other. To be a person is essentially to be in search of a person. For a person there must be a person."

Joan could never phrase it that way, but that is the way she lived it; for she actually found the only Person who could make her a real person. She found the Second Person of the Blessed Trinity. He, through the Third Person, led her to the First. The unfolding of her personality to fullest flower can be explained on no other grounds. Christ led her on, and she followed bravely.

Just three years after she first knew she had Hodgkin's, she was admitted as a patient in Mercy Hospital; for the disease now had sapped her strength severely. She was still "smiling Joan" and, after a visit with her, the administrator of the hospital had to exclaim: "In all my twenty-five years working with the sick, I've never seen anything like that girl, nor known a person quite like her. She has been a splendid nurse, and is now a wonderful patient. I have never seen her lose courage, nor manifest any real concern for herself. I just called on her to tell her that one of her former patients was dying, but that she had been received into the Church, and been given the last rites. You should have seen the joy in that girl's eyes! And you should have heard the way she said to me: 'Tell her to tell God that I'm coming; but not just yet.'"

Joan was right. She did not go at that time. She got out of that sickbed and carried on until late May. "Her hour" was not yet over. How like Christ that made her. "His hour" had come at that Last Supper. He stated the fact explicitly: "Father, the hour is come! Glorify your Son, that your Son may glorify you" (Jn. 17:1). But "His hour" did not end in the Cenacle. It ran through the dark of Gethsemani, then on through the dark of the Dungeon, through the Scourging, the thorns and the spittle, on through the trials before Pilate and the fool's robe from Herod, on through the stumbling Way of the Cross, then through the nails in hands and feet, and the Crucifixion with its mockery. Only when the world was darkened toward three o'clock in the afternoon did He cry out "It is consummated." So with Joan. She went on through May, on into June. Then, on the fifth day of that month dedicated to His Sacred Heart, she smiled her last smile on earth. It was consummated. She left what Cardinal Newman has so well called the "shadows and symbols" for the Substance — for Truth Itself.

The Owensboro paper carried a two-column obituary notice, if you care to call it such. It had been written by columnist Charlotte Baumgerten under the title *Sing No Sad Songs*. The author said Joan would not want them. Her article proved that we should not need them. But if the article would keep us from singing sad songs, it would not keep us from shedding tears; for the author told how Joan had kept all worries to herself save one — that about finances. After her second hospitalization, Joan knew her funds were low. She also knew that before "her hour" had run its course there would be a longer and more costly hospitalization. She let this worry slip her tongue in conversation with one of her intimates. Then happened what will profoundly move all who can call themselves human; for the very best in our God-made and God-remade human nature came to the fore. Joan's friends, a group of registered nurses and some technicians at the hospital, devised the plan of having what they would call "Joan's Bake Sale." The idea caught on rapidly. Cakes, contributions, help came from all sides. When these friends brought

the results of their idea to the sick girl, Joan Gasser cried for the
first time since that first night in Lourdes Hall, Louisville, after she
had heard the verdict of her medical men. But her tears now were
those of wonder, and gratitude, and deep humility. This young girl
never knew she had so many friends in Owensboro, nor how generous they could be. But now she knew that neither she nor her family
would have to worry about the mounting hospital bill, nor the expenses that would be incurred after her soul had gone to God.

The last task Joan performed on earth was to write thank-you
notes to those who had taken such a worry off her mind. When that
task was completed, she relaxed; and a few days later entered into
the fullness of life.

How aptly the columnist had titled her article: *Sing No Sad Songs.*
Why should we? This young girl had proved beyond all possibility
of doubt that suffering, when rightly accepted, can bring out human
nature's highest potential; she had shown that truest self-realization,
actual self-fulfillment, lies in self-sacrifice. Joan Gasser had thrust
her young life into the wounded hands of Christ, and let Him use
it, through His Spirit, for the glory of the Father. It was sheerest
truth she had expressed when she said she was always "coming alive."
For suffering, when shared, can be something of a joy. When the
Sharer is God's only Son, it is real glory. That is why it can be
said that the last three and a half years of Joan Gasser's life were
truly glorious.

She had not "made friends with pain," but she had taken pain
and used it for her and our changeless Friend. Deep within her was
the realization that God is God; consequently, everything and everyone lies under His plan and His Providence. Steadily to the surface
of her consciousness came the realization that, from all eternity, God,
in His love and wisdom, had decreed that before she was twenty-one
Hodgkin's disease should take hold of her, for her good and His
glory. Therefore, she would not only accept it gladly, but she would
use it for the purposes He desired. That was what she meant by
saying she "was coming alive." For Christ meant what He said when
He asserted that He had "come that they might have life, and have
it in abundance" (Jn. 10:10). As her physical, temporal life ebbed,
her real life, that share in God's own life, kept swelling toward the

flood. She came fully "alive to God in Christ Jesus" when the last tick of "her hour" was registered with her last earthly breath.

"Faith can stagger on the mystery of pain" — but Faith can also rise, walk steadily, and even run when one realizes, as Joan Gasser came to realize, that God is our Father who, as Cardinal Newman has observed "knows what *He* is about."

There is a *mystique* to suffering. It lies in the assent to the truth that we have died with Christ and consequently live with Him. But this assent must not be merely notional. It must be as real as was Joan Gasser's — an assent not only of the mind, but of the will, and the whole soul and being. Once that is made, we enter fully into the "Pascal Mystery" — that wondrous mystery of death and resurrection; that mystery which proves that sacrifice is creative. Christ's was, infinitely so. Christians can make theirs very close to the same. Then death is not the end, but the beginning; for life has been a liturgy, and what we call death is but the summons of God saying: "Well done, my good and faithful servant, come and share the joy of the Lord" (Mt. 25:21). That, undoubtedly, is what Joan Gasser heard June 5, 1952, as she "came fully alive." Indeed there was, and is, no place for "sad songs."

IV

A LONG HOUR—THAT WAS SHARED

To make life a liturgy, as did Joan Gasser, is the fundamental and final purpose of every human's life. But to many that will only be a puzzle or a problem, and not a plan. These will look upon Carl Miller and Joan as extraordinary people, or at least as people who did an extraordinary thing. Yet, if St. Paul tells us anything, it is precisely that: we are to make our life a liturgy — or fail to have lived. Hence, it is not Joan and Father Carl who have done the extraordinary thing, but only those who do not succeed in accomplishing what these two achieved; for they were but ordinary humans who lived the ordinary Christian life.

That is the fact which faces us with the question: How Christian are we Christians?

To bring this query into sharpest focus you have but to realize that that person who imagines he is being honest — and even humble — when he asks, "How can God, who knows all, ever love a person like me?" knows not what he is talking about. Perhaps you have asked yourself that question. Many people do. For they know they have been guilty not only of undignified acts, unworthy thoughts, and unbecoming words, but of thoughts, words, and deeds that are more than shameful; that are truly sinful. They know their meannesses, their pettiness, their small-souled jealousies, angers, and animal lusts. At such moments they want to echo Francis Thompson and ask: "Whom wilt thou find to love ignoble thee?" But they should go on as Thompson did and add: "Save Me, save only Me," and realize that it is the God of Truth who is speaking. He, the all-knowing God, not only does love you with all your ignobilities, but has "loved you with an everlasting love" — a love that was aflame before the daystar, and one that will not cease to burn unless you cause it to die.

That, of course, gives birth to a further question: one that will answer every other query about God's love. You do not now want

to know "How God can love you?" but *Why* does He love you?"
And it is Paul who has answered that question for you before it was
ever asked. He told his Corinthians, his Colossians, his Ephesians;
he told all his children, and through him it is the Holy Spirit who
now tells you just why God loves you. Hear him telling you today
what he told his Ephesians nineteen hundred years ago: "Out of love
he predestined us for himself to become *through Jesus Christ* his
adopted children, conformably to the good pleasure of his will, to
the praise of his resplendent grace, with which he has adorned us
in his beloved Son. . . . And this good pleasure he decreed to put
into effect when the designated period of time had elapsed, namely
to gather all creation both in heaven and on earth under one head,
Christ" (Eph. 1:5–10). Listen to him speaking to you as he tells
his Colossians: "He it is (God, the Father) who has qualified you
for a share in the lot of the saints in the light, and who has rescued
us from the power of darkness and transferred us into the kingdom
of his beloved Son. . . . He (Christ) is the image of the invisible
God, the first-born of every creature, because in him were created
all creatures in the heavens and on the earth. . . . All have been
created through him and for him. . . . Further, he is the head of his
body, the Church" (Col. 1:12–18).

Let Paul further clarify this matter of why God loves you by
allowing him to speak to you as he did to his Galatians, saying: "You
are all children of God through faith *in Jesus Christ,* since all of
you who have come *to Christ* by Baptism have clothed yourselves
in Christ. . . . You are all one *in Christ* . . . (for) . . . God sent
his Son . . . that we might receive the adoption. And because you
are sons, God sent the Spirit of his Son into your hearts, crying,
'Abba, Father.' You are then . . . a son" (3:26–4:7). Then hear
him saying to you what he said to his Corinthians: "All things belong
to you, and *you to Christ,* and Christ to God" (1 Cor. 3:23). (Em-
phasis added.)

With those inspired truths before you, you can readily understand
the man who says "God sees us through the red mist of His only
Son's Blood." But you can also realize that while such a man speaks
truth, he does not tell the whole of the wondrous truth. No. For
God sees you not only "through the red mists of His only Son's

Blood" but *in* that very Son. And note well that it is not in Him
as Babe of Bethlehem, nor even as Man of Calvary, but in Him as
risen, glorified, triumphant Christ who is at His side right now in
heaven.

That is the fact that turns you to Paul's Epistle to the Hebrews.
For it is in that letter that you will find this little Firebrand of God
giving a synthesis of sacred history and of the Christian life, which
he presents to you in a magnificent vision of one vast liturgy. For he
depicts the whole earthly existence of the faithful as an immense
procession toward that Sanctuary wherein God dwells, into which
they hope to be granted entrance so that they may see Him, know
Him, love Him, praise Him, and offer Him their sacrifices.

The center of this splendid vision is Christ the Priest. With what
vigor and vividness Paul portrays it all! It can serve as excellent
exegesis of those color-filled passages in St. John's Apocalypse in
which he tells of seeing "seven golden lampstands, and in their midst
one like the Son of Man, clothed in a long robe and girded around
the breast with a golden cincture. The hair of his head was as white
as snow-white wool; his eyes were like a flame of fire; his feet were
like burnished bronze smelted in a furnace; his voice was like the
sound of many waters. And in his right hand he held seven stars.
From his mouth there came forth a sharp two-edged sword, and his
face was like the sun shining in full splendor" (Apoc. 1:13–16). Or
again of that blinding fourth chapter wherein John tells of seeing "a
throne set up in heaven, and someone was seated on the throne. The
occupant of the throne looked like jasper and cornelian, and around
the throne was a rainbow like a vision of emerald. . . . From the
throne came forth flashes of lightning, and peals of thunder. . . . Before the throne there was something like a sea of glass, resembling
crystal." Then he tells you of hearing that song of heaven:

> Holy, holy holy, is the Lord God Almighty
> whose name is "He was" and "He is" and "He is coming."

Day and night, John tells you, that chant comes continually from the
"four living beings" who "had six wings" and who were "full of
eyes." Then he allows you to hear the chant of "the twenty-four
elders" as "they cast their crowns before the throne," and sing:

Worthy are you, O lord our God,
to reserve for yourself glory and honor and power,
because you created all things,
and by your will they came into being and were created.

It is all blindingly beautiful. God the Creator occupies that throne
and is adored by those twenty-four elders representing angels who
preside over the unfolding of history as God's ministers. But the most
personal scene, the one which tells you so much about your own
life and the liturgy you are to make it, even as it tells you why God
loves you, comes in the next chapter, wherein John tells of seeing

standing in front of the throne and in the midst of the four living
beings and of the elders, a Lamb as if slain, having seven horns
and seven eyes, which are the seven spirits of God who were given
a mission to the whole earth. The Lamb came and took the scroll
out of the right hand of him who was seated on the throne. When
the Lamb took the scroll, the four living beings and the twenty-four
elders prostrated themselves before him, each having a harp and
golden vials filled with perfumes, which symbolize the prayers of the
saints. They sang a new canticle:

You are worthy to take the scroll and to open its seals,
Because you were slain, and with your blood you redeemed for God
Men of every tribe and tongue and people and nation,
And you made of them a kingdom and priests for our God;
And they shall reign over the earth.

In my vision I heard a chorus of many angels and of the living
beings and elders who encircle the throne. Their number was myriads
on myriads and thousands on thousands. In a loud voice they said,

Worthy is the Lamb who has been slain
to receive power and wealth and wisdom and strength
and honor and glory and blessing.

In the same way every creature that was in heaven and on earth and
under the earth and in the sea, yes, and all things that dwell in
them, I heard saying,

To him who is seated on the throne and to the Lamb
blessing and honor and glory and dominion for ever and ever

The four living beings said, "May it be so." But the elders prostrated
themselves and worshipped him who lives for ever and ever (Apoc.
5:6–14).

How magnificent a scene! That is the liturgy of heaven. But what does it say to us of earth? Paul answers that question by telling you: "Now the main point in what we are saying is this: we have just that kind of a high priest. He has taken his seat at the right hand of the divine Majesty's throne in heaven. There in the sanctuary and the true tabernacle, which the Lord, and not man, has erected, he carries on priestly functions" (Hebr. 8:1, 2). ". . . It is not into a Holy Place made by human hands, a mere type of the genuine, that Christ has entered, but into heaven itself, where he now presents himself in the presence of God on our behalf . . ." (ibid. 9:24). "Therefore, brothers, we have confident access to the Holy Place, thanks to the blood of Jesus, by following the new and living path which he has opened for us through the veil – I mean his flesh; and we have a high priest in charge of the house of God. So let us draw near with a sincere heart, in full assurance of faith . . ." (ibid. 10:19–22). For ". . . he is able at all times to save those who come to God through him, living always, as he does, to make intercession on their behalf" (ibid. 7:25).

That passage practically speaks for itself. But to make surety doubly sure, more than one commentator has said that herein we find the essential themes of this Epistle. For it shows the Christian life as a liturgical procession of pilgrims who seek to approach the sanctuary and appear before God. This sanctuary, of course, is heaven where God is surrounded by tens of thousands of angels and those just men who have already reached the end of their journey. But the point is that even the Christians on earth have also attained the end of their liturgical pilgrimage in a certain way. It is an imperfect way, but it is also a real way. It is thanks to Him who said of Himself: "I am the Way." For Christ has purified us from our sins and sanctified us by the sprinkling of His Blood. He has introduced us, even now, into the sanctuary of heaven, uniting us really to the liturgical assembly of the angels and the saints; that assembly of which He is the eternal High Priest, sitting at the Father's right hand, the Liturgist "always living to intercede on our behalf."

Does not that tell you much about the Mass? Does not that tell you that there is only one Liturgist, Christ, and only one liturgy, that of the glorified Jesus? Consequently, can you not see that the true and

definitive world is the world of heaven, and that the one that seems
to be so real to us here on earth, is but its shadow, figure, and mere
imitation? The whole Epistle stresses the fact that the Jewish liturgy
was but a shadow and figure of the real liturgy performed by Christ,
and consequently, from the principles Paul so expressly stated, it
follows that our own earthly liturgy is a sign and symbol of the heavenly liturgy performed endlessly by Christ. In point of fact the
heavenly liturgy and our earthly liturgy are one and the same reality;
the only difference being one of visibility and invisibility. For in our
liturgy of earth it is Christ Himself who is acting under the veil of
rites and human ministers. The Council of Trent taught this apodic-
tically when speaking of the Mass: "it is one and the same Victim,
who by the ministry of the priests now offers Himself, and who
then offered Himself on the Cross" (D. 940). That is why Dom
Cyprian Vagaggini, O.S.B., could say so absolutely: "In the Mass,
in the sacraments and sacramentals, in the Church's prayer, Christ
is always the principal actor. The Christians, His ministers and His
faithful, are behind Him as His shadow; He carries them all in Himself, identifies them with Himself. The Father regards them as something of Christ. Only thus does He see them, hear them, and love
them. In the liturgy God does not see the action of men, but only
the action of Christ who has incorporated men with Himself."*

Those lines, expressing the truth about life and liturgy on earth
give deeper resonance to Newman's words about *"ex symbolis et
imaginibus in veritate"* (from shadows and signs into truth) and make
one want to capitalize that last word, for it is descriptive of the Word
who said of Himself "I am the Truth." They even clarify Joan
Gasser's life and liturgy, and the final lines about her "leaving shadows and symbols for Substance."

So now you see why God loves you: you are not only someone
He has made, and, consequently, loves as His creature, but some-
one He has *remade in His Christ.* And because He loves His Christ,
He loves you — both for yourself and for your place in His only
Son's Mystical Body. And you can now understand with greater
clarity the life and the liturgy of Father Carl Miller, who wanted to

---

* *Theological Dimensions of the Liturgy,* Collegeville, Minn., 1959, p. 147.

make the Mass his life and his life a veritable Mass. How truly it has been said that "it is the Mass that matters."

Of course there will be those who will argue that it was all relatively easy for a priest like Carl Miller, and a single girl like Joan Gasser, to live "their hour" as they did; for, after all, what earthly responsibilities did they have? No wife, husband, or family to care for – or leave behind. No dependents to cause them concern. So you will have to meet a man who had a wife and a large family – seven daughters and two sons – and learn from him how even those with dependents can make their life a liturgy, and spend "their hour" very like Christ spent His.

On October 9, 1952, John Leonard should have been feeling quite elated; for it was the feast day of his namesake who had been canonized just twelve years previously and whose feast had been added to the general calendar of the Church in 1941. Not too many know about St. John Leonard, founder of the Clerks Regular of the Mother of God. But it was only natural for John Leonard, now of Denver, Colorado, to take special interest in this priest of God who had died in 1609 on October 9, from a disease caught while attending the plague-stricken. As a young priest Giovanni Leonardi had devoted much of his time to the care of the sick in hospitals and those confined in prisons. He attracted many zealous young laymen to himself and set them working in a veritable lay apostolate. But soon he conceived the idea of a new congregation of secular priests for the Propagation of the Faith. As is the case in practically every good work undertaken for God, his provoked powerful opposition, especially in his native city of Lucca, in Italy, and throughout what was then the Lucchesan Republic. This opposition was mostly political, but it was powerful enough to keep John Leonard an exile from Lucca for practically the rest of his life. Yet holiness speaks for itself; and in 1583 the Bishop of Lucca officially recognized the Clerks Regular of the Mother of God with the approval of Pope Gregory XIII; but it was not until 1621, twelve years after the death of the founder, that the Congregation was granted its present name and allowed to pronounce solemn vows. During his lifetime John Leonard enjoyed the friendship and the encouragement of such saints of God as Philip Neri and Joseph Calasanctius. What may

bring him closer to us is the fact that he was very closely associated
with Mgr. J. B. Vives in the first planning of a seminary for foreign
missions, which was later instituted by Pope Urban VIII as the College *de Propaganda Fidei*. St. John Leonard is practically unknown
to us in America perhaps because there is only one house of his
Congregation outside of Italy while even in Italy, owing to the deliberate planning of the Founder, they never have had more than
fifteen churches. Today they are a very, very small Congregation.
But that does not detract in the least from St. John Leonard's very
great sanctity. His miracles and his zeal for the spread of the Faith
are referred to by the Roman Martyrology — which is no mean praise.

So, on October 9, 1952, his namesake should have been returning
to his home in Denver in a state of some elation. But he was far
from that. In fact, he had to practically drag himself into his house;
for he was suffering from a backache, a headache, a high fever, and
general malaise. Nor was this the first day of this miserable feeling.
Leonard suspected what it actually was — polio. He had reason to
suspect; for he had nursed his wife and his eldest child through the
disease which had by this time taken on epidemic proportions. He
told his wife, Mary, what he suspected. She hoped he was wrong,
but suggested a consultation with the family doctor, who ordered
immediate hospitalization. The members of the hospital staff did
not follow the advice of the more wise in the profession who always
insist that you listen carefully to the patient's own diagnosis; for,
frequently the patient is more nearly correct than the professionals.
They diagnosed it as a bad cold, bronchial trouble, maybe a touch
of the flu. But Leonard persisted in his own diagnosis; and time
proved him right. The medical men finally concluded that he was
suffering from spinal bulbar polio. So October 9 was the last time
John Leonard walked into his house. It was the last time he ever
walked at all; for the disease paralyzed him from the neck down. For
the next few months he lived in an iron lung. And during that time
his wife gave birth to their second son, David. That brought the
family total up to nine. John Leonard was then just past his fortieth
year of life. How he must have smiled to himself as he thought of
those who said "Life begins at forty." It did for Leonard; but it was
a mighty strange sort of life.

For the rest of that year of 1952 he lived in the iron lung. Then they moved him to Omaha, Nebraska, where they fitted him for a chest respirator. For the next three and a half years this respirator was his "home." In 1956, John Leonard became one of the first polio victims to be fitted with an intermittent hospital respirator. Surgeons made an opening in his throat and inserted a rubber tube into his windpipe. The opposite end of this tube was attached to an electrically operated bellows which fed a mixture of oxygen and air into his paralyzed lungs. That rubber tube served to keep him alive until April 20, 1961.

That is the story from the medical and the mechanical side. Now hear it from the real, the spiritual side.

"Johnny, you, I, and God can do anything." That is what his wife said to him a hundred times and more between October 9, 1952 and April 20, 1961. And that Trio did just about anything and everything. To some it may sound flippant, if not actually arrogant. But those some have never heard Paul say: *"Omnia possum in Eo qui me confortat —* I can do all things in him who strengthens me" (Phil. 4:13). They know not what real Faith is.

In late 1959 Mrs. Leonard was writing to a cloistered monk and saying:

I am sure there are no mere coincidences with God, so I see Special Providence in the fact that my good husband was stricken with spinal bulbar polio on the Feast of St. John Leonard, his namesake. Our eldest daughter was then eleven; our second son, and baby, "Beppo," was born five months after John was in the iron lung. At that time they performed a second tracheotomy, and the doctors said he could live only twenty minutes. Today, seven years later, he is still alive, still totally paralyzed, on mechanical respiratory aids, though no longer in an iron lung; and I am sure that he has done a greater job for God in his silent apostolate of suffering than if he had been the tremendous success in the business world he seemed destined to be when stricken. John is now forty-eight years old and has been an inspiration to all who have visited him — proof positive that if we accept God's will, He will sustain us solely on Divine Strength until our job or mission in His plan of redemption is completed.

Just last week he was anointed again after coming through a series of crises such as power failure, flu, ulcers — all just this past fall. A few years ago there was gall bladder surgery that made medical history. It seems he has been through just about everything — even fires! One in his own room here at home where we always have three cylinders of oxygen standing. But God has His finger on John's pulse, and, actually, I feel that we never had more security before in all our lives.

Can you picture the hazards while operating on a man while he is in an iron lung? Small wonder that gall bladder operation on John Leonard made medical history. It was something in the nature of a minor miracle. But as yet, you have not the full picture. The letter goes on:

"We have seven daughters, all named Mary, and two sons. That is why we always call our home 'Maryland.' . . ."

The names of the daughters is one explanation of the name of the home, but one wonders if there is not another. St. John Leonard called his Congregation "Clerks Regular of the Mother of God." Is it not likely that John Leonard of Denver would follow in the footsteps of his Patron and be most devoted to the Mother of God?

The letter continues:

. . . John has a brother a Vincentian, and I have a brother an Oblate of Mary Immaculate. He was here last Christmas and offered Mass in John's room, while the girls sang the responses, and our sons served the Mass. God has granted us this privilege not once, but many times. A year ago Bishop McSorley offered the Holy Sacrifice here after his consecration to the Episcopacy.

Now, Father, I have no business intruding into your life, but I am sure you will forgive me when I tell you I am a mendicant for prayers, and come to you begging a remembrance for my John. . . .

I will enclose a poem written by our eldest, now eighteen, and a freshman at St. Mary's College, Kansas — on scholarship, of course! We are the most popular paupers in Denver, but I don't think any of us would have it otherwise, as this is the road God has chosen for us to walk and work out our salvation. . . .

May the peace and joy of our Infant Savior be yours at Christmas and every day.

Gratefully in Mary Immaculate,
MARY A. LEONARD

That letter gives you insight into the heart of the wife. A few stanzas of the poem will give you insight into the heart of one of the children. It is entitled:

To Dad on His Seventh Anniversary
Oct. 9, 1959

For three long hours our Lord, Himself,
   Hung helpless on a tree;
But, dearest one, for seven years
   You've known your Calvary!

Your days have been so strained and hard,
   Your burden so immense:
How often you have ached to cry
   As did Omnipotence:

"I thirst! O God what I would give
   To play one melody;
To breathe one breath, to take one step,
   To raise my family!

"To do the many simple things
   I always took for granted:
To scratch myself, to turn in bed –
   O God, how can I stand it?"

The kindly answer came so soft:
   "Dear John, did you forget?
I ask My loves to suffer much
   Man's black sins to offset."

His Voice brings peace and calm again;
   Each pang becomes a gem.
You seek for pain with this one plea:
   "Father, forgive! Forgive them!"

The time will come when you will hear
   A whisper from the skies:
"Your work is done – today you'll be
   With Me in Paradise!"

You can be sure that cloistered monk was puzzled as to how he
should reply to such a bit of correspondence. These people were
suffering. But they already knew what any priest is supposed to tell
people about suffering: that it is wheat and wine for their "Sacrifice
of the Mass." The priest's function is to orient people to God; but
what could this cloistered priest do for these Leonards who were
already so fixedly God-oriented? He did what he could: he sent

them his blessing, promised them his prayers and those of his confreres, and wished them the joys of the birth of God.

Two weeks later he received a response which ran in part:

How good is the good God? Only eternity can answer that question fully. But we Leonards have a pretty fair idea of that answer.
Your Christmas card, with the note attached, including your blessing
and the news that the entire Community at Gethsemani (200 strong)
would be praying for us throughout the coming year, was just about
the most magnificent gift the Babe of Bethlehem could have given us.
Proof positive that He is aware of how badly we need His help.

He has never ignored our needs . . . and now, knowing that we
have a whole army of Trappist monks behind us with their prayers,
why 1960 will not only be the most glorious year for us, but should
the divine Master call John "Home," I'm confident he will be able
to take heaven by storm. . . .

Recently a Jesuit, visiting John, told him he had used him as
topic for his Thanksgiving Day sermon. I could see poor John squirm-
ing mentally, not wanting to be rude, but very eager to change the
subject — which he did without much delay. After Father had gone
I chided John a bit. . . . His answer, typical of his attitude throughout
the past seven years and more, was: ". . . The only compliment that
could ever impress me is the one I hope to hear on Judgment Day
from the good Lord Himself."

John is growing weaker by the day. He is having difficulty swallow-
ing now, and also talking. That's hard on an Irishman! But his spirit
is eager and ready to go to God as soon as He'll have him. Please
offer Mass, Father, that the journey "going" will be easier for him
than "staying."

                                        Joyfully in Mary Immaculate,
                                        MARY A. LEONARD

Those few lines from this one letter will leave the thoughtful
breathless. For that sign-off "Joyfully in Mary Immaculate" reads
like perfect summation of this woman's spirit. Mary Leonard was
joy-filled. There is no other explanation of the lilt in these lines.
The source of her joy is evident from the opening sentence. It was
God — His paternity — His providence — His love — His constant
care. Obviously, these were realities to this woman; more real than
the sun or the earth. In her complete worldly insecurity she had
found the truest of all security: the Fatherhood of God. Since He
is our Father, she knew He must provide. Here was Faith which

moves mountains; which, of course, gave her that for which so many
are searching in our fast-moving world: balance. Her appreciation of prayer, and of pain that has been turned into prayer, along
with her evaluation of time spent in pain that has been sublimated
into sacrifice, tells the vigor and vitality of her hope. As for the other
theological virtue. . . . Try to picture what life must have been like
for this wife and mother for seven and a half years, and you have
your answer. Were she not utterly in love — and the adjective is
chosen deliberately — with both her God and her husband, she could
never have kept her sanity, let alone her health and sense of humor.

But the thoughtful will also be set wondering who was carrying
the heavier cross out there in Denver: was it the polio victim who
for more than seven years could move only his head, or was it the
wife and mother who had to turn him, and even scratch him, as
the daughter had suggested in her poem, and make every other
single move for him? Those who know anything of the male of the
human species will have some inkling of what it must have meant
to this fairly young man (he was only entering his forties when
struck) to have to lie helpless amid his large family, and have his
wife take over practically all the duties of the head of the house.
How John Leonard must have burned all over — in his mind, imagination, emotions, and in all his body — as day, for him, dragged its
interminable length from east to west, only to drop down into a dark,
and a seemingly endless night, while all about him, even those within
his own home, sped on their ways with ever increasing speed. How
his soul must have ached to see his wife become ever more and more
burdened by him and his condition. How his heart must have almost broken within him as he looked on his nine children and saw
them suffering not only economically, and consequently, socially,
but even psychologically from the necessity that was theirs of living
with a father who was lashed to a bed.

You can see that John Leonard, as well as his wife, had to believe
in God with all his might, all his mind, will, soul, and strength. He,
too, had to have rocklike Faith if he was to stay sane. He had to
believe with all his being that there is divine purpose to pain, else
his whole manly being would cry out, as have some: "If there be a
God, He must be a Monster — a Molloch — almighty Cruelty!"

Seven young girl faces, and two of baby boys, would serve as irrefutable arguments for such a thesis. Then, when he looked into
the eyes of the mother of those nine — eyes he had wooed in wonder,
and something close to worship, not so many years ago — and now
found himself unable to lift a hand to touch her cheek. . . . But John
Leonard had eyes that looked and saw reality, not the mere surface
of reality, as was evident a few weeks later when a culture growth
disclosed that his inability to eat, or even to swallow so much as a
drop of water without feeling as if a fire had been ignited in his
mouth, was due to an excessive yeast growth in his mouth and throat.
When his medical men explained that this was the result of a
cumulative drug reaction which had killed off the normal bacterial
growth in his mouth, and that the fungus had taken over, John
Leonard laughed as well as his paralyzed condition would allow him
and said: "Begorrie, I'll most likely die of an excessive case of over-
medication. Who was the smart man who said something about a
cure being worse than the disease? Well, what next, Lord?" The
doctors looked at the smiling man and wondered. John saw their
wonder and added quietly: "I'll change that last question of mine,
Doctors. I won't ask the Lord what is next. It is His mercy that
conceals the future from us. I'll just ask Him for the courage and
trust to do the job He has assigned me. But now I'll ask you men:
What next?" The doctors prescribed. Mrs. Leonard listened carefully,
and when they had ended their directives, she cheerfully said: "We'll
follow your orders to the letter, Doctors. Now that we know what
we are fighting, we feel better. God will give us the strength we
need and use your medicines as He sees fit."

Just then the youngest of the family, young "Beppo" bounded into
the room, and with total lack of self-consciousness, despite the presence of the doctors, cried: "A million rosaries for you last night, Dad."

"A million?" echoed the father. "You must have been awake all
night, Beppo."

"Naw. Not me, Dad. But my angel was."

When the laughs had subsided, one of the medical men put his
hand on the boy's head and said, "I hope you'll be as good a man as
your daddy when you grow up." The child replied,

"I just hope I can suffer for God like he does."

That, from a seven-year-old boy, tells you the influence John Leonard was having on his children. They were all coming to see that suffering can be a mark of predilection. They were coming to an ever greater appreciation not of the cross, but of the Crucifixion. Christ's liturgy on Calvary was speaking to them of the liturgy they were to make of their lives — and they were listening attentively.

That they were making a liturgy out of their lives was shown by the Associated Press report that was released over the nation September 30, 1959. It told how a family fought to save its ailing father during a power failure. It read in part:

> Mary Colette Leonard, 13, roused from her sleep and stared at the white flakes whipping against the window pane. It was 3 A.M.
>
> The street lights were barely visible. Now, suddenly, Mary Colette could not see the lights at all. It was a power failure. Stunned, young Colette rolled out of bed and stumbled down the stairs. She reached the bedside of her father and quickly pressed a button which cuts in a portable equipment operated by batteries on his electrically powered respirator. . . .
>
> Mrs. Leonard, wakened by her daughter's flight downstairs, went to the basement and started a stand-by generator which furnished power for the regular equipment, vital to her husband's life. Once that was working she tried to phone the Public Service Company. The lines were jammed. She could not get through. She called the Police Department. A dispatcher in the police radio room answered. "John can't live fifteen minutes without his respirator," she told him and then explained her husband's condition. Within five minutes he called back to say that an emergency unit was on the way out. It was reassuring, but Mrs. Leonard kept wondering if her own emergency equipment would keep on working until the police car arrived. She hurried to the basement for another look at the generator. As she opened the door to the basement, smoke bellowed up and out into the kitchen — the standby generator had not only failed, it had burst into flames. She rushed back to John's room and switched back to the battery-operated portable equipment. It worked. John was able to breathe, but now she had no power to operate a suction unit to remove mucous from her husband's throat — another life-preserving necessity. She thought that if she recharged one of the batteries, she might be able to get the suction unit working; but while she bent over to recharge it, the battery exploded. She herself was unhurt, but the battery was useless. Then, as she bent over to check the oil, her dress caught in the fan. In the midst of all this excitement and

critical danger, she managed to say calmly enough: "Don't worry
Johnnie, you, I, and God can do anything."

Three neighbors who had been called, came in, all skilled me-
chanics. They managed to get the respirator working and keep
it working until the police car arrived with the emergency generator.
They were just connecting this when the sun broke through the
clouds, the snow stopped, and the power came on. All tensed for a
few anxious moments, wondering if that power would stay on. It did.
It was now three o'clock in the afternoon. Twelve hours of very real
crises had passed. "I guess the good Lord is still in business," laughed
the near-exhausted Mrs. Leonard. When reporters and photographers
gathered around John Leonard and asked him if he minded if they
took his picture, he smiled and said: "Mind? I'm just thankful to
God to be around to have it taken. He must have more work for me
to do on earth."

They had to have such faith in God and His paternal providence,
for just about this time the National Foundation came out with plans
to withdraw support of hopeless polio victims. The Foundation was
working on the very false assumption that a complete victory over
polio had been achieved by Salk vaccine. Caught in a financial
squeeze because of its entry into a costly research program into
arthritis and birth defects, the Foundation thought themselves justi-
fied in withdrawing from the field of full medical care for polio
patients.

John Leonard had been invalided for seven full years. His daily
drug bill was twenty-four dollars. Aid from Social Security and Welfare was under three hundred dollars a month. Mrs. Leonard had
reason to recall the advice about "when the outlook is bad, try the
up look." She looked up to God and asked: "What now?"

God answered by inspiring State Welfare Director, Guy R. Justis
to denounce the National Foundation. He told them that he considered it unfair to the taxpayers, who pay the bill for public welfare,
for their organization to relinquish responsibility in the care of
severely handicapped individuals. He pointed to the fact that since
the Foundation had funds sufficient to enter into other health fields,
dropping the health care of the chronic polio victims could not
have been based on failure in the Foundation's financial campaigns.
It was on behalf of victims who will need medical services for the

balance of their lives that the foundation funds were obtained.

Justis had a point there; for the National Foundation, which had recently taken this name and entered other fields of research, had originally been called the National Foundation for Infantile Paralysis. Both U. S. Senators from Colorado gave strong support to Justis' complaint. That did it. The Foundation reconsidered its decision, and John Leonard received the help he needed. John, his wife, and his children thanked Justis after they had thanked God.

It was this continual God-consciousness that enabled them to make a liturgy out of their lives, and this consciousness was alive in every member of the family as is instanced in the case of young John Jr. A group of boys had gathered in the Leonard yard, for if one thing could be predicated about the Leonard youngsters it was geniality. The children were not only well liked, they were admired, sought out, and quite generally loved. At any rate, John stood in the midst of his playmates tossing a ball in the air as they talked among themselves. An elder listening would have been prompted to think that youngsters can be unconsciously cruel, for one of the group had begun to boast about the activities of his dad. That led others on to the same kind of boasting. One boy told proudly that his father worked for the Government, another boasted that his father worked for the air lines, a third that his dad was chief engineer at one of the local power plants. Young John kept tossing the ball into the air and catching it as it came down, listening all the while to the various boasts. An older person might have wondered what he could say about his dad who was lying in bed paralyzed from the neck down, and secretly sympathized with the boy. But that would have been misplaced sympathy. As the conversation quieted, John very simply, but very proudly stated, "My dad works for God."

But let no one get the idea that this process of making life a liturgy means that a family is to make a "church" out of their home. The Leonards never did that; John would never allow it. His large sunny room, specially equipped for him, was the center of activity in the Leonard home. Around his bed the children gathered to discuss their problems, air their troubles, tell of their ambitions, ask advice, and get direction. John had lost all power of physical motion except that of moving his head, but he had lost none of his wit, humor, or intellectual curiosity. And his confinement gave him closer and more continual contact with his children whom he loved with all his great heart. Yes, he was Irish and a lover of good music and good company. Before he was stricken he had always made March 17 a gala day. He would don his top hat, white tie, and tails, and put on a family show, well rehearsed by his little troupe of performers — the children. The costumes on the youngsters, though simple, gave the theatrical atmosphere so loved by children. Now that he was flat on his back was no reason, according to him, for not continuing the custom. So every St. Patrick's Day the family dressed in Irish costumes, sang Irish songs, and spoke Irish "pieces," as they put on a little Irish skit in Dad's room.

But it was not only St. Patrick's Day that found the Leonard home throbbing with life, ringing with laughter, and resounding with good music. For while John could no longer play his beloved piano, he could still talk, sing, and entertain visitors. He delighted in company — and was seldom without some; for if he delighted in having visitors, most visitors were more delighted in having him. On entering his room for the first time, some felt nervous and quite self-conscious. But they were not there long before this feeling was completely dispelled; for they soon found that this man, held fast to his bed by practically total paralysis, was getting more out of life than they, or the million others, who frantically rush about seeking material happiness. His cheerful, friendly attitude, his quick wit, his lively intellect soon had them forgetting the petty problems that plagued their lives and set them counting their blessings.

Many wondered at his store of information on all the lively topics of the day and at his profound grasp on so many different subjects. But their wondering ceased when they learned he was able to read and that he used this ability daily; then that he obtained all news reports from his television. When talk veered toward politics, visitors received their greatest surprise for they soon learned that John Leonard was not only versed in politics, he was deeply concerned with statesmanship. If anyone spoke disparagingly of any of his "idols" the person immediately found out that there was plenty of "life" still left in this invalid; for John Leonard could grow eloquent, and argue with all the fire, force, and feeling of a true Irishman.

But as visitors left the Leonard home they had to confess that while they may never have spoken a single word about God, religion, or holiness of life, they always went away inspired and even awe-stricken. For there was an atmosphere in the house, about the children, and especially around John Leonard and his wife, that set them thinking on God and on life's real values and purpose.

You have heard Leonard himself speaking of "his work for God." Were you to listen to some of his visitors you would get a very clear idea as to the nature of that work. Lawrence Welk, the popular orchestra leader, visited him, and the comment on leaving was typical of many others. "It is a meditation just to see him," said Welk. That "meditation" for most took the form of looking at their own "unbearable crosses" again and seeing them in proper perspective; for all, it took the form of returning to life and living with a greater consciousness of God. Those in good health knew a renewal of gratitude to God for His gift. Those with family or domestic problems blushed at their own concern when they saw the unconcern of this paralyzed man and breathed the atmosphere of this home. Others left with a determination to really find God or to return to Him. No one left without being spiritually refreshed. John Leonard's wide-open human heart became the receptacle for a countless number of "troubles," "burdens," "perplexities"; and all who dropped their concerns into that heart left the Leonard home more in love with God because of the almost tangible love for Him found among the Leonards. They also left more in love with their fellowman because of the love that had been shown them by this stricken man and his family. John Leonard knew he had a work to do for God, and he knew how to do it.

When one visitor mentioned John's wonderful courage, the invalid laughed and said: "Courage? What are you talking about, man? Courage connotes a choice. What choice did I have to make? This was given me by God. I only have to accept. And that is the easiest thing we humans do."

As one magazine writer put it: "Through sheer immobility, John Leonard has attained a more far-reaching apostolate than most men with full health and independent action ever dream of attaining." That apostolate ran from prelates, priests, and politicians to nuns, and ne'er-do-wells; for it seemed that it was always "open house" at the Leonards, and countless folk from every strata in society knew it.

When Robert Kennedy, while campaigning for his brother, John, visited the Leonard home, John Leonard said to him: "I'll gladly take ten more years of this," bowing to his paralyzed body, "if God will get your brother into the White House." Then he told how closely he had followed the presidential campaign and how much respect he had for John Kennedy.

As soon as the election was over both Mrs. Leonard and her eldest daughter were heard to say: "I hope God wasn't listening when Dad spoke about ten years more." Who could blame them?

By this time John was operating his household through the aid of an intercom system which carried his voice to every room in the house. One day Mary Agnes, the eldest daughter, heard him calling her. When she went to his room she was asked: "What's this I hear about you having your heart set on going to college?" Mary Agnes admitted that a college education was the desire of her heart. "How do you think we are going to finance that?" asked her father.

"I hope to care for that myself, Dad. There's a Gates Foundation Scholarship which allows a girl to choose whatever college she likes and pays all the expenses. I plan to win that Scholarship."

"How many will be competing?"

"I suppose about eight hundred or more."

"And you expect to beat that crowd?"

"Mommy always says 'You, I, and God can do anything.' So why can't I say the same? You offer your sufferings. I'll pray and work. God will do the rest."

"Hmm. Well, all I've got to say is that you'll have to work like the devil."

Mary Agnes laughed. "I've already been working like the devil, Dad, if he plugs, and plugs, and plugs. Will you offer some of your suffering?"

The stricken man looked long at his daughter. But before she began to feel uneasy under that gaze, John Leonard said: "Mary Agnes, I'll offer all of it. But don't you forget that it is God's will that we want, and not just yours."

"Maybe those two wills will be the same, Dad."

"Maybe," was all her father would say. But before that summer had arrived, there came to the Leonard home the announcement that out of eight hundred and fifty applicants, Mary Agnes Leonard had come out first. The full scholarship was hers. When she laughingly reminded her father that she had "worked like the devil," but felt sure it was his suffering that won the contest, he muttered: "Nonsense. It is just God's will. But let me say I'm proud of you, girl. Thank God, and do it by deeds. Become a scholar. Have you thought of any college as yet?"

"Oh yes! St. Mary's, Kansas, near Leavenworth."

"Well, there's a prison nearby, so I guess you'll be safe."

Whether it was an excess of joy, or the depression that so often follows on great elation, no one can say, but that same evening John Leonard said to his wife: "Mary, I wish I knew some way I could love God more. I feel so helpless this way."

At first these fluctuations of spirit had frightened Mrs. Leonard; for she feared her husband was losing his courage and weakening in Faith. But soon she came to recognize them for what they were: the very human swing of emotion, now up, now down. Her antidote was usually a laugh and the reply: "Johnnie, you, I, and God can do anything." But this evening she herself was conscious of a physical weariness she seldom felt. Little did she realize it was the reaction to the thrill that had been hers when she learned of her daughter's success. So it was with real seriousness that she pondered his question, and found answer only after she had looked deep into her own heart and saw there what real love is. Then she quietly bent over the bed and said: "Johnnie, I think I know what you mean. But isn't it true that there is only one way to love God perfectly? Isn't it all a matter of doing the one thing He asks us to do this one moment? If that is the case, don't you see that you could never please God any more than you are pleasing Him right now by lying here helpless just because that is His will for you at this moment?"

The profoundest theologian could have given no better, nor more correct a reply. Omnipotence needs our impotence in which to exercise His power. That is what Paul learned when he begged to be freed from his infirmities. That is what every Christian must learn if he is to live "his hour" aright. John Leonard may have yearned to conquer worlds for Christ, but all Christ was asking him at the moment was to lie impotent. By doing that "in Christ," he was, in his own way, "omnipotent"; for he was "filling up what is wanting" to that omnipotent Sacrifice of the Christ.

Early in 1960 John Leonard was shown how he was "to love God more"; for when the doctor came one morning in late February to take some blood specimens he found his patient with a distended abdomen and seemingly in greater pain than ever. The medical man stood by the bed in perplexity for a few moments. He decided to forget about the blood specimen; for it would only cause the patient more pain. But what was he to do about that abdomen? The symptoms looked like those of uremic poisoning, but what was he to do about it? He could not give John Leonard any antibiotics lest that fungus in his mouth and throat flare up again. He examined his arms and legs and shook his head. No place even for a hypo — scar tissue from so many injections was too thick. He spoke a few words of encouragement to the patient, then nodded to Mrs. Leonard to see him outside John's room. Once there he said to her: "You'd better have John anointed again, Mrs. Leonard. If this thing is what I think it is — uremic poisoning — I don't see how he can last more than a few weeks."

That sent the woman to the phone not only to call the priest but also to call her four eldest daughters who were away at boarding school. She gave them the doctor's verdict but quickly added that no doctor is infallible and that they had already seen many a similar verdict voided by God. Nevertheless they were to renew their efforts, prayers, and sacrifices. Then she wrote to her cloistered friend telling him the latest developments and asking him to offer a triduum of Masses "for a happy death for John." She closed that letter with "Don't think I've given up hope. I still believe in miracles; for I'm living with one every minute of the day. Yet one must be realistic as well as hopeful as we let God do with us as He pleases."

By this time that cloistered priest knew that Mary Leonard was no alarmist, so he offered those three Masses immediately and prepared himself for word that God had heard the request offered with those Masses and that John Leonard's long "hour" had passed into the endless *Now* of bliss. But weeks went by without that word. Winter melted into spring. Easter was nearing when a letter arrived from Xavier, Kansas. It was from Mary Agnes, the eldest of the family, who was now at St. Mary's College. "Wednesday," she wrote, "begins an Easter vacation which I can't help but feel will be unforgettable; for Daddy has been suffering more than ever lately – something I thought impossible. He was anointed again last Friday, for the doctor says he has uremic poisoning to a normally fatal amount. I can see from Mother's letter that she herself is in a daze. So pray for her as you pray for Daddy. Pray for all of us. I think we are ready and even hope that we will all rejoice should Daddy depart during this season that marks His departure and His resurrection."

But Mary Agnes had no sooner arrived home from school than John's Vincentian brother, Father Lawrence, arrived from San Antonio. He brought Holy Communion to John and the entire family Holy Thursday night and each day thereafter until Easter Sunday, when he offered Mass in John Leonard's room. John Jr. and young Beppo served him while the girls formed themselves into a choir. John Leonard rallied after that. Unquestionably the Mass and Communion account for his spiritual renewal, but his emotional elation also came from the fact that on Holy Saturday night young Mary Agnes had asked him if she could enter the Convent in the coming fall. The paralyzed man closed his eyes for a moment. When he opened them again they were misted over with tears, and his firstborn heard him say: "There have been many selfish elements in my 'cross,' Mary A. One of the deepest was that I might see some fruit from my sufferings before I went 'home.' This decision of yours has given me more than I ever expected, and much more than I have ever deserved. Now I can truly say: 'Any time, dear Lord.'"

Easter passed amid much calm joy for the Leonard household. But Easter Monday morning found John Leonard again with an excruciatingly sore mouth and throat, so sore that he could not receive Holy Communion or even say "Good-bye" to his brother, Father Lawrence. That departure was packed with emotion. But that very afternoon God changed the atmosphere in the Leonard home by a phone call from New York City: Mary's Oblate brother, Father John, was calling from the dock. He had just arrived unexpectedly from Rome. He flew to Denver the next day and ten minutes after his arrival the family sat in to its one and only family reunion dinner of the vacation. It was a noisy affair at which everyone talked at once, time being too hurried for anyone to listen. They were celebrating Father John's 43rd birthday, Mary Kathleen's 10th, and Mrs. Leonard's 45th. Two hours later, the family was separating again; as Mary Agnes had to get back to her school, and the three next girls were due at St. Gertrude's Academy, at Boulder, Colorado. John Leonard found his voice again as they were leaving and after the last had noisily gone out the door he turned to Father John with the remark: "Isn't youth wonderful! As has been so well said, 'Too wonderful to be wasted on the young!' "

There was Mass in John's room the next four mornings with the two boys serving, as Mary and her three youngest daughters assisted from the side of John's bed. Father John enjoyed those days as he had enjoyed few in his life; for this was his first semblance of a vacation in over seven years. No one knew where he was, so there were no phone calls to answer, no schedule to meet. Nothing to do but relax with his only sister and her inspiring husband. Yes, Father John Walsh, O.M.I., found John Leonard inspiring. As he was leaving to resume his arduous task as American Visitor to the various missions the Oblates conduct in foreign lands, he said to his sister: "It's stupendous, Mary! I've never seen such composure in all my life. I can carry on now, and God help me if ever a complaint passes these lips of mine again."

He could carry on with greater confidence, for in one of their quiet chats John Leonard had told him how he had consecrated every Monday, with all its sufferings, to be offered with every Mass for the missions. He had instructed the children to do the same. Then he chuckled as he added: "Mary, of course, wants all those offerings channeled toward the Oblates' missions."

You will wonder what size hourglass God had chosen for this man in Denver when you learn that he not only conquered the uremic poisoning, lived through that spring and summer, but well into the fall before another crisis came. This time it was his liver that had swollen. This, of course, gave him intense abdominal pain. But what caused him the greatest distress was that fact that his body itched from head to foot. He could not move a finger to ease that itching. His wife and his children did what they could to relieve him. But often they scratched until blood came and yet the sufferer had to confess he was still itching. After one such session John Leonard spoke words that reveal the secret of his success. A priest had exclaimed: "How does he stand it?" John overheard, and smiled. He beckoned the priest nearer his bed and quietly explained: "I say much the same as you say at every Mass, Father. I say 'This is Your body, Lord. This is Your blood.' I can do that, can't I, Father; for I *am* His member."

Many had compared John Leonard to Jesus Christ on the cross; for all either could move was his head. But how many ever realized how like Christ this paralyzed man was? His words to that priest show how truly he was making his life a liturgy – a veritable "Mass."

Advent of the year 1960 came. Eight full years had passed since John Leonard had come home on his patron's feast day feeling ill. Then on Christmas Eve his brother, Father Lawrence, arrived from Texas with permission to offer Mass in John's room every day of the Christmas season. The Leonards had a Midnight Mass of their own that year; and it was followed by the Mass of the Aurora, and then the Mass of the Day. John Leonard was very happy that Christmas Day; for in less than twenty-four hours four Masses had been offered in his own private room. He knew he was God's son, and even God's favorite son. But that evening he was all father; for the family gathered in his room to produce a Christmas play that had been written, directed, and staged by the older girls with the youngsters in the starring roles. Mary Kathleen, aged eleven, played Mother Mary, while Beppo, aged seven, played St. Joseph. John Jr. was the narrator, and Mary Dorothy, aged nine, looked lovely as an angel with wings made from coat hangers covered with tin foil.

During the following week the family gathered in John's room every evening for a celebration of some sort; and since he was feeling comparatively well, all enjoyed the week immensely.

Before the end of that vacation the Leonards had something really new in their home. A local construction contractor had sent a man over to – as Mary Frances put it – "literally 'raise the roof.' " The man inserted a plastic dome about forty inches square in John's room. The invalid could now have his fill of stars and the night sky. Lights went out early in John's room the last few nights of the year 1960, and you could find the family there, some huddled on the bed with John, others crowding around it; all with eyes uplifted to the stars.

On New Year's Day Mrs. Leonard was writing to friends: "I can't believe that God has given John and me another year to start out together. This is the ninth of his sickness. All I can do is keep on saying 'Thank You' to God — and I say it in Chinese, as a friend of mine told me that in that language 'Thank you' means 'Do it again.'"

But God was not to hear that "Thank You" in Chinese; for, from all eternity, He had decreed that, before 1961 had known the full glory of spring, John Leonard's "hour" would be ended.

Easter that year, fell on April 2. The lilies for the feast were just fading as Mary Agnes was hurrying off night letters which told how her daddy had met death with the words "My Jesus" on his lips at 9 P.M. April 20. Did she realize all the truth she had put in those words? Christ said "I shall come like a thief in the night" and He had been speaking of death. So the Angel of Death is no other than Christ Himself. No wonder John greeted Him by name, and even called Him "My Jesus." Mary Agnes had promised to follow those night letters with full details, but before she kept her promise Mrs. Leonard herself had written to her cloistered friend saying:

> On the Saturday preceding his death, Msgr. Campbell visited. John told him he felt the end was near. No great change was evident to me, so it was not until Wednesday that I called the Doctor. Several times that day John had mentioned that he was sure that this was the end. When I described the change which had begun that day to the doctor, he said that John was suffering from oxygen starvation. I increased the pressure on the respirator. When I noticed a glassy look in John's eyes I phoned the rectory to ask the Monsignor if he would anoint John again. He had one of his assistants here in five minutes. As the four youngest came in from school that day they were somewhat surprised, but I was happy to have them present for the administration of the sacrament. Then, as always before, John gained strength; we could see color returning to his cheeks. The delirium left him, but he seemed to grow weaker during the night. Thursday morning the assistant to the pastor brought John Holy Communion.

As the day wore on I decided to call the girls from the Mount in Boulder and then put in a call to Xavier, Kansas, and told the head of the drama department to get a "stand-in" ready to take Anne's part in the play that was to go on Friday and Sunday night. At five in the evening Mary Agnes called the Dean and told her to put Mary Anne on the first plane available – which meant Friday morning for poor Anne.

The girls came in from Boulder about 4 P.M. John recognized them all. They were shocked by the way he looked. He had been unshaven for two days, and his color was bad. We had two tanks of oxygen on now; one into his trachea and one into his mouth.

We spent the evening around his bed saying the Rosary and aspirations. Finally I started the Prayers for the Dying. This was the third time I had said them for my husband, and I felt that the third time would be the finale. I couldn't quite make it kneeling on the floor, as I wanted to be up by the bed, breathing the prayers into his ear, so Francie took over. She couldn't make it at all. So Joan took over and went right through, leading the Litany for the Dying down to the last Amen. God bless her!

About an hour before he left us, a great peace and tranquillity came over him. The struggle was over. We had said the prayer to St. Michael the Archangel to defend him in the battle, and the angel did his job well. My arm was around his head with my finger on the pulse in his temple. When the pulse changed I had the girls call the Monsignor, Father Dan, the doctor, and John's brother, Pete, who had just arrived in town that morning on business from Chicago. God had arranged that he be here. They all made it on time with the exception of Father Dan. The pulse stopped, but Doctor Phil Clarke said he could detect heart action for some time. We continued to pray. No struggle, no final gasp, no death rattle. Doctor Phil turned off the respirator, and we knew it was over.

"Daddy is in heaven." – It seemed to chorus throughout the room through the tears of human grief. Theirs was no hysteria – grief and sorrow, yes, but *joy* commensurate with it.

Why wouldn't there be joy – this family had shared the long, long "hour" of a man who was their father and who had lived and died "in Christ Jesus"; and it was He who had prayed to His Father the night before He died that "they may taste my joy made perfect within their hearts" (Jn. 17:13).

That Mrs Leonard was telling of fact is evidenced by her closing lines: "My sentiments are those written by Mary Agnes in the enclosed poem which was attached to nine roses on top of John's casket. They had tried all over town to get white roses, with no results. Then in the late afternoon a florist called to say he had obtained just nine — would they do? Would they!"

The poem read:

> Daddy, love, you made it home;
> You won your battle strong!
> A tribute? — No, you have our hearts;
> For with you they belong.
>
> Yes, our hearts are all united
> With your own, so stanch and brave.
> So we bought these nine white roses
> As symbols for your grave.
>
> They simply say: "We love you."
> For your Irish, selfless deeds;
> But most of all they thank you
> For planting them as seeds.
>
> They beg, too, Daddy dearest,
> That you prune them from above,
> So their lives will also blossom
> Into *paralyzing* love!
>
> Then, as the almighty Gardener
> Reaches down to pluck each bloom,
> We will hear our Daddy calling:
> "Come, my darlings, I've made room!"
>
> Again we'll be together
> Free from pain, and space, and time,
> To live and love together —
> Daddy, Mom, and roses nine!

In our so-called realistic age there will be some who will call that "sentimentality." But others who are more realistic may well ask: "What is wrong with sentimentality — especially with this kind?" To them it will be seen that Mary Agnes is only saying in her own words what the great St. Paul said in his to the Romans: "I exhort you, therefore, brothers, in view of the mercies of God, to offer your bodies as a sacrifice, living, holy, pleasing to God — such as is the worship of mind and soul . . . be transformed by the renewal of your mind, that you may investigate the will of God . . ." (Rom. 12:1, 2).

That is exactly what John Leonard had done: he had "offered his body as a sacrifice"; he had made his life a liturgy; for he had made it a "Mass." His children would do the same, and thus make life the only success that can be called success.

V

A LITTLE CHILD SHALL LEAD THEM

God never makes a mistake. That irrefutable truth is one that is too often refuted by our attitudes and sometimes even by our actions. Yet it is the one truth that can stabilize our world for us no matter what upheavals are shaking it. Cardinal Newman with his remark that "He (God) knows what He is about," has given us the most potent tranquilizer obtainable. But, alas, how often we fail to use it!

The fact is that dust gets in our eyes, the dust of this world, and we cannot see clearly. That is why we need Faith; for, far from being "blind," as is too often said, Faith is an eye-opener. St. Paul put it plainly enough: "Faith is the foundation of the blessings for which we hope, the proof of the realities we do not see" (Hebr. 11:1). But those are the true realities, and the ones we need to see! "By faith we understand that the world was fashioned by God's word in such a way that what is visible has an invisible cause" (*ibid.* 1:3). That invisible Cause is God. So how can we avoid the conclusion that every creature, without exception, has place and purpose in God's plan; an important place, and an infinitely wise purpose?

Once we have arrived at that conclusion, and have given it a "real assent" and not merely a "notional" one, then we can do as Paul exhorted in this same vital Epistle; we can "eagerly throw ourselves into the struggle before us, and persevere, with our gaze fixed on Jesus, the pioneer and perfect embodiment of confidence. He, in view of the joy offered him, underwent crucifixion with contempt for its disgrace, and has taken his seat at the right hand of God's throne. Meditate on him who in his own person endured such great opposition at the hands of sinners; then your souls will not be overwhelmed with discouragement" (*ibid.* 12:2, 3).

Faith in Christ gives the answer to every difficulty, but to none more clearly than to the puzzling one called "suffering."

Christ, and our relation to Him, as members of His Mystical Body, solves the otherwise insoluble mystery of pain not only for the aged, the adult, the adolescent, but even for newborn babes.

The liturgy of the Church teaches truth with such tangibility that no one can fail to grasp it if he will but open his eyes and see, and not merely use his eyes to look. Christmas Day, with its lessons from the birth of Christ, is not over before there is an announcement of a death which is to be commemorated on the next day. In point of fact, holy Mother Church, changes the white of Christmas Day for red on the days immediately following Christmas as she has us celebrate the feasts of the first martyr, St. Stephen, then of the last living Apostle, St. John, and the slaughter of the Innocents. This last commemoration is the one that puzzles those whose eyes are not made clear-sighted by the light of surface-piercing Faith. "The cry heard at Rama — the weeping and the sore lament; the unconsolable Rachel who wept for her children because they were no more," not only deafens them to angel song that shepherds heard, but blinds them to the reality Magi found. They lack Faith. Hence, they are without "proof of the realities which they do not see." They weep with Rachel instead of rejoicing with Augustine who cried: "O how happily born were they whom eternal life met on the threshold of existence" (1st Sermon on the Innocents). The Bishop of Hippo had Faith. He saw; he did not merely look. Hence, he could say: "Behold, the profane enemy could never have benefited the little ones with kindness as much as he did by hatred. Do you ask how? Simply because he gave them the dignity and glory of Eternal Life almost before they had received the temporal one." The liturgy for this feast opens with the words: "Out of the mouths of infants and sucklings Thou has perfected praise, O God, to confound Thine enemies" (Introit of Mass of Holy Innocents). You have no greater enemy than that world which stirs up so much dust and clouds your vision. So you need to learn from infants. Here are a few who are magnificent teachers. . . .

Kay Trotter was in her early seventies. She sat in her Seattle apartment just ten days before Christmas, 1960, thinking of her scattered family. They were all married now and settled along the Pacific slope: three in Washington, one in Oregon, and the last two in California. She smiled happily as she thought back on those

Christmases when her big concern was dolls and toys for her own youngsters. Actually those years did not seem so far away from her as she sat in the gathering dusk of this December afternoon, and yet not only the figures on the calendar but the fact that she now had to busy herself about dolls and toys for great-grandchildren told her they were very far away. Kay started to count quietly to herself. As she softly said "And Betty's next will make my twentieth grandchild, while young Margie-Kay is due to give me my fourth great-grandchild," she rose from her rocker and started toward the kitchenette, adding: "I *must* be getting old — four great-grandchildren!"

But before she had plugged in her percolator, the phone rang. It was one of those long, insistent rings, which so often tell of a long-distance call. Kay lifted the phone and with a quizzical lilt in her voice said: "Yes?"

"Grandma?" came a young voice, edged with excitement. "This is Mickie, down in Pacifica, California. Daddy told me to call you and tell you Mother had her baby. He said he wished you could be here."

"Why, child, doesn't he realize that Christmas is almost on us?"

"I don't know, Grandma; he just told me to tell you that. He is at the hospital with Mother. I am all alone. The kids are all out playing."

"Is it a boy or a girl, Mickie?"

"Daddy didn't say, Grandma. He was in an awful hurry. He was real excited. Maybe he'll call you later."

"I wish he would. If he calls you again, Mickie, tell him I'm very proud of him and Betty, and that I'd love for him to call."

The child, Betty's second eldest daughter, hung up. Kay Trotter placed her phone back on its cradle thoughtfully. Could anything be wrong with Betty? she wondered. It was not like her son-in-law, Bill, to do things this way. What could he have meant by saying he wished she could be there? He had never said anything like that at the other births — and there had been seven of them. Slowly she made her way back to her kitchenette and rather distractedly resumed the preparation of her light supper. That "wish" of Bill's haunted her.

She was just washing the last of her few dishes when the phone rang again. Surely, this could not be Bill calling from California so soon. It wasn't. It was another son-in-law, Pat Campbell — the ever cheerful, always practical Pat.

"How you feeling, Mum?" was his greeting. She had not really answered before he went on with, "How would you like to take a plane ride tomorrow?"

"Pat! What in the world are you talking about?"

"Airplanes, Mum. Look, I just got a ticket for the 8:15 tomorrow morning. That ticket will allow you to ride down to 'Frisco. It's excellent flying weather, and I know it's high time a young girl like you should be going places."

"Pat, get serious. What's this all about?"

"About you and a plane ride to 'Frisco tomorrow morning. You see, Mum, Betty wants a special Christmas present. She wants it early. And you're it."

The voice was cheery, but Kay Trotter had known Pat Campbell a long time; his cheeriness did not fool her. "Is Betty ill, Pat?"

"No, Mum. Not really ill. But she's not feeling too well. I just got a call from Bill. He said there's nothing to get excited about, but that you would be just the medicine Betty needed. So be a good Mum and get packed. I'll be over for you early in the morning."

They chatted for a few moments more, but no further information was given; for Pat Campbell did not have any more to give. But he had hardly hung up when Kay Trotter's phone rang again. She picked up the phone with an energy that bespoke excitement. She immediately recognized the voice that came from the other end of the line. It was that of Margie-Kay, Betty's eldest daughter, married just over a year and expecting her first child within a few months. "I'm in 'Frisco, Grandma. . . ."

"What are you doing there, child? Is something terribly wrong with your mother?"

"No, Grandma. It's the baby. Daddy called me early this after. I came right up. . . ."

"What's wrong with her?"

Sobs broke from the other end of the line. "She's a mongoloid. . . ."

"Mongoloid!" repeated Kay Trotter. Stunned, she stood there with the phone to her ear, wide eyes staring straight ahead. Then those eyes snapped and Kay Trotter spoke in a strong, steady, kindly, but commanding voice. "Don't cry, Margie-Kay. God never makes a mistake. He knows exactly what He is about. Tell your mother I'll be down the first thing in the morning. Pat got me a ticket for the 8:15 plane. Please stop crying, child. Go out to your mother and tell her God knows what He is doing. . . ."

"She does not know," came the tear-choked words.

"What do you mean? Haven't they told her?"

"Not yet, Grandma. I think maybe Daddy wants you down for that purpose."

Kay Trotter caught her breath at that announcement, but Margie-Kay would never know what her words did to her Grandma for it was almost a cheerful voice that said: "O.K., child. That's what mothers are for. I'll be down. You'll be there, won't you?"

"Yes, Grandma. Stuart and I are staying over. Pray for poor Mother. . . ." It was the mother-to-be in young Margie-Kay crying out.

The older, wiser woman answered: "Of course I'll pray, child; but don't call your mother 'poor.' She has a treasure from God. She's infinitely rich."

Margie-Kay hung up. Kay Trotter placed her own phone back on its cradle shakily as she softly asked: "O dear God, why . . . ?" But then she caught herself. "Forgive that question, Lord. I know You could have given Betty the most brilliant child in all the world. But this is Your child every bit as much as that other one would be. Help Betty. . . ." Then she herself sobbed as had Margie-Kay.

It was a long night for Kay Trotter, but one of very little sleep. She tossed from side to side thinking of Betty, and all this would mean to her and her seven growing children. She thought of Bill, Betty's husband who was a convert to the Faith. Would this shake his new-found beliefs? She thought of the child. . . . She had never seen a mongoloid, so she knew not how to picture this child. In fact she knew next to nothing about such children, save that they were often imbecilic. She tossed some more and managed to talk to God about Betty, Bill, their children, and their newborn babe. She was up early.

"What a lucky mother I have," was Pat's greeting as he strode into the apartment with hardly a knock. His quick eye took in the suitcase and the coat laid out ready to be snapped up. His smile broadened. "When I stopped to pick up your ticket, Mum, they told me that a cancellation on the jet had just come in. So now you go to 'Frisco in real style."

"A jet! Planes are bad enough. But a jet. Oh, Pat!"

"You'll love it," said Pat as he helped her into her coat. Then snatching up her bag he continued, "It'll have you in 'Frisco before you know it. Yes, you'll love it."

Getting on the huge plane she was actually scared. But once it had shot up through the clouds and leveled off, Kay Trotter sat back and began to enjoy herself in a way she never expected to. The sun was brilliant in the high blue. Below her was a world of fluffy whiteness such as earth never shows, with, here and there, cloud curls tinted gold, looking very like crested waves breaking into sun foam. She had just settled back comfortably and was taking in the endless stretches of this shoreless sea when it was announced that they were over Portland. Kay could not believe it. She looked down, and through a break in the cloud field saw the silver path of the Columbia River. Beyond that was the city. How tiny it all looked. How tidy! Her son, Bob, lived there. She wondered if he knew about Betty. Could that be snow on those mountaintops? It was. The jet was knifing its way south. Salem, Eugene, Medford appeared very little apart. Kay Trotter found herself gasping in surprise and praying in admiration. God seemed very near. The worries of earth seemed remote and trifling. Everything about her spoke of serenity, sovereignty, divine Supremacy. Kay Trotter was actually adoring, but with such joy and ease that she had to whisper: "O, dear God, would that it was always as pleasant to pray as this! You seem so near, so real — the only Reality! — so good, powerful, beautiful!" She closed her eyes in sheer delight. When she opened them she looked down on what appeared to be rumpled green velvet. She knew she was over California, yet she could hardly believe it. She was not out of Seattle more than an hour!

With something like a start she looked around. She had not noticed before that the plane was completely filled. She had been too frightened at first. Then, too absorbed in God and His beauty. She noted now that most were fastening their seat belts. Could that mean that they were nearing San Francisco? She looked down. Yes, there was the magnificent Bay. How small it looked from this height. There were the bridges — tiny silver gray threads stretching from land to land. They were now descending — or was the earth coming up to meet them. This plane was so quiet in its flight! There was the air-port. A glance at her watch told her it was not quite 9:45. Not an hour and a half ago she waved good-bye to Pat up at the other end of this Pacific slope. "How wonderful!" she exclaimed to herself, then followed the other passengers down the steps. She looked toward the gates. There was Margie-Kay — but where was her smile of welcome? There was her husband beside her. How serious he looked! "Oh Grandma!" cried Margie-Kay and tears were in her eyes.

Kay Trotter kissed her, held her off a bit and asked: "What are you crying about child? Has anything new happened?"

"No. But isn't it awful?"

"Birth is never awful. What are you thinking about, child?" and Kay Trotter turned to Margie-Kay's husband. "Where do I get my bag?"

During the ride out to the hospital the wise grandmother kept Margie-Kay talking about herself and her own pregnancy, once she had learned her own daughter, Betty, was doing all right. It was a successful subterfuge. But once they arrived at the hospital, Bill, Margie-Kay's father and Kay Trotter's convert son-in-law, met them at the door. He broke down in sobs.

"Grip yourself, boy. How is Betty?"

"She's just been told. . . . Thank God you're here."

"Can we go right up to see her?" asked Kay. She knew the value of action in such a crisis. Bill wiped his eyes and led the way. Outside the maternity floor they met Betty's obstetrician. He bowed to Mrs. Trotter and said something about Nature's strange ways, adding "I've just suggested to your daughter that she place the child in a state institution. She did not seem to understand. I hope you will orient her. . . ."

Kay Trotter's look silenced him. He bowed the little party into the maternity ward. At the desk Bill greeted the family doctor. He introduced his mother-in-law, and the entire group headed for Betty's room. The girl sobbed brokenheartedly and clung to her mother. Kay quieted her quickly with "Hush, child, we're all here now and will care for you and your little angel."

That last phrase was the one the family doctor took up as he practically took over the whole scene. Speaking directly to Betty with an occasional turn to Bill he asked that no decision about the child be made until he had brought them a book by a Redemptorist, a Father Breitenbeck, who had written *For Parents of Retarded Children.* The very title seemed to fascinate Betty. She vaguely awoke to the fact that she was not alone in this predicament. There must be others, else no such book would ever have been written. She paid more attention to her family doctor. Bill, too, was eagerly listening. "Have you seen the baby yet?" the doctor asked.

Betty shook her head. The doctor saw the fright in her eyes and very quietly but enthusiastically said: "I'll bet she's beautiful. Many of these children are. And have you two realized that this child will never offend the good God? Most likely she will never know right from wrong. So, once you have her baptized, you'll have a living 'angel' in your home."

Kay Trotter silently blessed the doctor for having said such a thing. Betty's face had completely changed as the truth of his words made their way to her stunned brain. "I never thought of that," she confessed slowly and looked at her husband.

The doctor turned to Bill and said, "Your love and care of this child could very well be your through-ticket to heaven."

Bill brightened. "Bring the book for Betty if you like, Doc. As far as I'm concerned my mind is made up. The child comes home. We'll name her as we planned, Betty. She'll be our angel, Melissa Maureen."

Betty smiled for the first time that day. But then hesitantly asked, "But . . . how about the other children? Won't this child influence them?"

"Indeed she will!" said the doctor. "She might very well make saints of all of them. They will love her, Betty. Take my word for it. But let me have them bring the baby in."

"Isn't she beautiful!" exclaimed Betty as she held the child out before her, then cuddled her to her heart.

"Beautiful is the word," cried Bill even as his eyes misted again.

Mrs. Trotter, who had maintained a discreet silence throughout the scene, now moved to Betty's side. "Let me hold her!" she said.

Betty's eyes were alive with joy as she lifted the infant to her mother. "She is beautiful. Melissa Maureen. . . . She's as beautiful as her name."

"She'll be even more beautiful once you have her baptized," said the doctor as he bowed to the nurse to take the child back to the nursery. He then excused himself. When Bill followed him out of the room to thank him for what he had just accomplished with Betty, the doctor talked to him even more earnestly about taking the baby home.

"You don't have to argue with me, Doc," said Bill. "That has been my desire all along. Down deep in her, I think it is Betty's too. But she was afraid for the sake of the other children. There are six still at home, you know."

"Youngsters today need to learn selflessness. Melissa Maureen will give them that lesson almost hourly. I believe you are right about Betty, too, Bill. That look on her face when she saw the child. . . . She would not be happy without it."

Before Christmas had come, Melissa Maureen had become a member of Christ, a child stamped indelibly as belonging to God for all eternity. Baptism had worked its wonder, and Betty and Bill had their "living angel" under their own roof.

Kay Trotter spent Christmas in Pacifica, California, contrary to all the plans she had so carefully laid. But she admitted to herself that it was one of the most enjoyable Christmases she had spent in many a year. Betty's youngsters, with their excitement over the new baby, and all the usual commotion of a young and large family at this happy season, took her back to the years when her own were the same age as Betty's, and had been just as noisy and excited. Happy childhood and happy parenthood of such children, were the thoughts that filled her mind and heart each evening as she helped prepare the children for bed. But every evening, too, she would look at Betty and look long at Melissa Maureen. The child was beautiful now she realized, but she also realized all that any normal child takes out of a mother during the years of babyhood, and then reflected on the fact that Melissa would always be a baby and always a care for Betty. She conjured up the heartaches and the near heartbreaks ahead and quietly, but very earnestly turned to prayer.

She resolved to enlist others in this apostolate of prayer for her daughter and her grandchild, who undoubtedly could be called an "angel," but one who would demand constant human care. She wrote to her friends in religion and all her clerical friends telling them about Betty and the child, and asking them to pray God for all the graces necessary to care for this "image of Him" whose surface was misted, as it were.

These letters were written from the heart, and they appealed to the hearts of each of the recipients. They were alive with that "God-consciousness" that makes of life what it was meant to be by God: a divine romance. Hence, they not only showed Kay Trotter's living Faith, but aroused the Faith in all her friends to greater life; for most of those missives ended with the words: "They are all now not only resigned but very happy with Melissa. Thank God with me."

"Thank God" for a mongoloid? How many humans could measure up to that request? Yet, not to do so shows how false a concept of God, His Fatherly Providence, His Wisdom, and His Love so many of us have.

From the reactions of acquaintances to the news of Melissa's birth, Kay Trotter came to understand why saints like Philip Neri would go about lamenting in the phrase: "Poor Jesus Christ! Poor Jesus Christ!" For so many of them greeted the announcement with exclamations such as "Oh, what a shame!" or "How terrible!" Hence, she was greatly consoled by letters from her friends in religion who saw both the human and the divine sides to this gift from God.

One told her of Nancy Hamilton, the child who had been visited by God with that strange disease which kept her from walking, and about which her mother, Marguerite, had told the reading world in her magnificent books *Red Shoes for Nancy* and *Borrowed Angel.* The title of the last book spoke very directly to Kay, and she relayed all it told her to her own daughter, Betty. The story of Nancy, told so touchingly by her mother, turned out to be, for the thoughtful reader, the story of God's tender Providence. Through this peculiar disease He not only gave Nancy a very exciting life, but brought her to everlasting life as the pathology brought the child into contact with Catholic nursing Sisters whose total dedication spoke to the child about God in a way nothing else could have spoken. Their example led her on to Him for whom they lived their lives of sacrifice. Little Nancy was received into the Mystical Body of Christ and the new life given her by baptism, the Eucharist, confirmation, the Mass and prayer brought such joy to the child that she radiated God's own goodness and finally brought her own mother, Marguerite, not only into the Catholic Church, but to peace of mind and happiness of heart. Kay knew that what Nancy had done for her mother, little Melissa could do for Betty and for Bill — her own parents.

Then came an introduction through letters to the parents of another retarded child who had written their story in a magazine article which they had entitled *Blue Angel*. The recurrence of that word *Angel* in reference to such children struck Kay forcibly. She wondered if Betty's family doctor had coined the title for Melissa, or whether he had borrowed it from such books and articles.

As so often happens, the affliction of one brings all connected with her into contact with others who have had some similar affliction. Thus Kay learned of a couple in Louisville, Kentucky, Marguerite and Pat, who had had two children born in much the same condition as Melissa. One had died very close to the day Melissa had been born, after fourteen years of earthly existence. The other was still living at the age of sixteen, and was a constant reminder to his parents of the immortality of the human soul, as well as of God's wisdom displayed in ways that seem so strange to us humans. But the fact that lifted Kay's heart was the one which told of the joy these parents felt in having been entrusted by God with such rare treasure. The love they had lavished on these two children, who could never give them a single human response to that love, had served not only to increase the mutual love of Pat and Marguerite, but had kept them ever conscious of the God of love.

But then came some revelations that showed Kay that not all parents were as keen as Marguerite Hamilton had been, nor as this couple in Kentucky. For she learned of a couple in Maryland who had reached the verge of despair as they went from doctor to doctor for years, laboring to find one who would tell them that their child was normal. Almost at the same time she was told about a couple in Massachusetts who stubbornly refused to admit to themselves, or to anyone else, that their son and daughter were definitely retarded. Reflecting on such letters, Kay came to see that one of the most important words in the English language for tranquillity of mind and harmony in life is the word *acceptance*. If these parents would only *accept* their children as they were, and realize exactly what they were, "images of God," then all would be well. She prayed often after such revelations: "Oh, dear God, give us more men like Betty's family doctor. Men who will recognize You in all Your works — especially in those we poor humans consider defective!"

She was using all these letters to cheer her daughter and son-in-law, pointing out to them that God had blessed others the way He had blessed them, and that some of these others had used their blessings as God wanted them to be used: as means to obtain ever greater blessings for themselves in the way of Faith and "God-consciousness." She even reminded them of the family doctor's remark about Melissa being a "through-ticket to heaven" for them, and showed how other children similarly brought forth by God had served that purpose for their parents.

The replies she was receiving from California had Kay thinking that, perhaps, she was wasting her time; for Betty and Bill seemed far happier with their Melissa in these first two months of her life than Marguerite Hamilton had ever been with her "borrowed angel" Nancy, until the very end of that little one's days. All seemed joy down in Pacifica. But Kay Trotter had lived the biblical age of "three score and ten." She knew much of human nature. She well knew that she must keep on encouraging both Betty and Bill; for she knew with Longfellow that "Some days must be dark and dreary."

Kay had to admit to herself that Melissa was serving to increase her own Faith as she was led on to ever greater consciousness of God's absolute dominion over His creatures and our utter dependence on His good pleasure. The abnormality of this child gave her a far greater appreciation of that normality which humans take so much for granted and with such little gratitude. She found herself thanking God daily with much warmer heart and keener joy for all the generosity He had shown through the years to her own children and to herself. She marveled that she had been so unappreciative and even unconscious of how dependent we human beings are on

Him for everything, even such simple things as breathing and,
walking. To all her prayers now she found herself adding "and
thank You for Melissa."

One of her latest contacts was with a cloistered priest who answered her request for prayers with letters that caused her to look
into herself and realize that her great gift of faith actually covered
everything in life, and accounted for many things humans considered
utterly unaccountable. One day he set her staring at the truth that
Melissa, or any other mongoloid, presented a "mystery" nowhere
near as profound as the Mystery of a Consecrated Host, and a chal-
lenge to our Faith nowhere near as great. He had pointed out that
it requires tremendous faith to see in a tiny wafer of wheat matter
that can yield its substance so that God can live under its appearances. Yet we all believe it without blinking. Why then should
anyone blink at the fact that infinite Wisdom lives within the flesh
and blood of a child who is witless? One Presence was Sacramental;
the other, mystical. Both were real! Kay Trotter now saw why this
same priest had asserted that the family doctor in San Francisco,
who had promised Betty and Bill that they would have a "living
angel" in their home once they took Melissa with them and had
her baptized, had spoken only half the truth. He had insisted that
Betty and Bill had in their home Him whom angels worship; Him
at whose throne ten thousand times ten thousand angels minister.
For if in the consecrated Host we have "the Body and Blood, soul
and Divinity" of Jesus Christ, just as certainly have we in the baptized, sinless soul of mongoloid, or mighty genius, Father, Son, and
Holy Spirit dwelling as in Their abode. Melissa, then, made of that
home in Pacifica, California, a veritable sanctuary where God Almighty dwells.

These letters from this cloistered priest read easily; they seemed
to have been effortless compositions, and Kay began to think that
cloistered souls had special gifts. She did not know that her letter
had set this same priest pondering on the mystery of it all; and it came
home to him that witless mongoloids are actually witnesses to the
wisdom of God, and breathing condemnations of the senseless super-
ficiality of present-day human sophistication. As he wrote to Kay
Trotter, he recalled a small book written by the gifted Caryll House-

lander entitled *The Passion of the Infant Christ,* in which she had shown that Christ is being incarnated hourly in humans, to live again His torrent of passion and pain. She had claimed that "the Christ-Child can suffer nothing that is not the redeeming Passion of Infinite Love." Taking that as starting point, the priest told Kay that it appeared to him that immortal souls, images of God Almighty, shackled at birth, as had been these souls in mongoloids, once they were "baptized into Christ's Death and Resurrection," became, for those who would look until they saw, striking manifestations of the sanity of God in a world gone well nigh insane. For they reminded the thoughtful of the infinite worth of each immortal human soul as they became palpitating arguments that drove one on to the conclusion that none of us are of worth save only in so far as Christ can live in us, and, through us, somehow "fill up what is wanting to His Passion." He prudently added that these shackled members of the Mystical Christ would be for many moderns what the physical Christ, shackled before Annas and Caiphas, Pilate and Herod, and finally spiked to a cross, had been for the Jews of that day and the Gentiles shortly after: "stumbling blocks and absurdities" (1 Cor. 1:23). Then he added the rest of Paul's text: "but to those who are called . . . the power of God and the wisdom of God"; then pointed his argument by adapting Paul's lines to Melissa Maureen and others like her, saying: "Why, there is more wisdom in these 'absurdities' of God than in all the 'wisdom' of men, and more might in these 'weaknesses' of God than in all the might of men" (1 Cor. 1:24, 25).

Truth had seldom been presented to Kay Trotter in this fashion before. It prompted her to read her Bible with keener consciousness that practically every word therein had personal meaning for her, and very practical, personal application for her great-granddaughter Melissa Maureen. The fact is that this priest in his cloister so many miles from the Pacific Slope was opening the eyes of many on that Slope to the thrilling truth of the Mystical Body of Jesus Christ.

While acknowledging a stipend for some Masses that Kay had requested, he one day enclosed a poem that had come to him from the Leonard family in Denver, Colorado. "This should speak to you and your daughter, Betty," he wrote, "for it was composed on behalf of one who had to look as you and your daughter have been forced

to look, and keep on looking until she saw." Then he recounted
how this woman, a relative of Mrs. John Leonard, had just given
birth to a mongoloid child whom she had named Bernadette at
baptism. "But before you will grasp the poignancy of this poem,"
he wrote, "you must first know that this woman had found her third
child, named Regina, dead in her crib the very day she had brought
her home from the hospital, and that her fourth child, Germaine,
had gone back to God after a brief nine months on earth. Mary
Agnes, the eldest of the Leonard children, has seen into Reality.
Read her poem carefully, and send it on to Betty and Bill."

> Rejected and scorned;
> Calvary with her first baby breath!
>   Cringe, if you will, Oh, moron world:
>   I *love* her —
>   My Bernadette!

> She's more mine than most:
> Not hair, eyes, or feature-wise;
>   She's *mine* — for she's a product
>   Of my pain, my hurt —
>   She's my "Little Sorrow."

Kay Trotter could read no further; for tears blinded her eyes. How
her own daughter, Betty, could feel the same way! Later that day
she went back to the poem and found her heart aching with sympathy for the mother of these three children, even as it expanded
with admiration for young Mary Agnes' faith; for after speaking of
Regina, the child found dead in her crib, as a "snowflake, too lovely
and delicate to linger among mere mortals," and of Germaine, the
baby who lived outside her mother's womb only as long as she had
lived inside it, as "a little rose, once budding sweet for us, now
blossoming for Him," she went on to speak of the mongoloid as
"Little Sorrow, even closer to her mother's heart because of deformity
— yet all the more Christlike therein." Then she boldly stated:

> Sure — a torn and twisted body
> Always brings the spit and scorn;
> Think of Calvary's Asylum:
>   God Almighty rendered *Idiot*
>   By explosive, infinite Love.

Kay Trotter might have been shocked by that daring epithet had not her priest-friend explained that Mary Agnes was being more true than Francis Thompson had been when he called God "The Hound of Heaven," and that Jesus, Infinite Wisdom, had been taken for an "Idiot" long before He reached that Asylum called Calvary. Herod, with the white robe, had sneered with this symbol which everyone read as "Fool!" And long before that, Christ's own "brethren," as they are called in Scripture, had thought Him out of His mind (Jn. 3:7) and the Jews claimed that He was mad (Jn. 10:20). Kay read on with greater interest and understanding, and found the mother of this mongoloid, Bernadette, calling our Lady-Mother the "Mother of Seven . . . 'Little Sorrows' " and asking her, the Mother of Grace, to

> Grant me the strength of your example,
> The consolation of your courage.
>   Stand with me *here!*
> Grant we stand together
>   Some day . . . *There*
> As proudly to your dear Son
>   My credentials I present:
> My God —
> My Trinity of trial:
>   Regina . . .
>   Germaine . . .
>   And the grace you let me borrow:
> Pure, and precious, "Little Sorrow" —
>   *Bernadette!*

"Calvary with her first baby breath" — "her hour" struck at birth! Yes, for Melissa, Bernadette, and every other child similarly born. And for the parents of such? — A lifetime of care which the nonseeing ones of earth would call a lifetime of misery, but which the open eyes of faith see as a lifetime of mystery — the mystery of the Passion of the Infant Christ. Looking upon their children rightly, such parents can see not only the Christ of Calvary, but the Christ who was born, as it were, from Calvary — the Christ of Easter — the glorified Jesus; for it is the glorified Christ who lives on in such infants. He is a wounded Christ, but His wounds shine like suns. They are His "credentials" — just as these children will be the

"credentials" of such parents! Truly, mongoloids, who are loved can
be what Betty's doctor claimed: through-tickets to heaven. For in
accounting for the way mankind will be separated at the Last Judgment, Christ, Incarnate Truth and Infinite Justice, showed us but
one scale. He revealed to us the fact that we go to heaven or to hell
for all eternity because in time we ministered, or failed to minister,
to Him in His members: "I tell you the plain truth: inasmuch as
you did this to one of these least brethren of mine, you did it to me"
(Mt. 25:40).

That is why Kay Trotter learned the truth that when "the hour"
is sounded for a child at birth, as it had been for Melissa Maureen,
the parents of the child can rejoice! For, in such little ones the only
Son, "the Splendor of the Father's Glory," has chosen to be "incarnated" anew. Omniscience selected these little ones to be His
members, though we will never know with fullest clarity just what
He was doing until after "our hour" is ended. But we must never
forget that such children, by their very breathing, are a continual
Act of Obedience to God's creative and continuing *Fiat* — and it was
obedience that saved the world, and will yet sanctify it. What a
consolation to such parents to realize that Christ is in their little ones
just as really, and for the same purpose, as He is in every Host:
to love and be loved!

These little ones, in whom intelligence is not awake, can awaken
us, who have intelligence, to the wondrous truth Caryll Houselander
told toward the end of her little book: *The Passion of the Infant
Christ*: "The Holy Spirit is descending upon the world. There is
Incarnation everywhere — everywhere the Infant Christ is born; every
day the Infant Christ makes the world new. Upon the world that
seems so cruel, mercy falls like summer rain; upon the world that
seems so blind, light comes down in living beams. The heart of man
that seems so hard, is sifted, irrigated, warmed; the water of life
floods it. The fire and light of the Spirit burn it. The seed of Christ-
life, which seemed to have dried up, lives and quickens, and from
the secret depth of man's being the divine Life flowers."

Who could despair of such a world, or of the men in such a world,
when mongoloids, like Melissa Maureen and Bernadette, carry such
mystery — and unravel so much more? Mary Agnes Leonard was

sure, with the surety of faith, that mongoloids, who will never know how to tell time, will, because of baptism, know God for all eternity. She was also sure that the parents of such children would never know eternity unless they did in time what she had the mother of Bernadette doing in her poem: pray the Mother of "Seven Little Sorrows" to stand with them throughout the Passion of the Infant Christ within their children even as she had stood throughout the Passion of her grown Son. Once they pray that prayer and have it answered, they will see the Passion of Christ for what it was: a blotting out of sin. For while they well may have worries about their so-called normal children, and wonder often if Christ be living within them — for it is a sin-filled world, and all normal mortals are ever prone to sin! — they need never wonder or worry about children like Bernadette or Melissa Maureen. They can be sure He is always there. Hence, ministering to such children, they are as surely ministering to God's Only Son — and to God Himself — as were Mary and Joseph at Bethlehem, in Egypt, and within that holy home at Nazareth.

In early January of 1961 Kay Trotter had written: "there will be heartaches ahead." Of course! Heartaches that very nearly are heartbreaks. But that only proves how deeply Mary Agnes Leonard had seen into Reality when she turned the mother of Bernadette to that other Mother who had her heart pierced by "seven swords." Was it not the scabbarding of these seven sorrows within that heart that made her Coredemptrix of our fallen race and, with her Son, "Recreatrix" of our shattered world? Have modern parents any other role to play? Hardly, when life's drama is seen to be what it actually is: the continuation of His Incarnation, and the completion of His work of Redemption — a drama played in time, but with eternity as the backdrop.

In early March Kay's words proved that her daughter, Betty, and her son-in-law, Bill, knew their roles. "Betty just called," she wrote. "I get impatient with her for phoning and not writing, but this phone call made up for much. Melissa has been very ill. As Betty described it: the tube from the stomach to the intestines had grown together. While the doctors were preparing to operate, the darling child became dehydrated. Betty said her tiny veins were too small to allow for any injections, so the doctors had to put needles, Betty called them, into Melissa's little head. They gave the child one chance in four of surviving the operation. They had to reroute the digestive system. When Betty called she said the doctors considered Melissa out of danger. They had allowed Betty to hold her child for three minutes the day before, and Bill had called Betty just before she called me, and said that he had been at the hospital during his lunch hour, and the doctors had allowed him, also, to hold the child. I thank God for 'Missy's' recovery, but I thank Him even more for the *sheer joy* in Betty's voice.

" 'Missy' is at Sacred Heart Hospital, and 'the dearest little nun,' as Betty put it, thanked her and Bill for having brought the child there. She said: 'Now I can write Sister (Betty couldn't remember the name) and tell her that I, too, have been privileged to care for one of God's little angels.'

"Someone, not in the family, said: 'It might have been better if God had taken her.' I was furious. But I spoke calmly, I hope. Afterward I was very ashamed of my fury; for I realized if God had not gifted me with faith enough to see through appearances, I might have felt the same way; and with much less reason, for this person, while a Catholic, has never been a mother."

"Better if God had taken her" — When will mortals realize that God knows His business? When will they cease posing as knowing better than God Himself? What if God Almighty had allowed His Only Son to be "taken" with the Babes of Bethlehem? Humanly speaking, how much His mother and foster-father would have been saved. The world, undoubtedly, could have been redeemed by such a slaughter, but oh! what the world would have been deprived of: no gospel stories of the hidden life, the public life, the Crucifixion; no teachings from the lips of Omniscience; no parables about the Prodigal Son, the Good Samaritan, the Good Shepherd. Could we live without these? Possibly . . . but how could we ever have faced the Judgment had we not heard how we are to be judged? "I tell you the plain truth, inasmuch as you did this to one of these least brethren of mine, you did it to me" (Mt. 25:40).

The religious to whom Kay addressed this latest letter replied by giving her extracts from a letter that had come in the same mail from

Marguerite, the mother of the Louisville children, Danny and Michael, who had been so retarded. "I was talking to Danny on the fourth anniversary of Michael's death, telling him that, most probably, Michael was then running about heaven; and that he would be doing the same as soon as he died. As soon as he heard Michael's name his whole face lit up and was wreathed in smiles. This thrilled me, for it told me that he had not forgotten his brother despite the four years' absence. It is strange about these children: you never know how much they comprehend. I feel sure that Danny understands almost everything I say to him, but he is damaged in whatever it is that helps us communicate with one another. God will make it all up to him hereafter — of that I am sure."

That such children can understand some things gave Kay Trotter a new hope for Melissa. But what consoled her most was the truth this same religious told when he wrote: "All of God's works are perfect works. They could not be otherwise and He still be God. Everything that lives shows forth, in some degree, His perfection and His love. When will we sophisticated humans think theologically and realize that what we so arrogantly term 'defective' is a perfect work of Him who is All-perfect? . . . Maybe Betty and Bill will profit from reading the following poem by Eithne Tabor, a talented girl who has suffered off and on from what our learned medical men term *mental illness*. Eithne is a poetess of real worth."

> My wish —
> It is not for my freedom
> Nor my sanity —
> Not to be once more whole
> and clean again,
> Free from that which hurts
> Far, deep, inside my brain.
>
> My wish —
> Is but to tell my story
> to humanity,
> To let them know that God
> lives closer to the minds
> whose self-shields are destroyed.
>
> My wish —
> Is for His love

Even in insanity.*

"If we have His love" were the letter's last words, "can we be insane?"

* From *The Cliff's Edge*, by Ethne Tabor. Copyright 1950, by Sheed and Ward, Inc.

VI

"UNTO THE END"

Father Matt Brennan laid the morning paper down after merely scanning a few headlines. He had heard most of what it contained in last night's newscast, he felt sure. Further, he was preoccupied with the question put to him by his friend from a nearby monastery during the latter's last visit to the hospital of which Father Matt was chaplain. "What do you see when you look at this hospital?" the monk had asked. Father Matt knew his friend had something worthwhile behind the question but, as usual, answered him offhand and with a touch of flippancy: "A lot of work!" It was a realistic answer; for St. Joseph Infirmary held five hundred beds, and few were left unoccupied for any length of time. There were miles of corridors that Father Matt had to cover daily, and countless difficulties he had to straighten out. Patients had to be comforted, consoled, oriented correctly toward their sickness. Relatives had to be calmed or given sympathy. Doctors, nurses, nuns, members of the huge staff of workers had to be solaced in their own perplexities — and through it all, and in it all, God had to be served. Indeed, he had "a lot of work."

But the laugh on the monk's lips and the light in his eyes told Father Matt that he had not even heard the question right, let alone answered it. He was still wondering what was behind the query when he snapped out his second reply: "Expense!" He had gone on to tell how the latest survey showed that the cost per patient had risen in the past twenty years from $5.08 to $29.71 per day. "That means it costs a patient, on the average, $1.23 an hour each hour of the twenty-four. But that expense in currency is nothing compared to the expense on the person — the psychological and physical expense is incalculable. That is what I see, and what most people see when they look at this hospital. Why do you ask?"

"You're only looking, Father Matt; you're not seeing yet. What do you *see* when you look at this hospital?" asked the monk.

"Trouble," said Father Matt.

The monk said: "I see a chalice filled to the full with fragmented Hosts. . . ."

"I knew it!" cut in Father Brennan. "I knew it would be something out of this world. When will you be realistic and see things as they are?"

"It is you who are not realistic, Matt. Be true to your nature. You were made to be 'like unto God,' and He sees every hospital for what it is: the Upper Room, Holy Thursday Night; Golgotha, Good Friday afternoon; the Garden, glorious with the Easter dawn and the Empty Tomb; heaven, made radiant by the five wounds of that Man who died that men might never die."

That precipitated a long discussion during which they had dwelt on the meaning of words. They had agreed that language is a living thing, and that it, like all other living things, changed as time went on. But the point had been made that things never change essentially. A human being changes greatly as time goes on, but he always remains a human being. A boy may become a bully, but he never becomes a bull. So, too with words. If we go back to their roots, we often get revelation; for by tracing down their history, we often lay hand on holiness. That had been the monks' contention, and he proved it quite well regarding the word *hospital*.

Father Brennan recalled it all now as well as he could. He had laughed when his friend had claimed that "there is nothing new under the sun" then went on to take Socialized Medicine as an example. That, certainly, looked new; to many on the medical staff, the chaplain well knew, it looked like today's newborn bugbear. But Father Joe, as the chaplain always called him, told how it had been practiced by the Romans and Greeks long before the time of Christ. City hospitals seem modern; some of them ultramodern. But the historical fact is that, over sixteen centuries ago, St. Basil had erected so many buildings at Caesarea in Cappadocia for the care of the sick, that his institution took on the dimensions of a city. There were regular streets, separate buildings for various kinds of diseases, special residences for the doctors, and houses exclusively for the nurses. What is more, in this *Basilias,* as it came to be called, there were workshops, or what today would be called "Physical Therapy Departments." As for our supposedly modern discovery of "occupational therapy," there were so many different occupations practiced as therapies within the confines of this *Basilias,* that veritable industrial schools were founded.

This had been news to Father Matt, but when his friend told him that when St. Gregory of Nazianzen visited this *Basilias* he called it "The Easy Ascent to Heaven," the discussion took a new turn and they had gone back to the word *hospital.* When first used, this word had nothing at all to do with the sick. Following this word down to its roots, in place of a sick man, they found instead a jovial host with his happy guest; for *hospes* is the root from which our word has sprung, and *hospes* means a guest. But you cannot have a guest unless there is a host. Thus the first shoot from this root was *hospitium,* which designated a Guest House. He who received guests and entertained them generously was a *hospitable* person — the right kind of a *host.*

Father Matt saw where the discussion was leading, but he wondered how it was that our word *hospital* came to have such a restricted meaning. He was told that, originally, our word designated a place where guests and strangers were received kindly and entertained generously, and reminded that, even today, there are places in the Alps named *hospices,* which bespeak no reference whatsoever to sickness, let alone to death. They exist for those who would rest and have some entertainment. Our word began to take on a restricted meaning only when some military monks began to devote themselves exclusively to the care of pilgrims to the Holy Land — some of whom did fall sick. These monks were known first as *Knights of the Hospital;* for it was in the hospital, or guest house, that they worked. The first of these Orders was that of John of Jerusalem, founded about 1048 in the Holy Land. Their direct descendants are among us today known as the Knights of Malta. Later it was war that brought into being other Orders made up of knights who dedicated themselves to the service of the wounded and the sick. The general name given these men was *Knights Hospitallers.* From this term our modern word *hospital* is taken, and restricted to those institutions which receive and care only for the sick.

Father Matt had been taken by the religious elements in the origin of our modern word. It was in the Holy Land that these Orders first knew birth. They were religious Orders. When he asked about the modern Red Cross, which we so universally associate with the sick and care of the afflicted, he learned that we have to go back further than the past century and the Geneva Cross, if we are to get at its roots. These we find in the Crusaders and their red crosses, which were symbols and reminders of that reddest of all red crosses, the one made red by the Blood of Him who cured the deepest and most prevalent of all human sicknesses, that of sin, and on that cross became the Savior of mankind.

That led the two priests to the fact that every hospital is a monument to sin and to Him who saved us by "becoming sin," as St. Paul so strikingly put it. At this point in the discussion they recalled the term the French have for a hospital; an *Hôtel-Dieu* — a House of God. Hence, when men think theologically, and that is the only way to think realistically, they see that every hospital is really a house where God is host to guests. "If modern man would only realize that," the priests concluded, "they would never shy away from sickness and suffering."

That, quite naturally, brought them to the matter of death. But the monk insisted that hospitals were places where life is found, not death. He pointed to the fourth floor west in St. Joseph's Infirmary and said that is where humans are born to earthly life. As for the other floors, he said that on each of them humans have been born to eternal life. Hence, we should think of life rather than of death, whenever we think of a hospital.

When he got this far in his reflections Father Matt chuckled, for he now recalled the liveliest part of the discussion; for he had begged the Monk once again to be realistic, insisting that men do die; that death is all about us, and the term toward which each of us is hurrying. When Father Joe quietly said: "Think theologically, Matt," the chaplain had retorted that that was exactly what he was doing; for death is a consequence of sin, and sin is a theological reality. He had even quoted Scripture to the effect that "it is appointed for all men once to die." But the Monk had subsumed on him and claimed that too many men find reality only on the surface of things. But on surfaces there is next to no reality. Reality is as deep as God; and apart from Him there is no reality. God is above us and below us, within us and without us; God is all about us. Hence, when we think theologically, we can find Him in everything from the almost painless twinge of a nerve to the angry clutch of a coronary thrombosis. What is more, we can find His love in every pinch of pain, and read His anxiety to give us fuller, richer life in everything from a common head cold to a terminal cancer.

"Christ came to give us life," continued the monk, "and He succeeded in His mission. That is why you can say that no one ever goes to a hospital to die. No one! For since the day the God-Man died, no man will ever know death, but only a transition from one kind of life to another. Jesus Christ conquered death; and, like all His victories, this one is irreversible. So you can tell your patients that they have been brought here to get life — and get it more abundantly."

"Too poetical!" had been Father Matt's comment. But his friend said that the "function of the poet is to remove the veils of familiarity, and give us back the world in all its native strangeness." Then he quoted from Gerard Manley Hopkins a passage with which the chaplain was not familiar. ". . . the just man," said the monk,

> Acts in God's eyes what in God's eyes he is:
> *Christ* — for Christ plays in ten thousand places,
> Lovely in limbs, and lovely in eyes not His,
> To the Father through the features of men's faces. *

When they had talked that bit of poetry over, the monk surprised the chaplain by saying, "You know, Father Matt, there are times when I envy you your job. For it seems to me that if there is any one place in the world, outside the sanctuary, where a priest can be all priest, live ever in the presence of God, and do the most for God and humans, it is in a hospital. I see this place as a monument to sin and the Savior, as I've said. But I also see it as that chalice I told you about, filled to the overflowing with the Blood of Christ, and as a huge Corporal on which lie living particles of the broken Host. For Calvary is forever, you know, and His Mass is always going on."

"I envy you your eyesight . . ." said the chaplain, only to be

* *Poems of Gerard Manley Hopkins*, Oxford University Press, 1948. By permission.

interrupted with: "Matt, this place, and every other hospital in the world, is holy with the very holiness of God. It is sacred with the very sacredness and sanctity of the only Son of God. For if we humans are meant to be the *Pleroma Christi* — His members who fill out the fullness of Jesus Christ — then it is here that the greatest work of Christ is carried on. I believe that every hospital has been designed by the eternal Architect to serve the selfsame purpose the skull-shaped mound of Calvary served, and the triumph achieved there is to be achieved here. Redemption is ended, but salvation goes on. The first was accomplished in what He called 'His Hour' — the second will be accomplished by us, if we are alert, in what we may very justly call 'our hour.' Life's greatest work, and, in one sense, life's only work is to 'fill up what is wanting to His Passion' (Col. 1:24). Where can it be done more surely than in a hospital? As you see I am back to my old theme: the Mass. That was Christ's great Act. That, too, is to be our greatest. . . ."

A call for the chaplain ended the discussion, but Father Brennan had been over it again and again in the intervening weeks and months, and he had concluded that most of us humans look but do not see; think logically enough at times, but not nearly theologically enough at any time. As he arose to begin his morning's rounds he was wondering if he could get a dying patient on the third floor to see his bed as an altar and himself as a Host in the hands of the New Law's only High Priest, Jesus Christ. It would be worth a try, he concluded, and headed toward the nearest elevator.

Twenty minutes later Father Brennan was back on the first floor, happy over his success with the patient he had just visited, happier still to be about to share his joy with one of his closest clerical friends, Father James Lehmann, who had recently been operated upon, but whose spirits were never lowered by hospitalization. The Chaplain knocked on the door loudly, and without waiting for an invitation, strode in, calling "Anybody home?" But as he crossed the threshold he stopped. His whole attitude changed. He chuckled softly, turned to the priest in the bed and in a greatly modulated tone said: "Father Jim, it's true: think of the devil and you'll smell fire. I've been thinking of your visitor here all morning, but never thought I'd lay eyes on him again today. Father Joe, hope you are as well as you look. What do you think of our busy pastor, Father James Lehmann? Doesn't he look comfortable there in that bed? 'There ain't no justice.' Believe me. Here I am just a hardworking chaplain, getting vericose veins, fallen arches, and gray hairs running all over this hospital. While the illustrious Pastor reclines. . . ."

"But tell me why he is reclining, will you, Father Matt? He doesn't seem to know anything about his condition though I have been questioning him here for ten minutes. What did they find when they took this man to Surgery? . . ."

"Just more of the same, Joe. Father James likes the disease you seem to have been relieved of. Some six years ago they excised a fine cancer from his anatomy on St. Patrick's Day. This year, on Washington's Birthday they went in again and found more of the same. At least the busy pastor chooses good days. He's patriotic and loyal; for despite his name of Lehmann, he's as Irish as you or I at heart. . . ."

"I know all about the world being divided into two classes of people, Matt: those who are Irish, and those who wish they were. But, tell me, did they get it all this time?"

"All the Ca.? — Never. Jimmie's hoarding on us. He wouldn't give them any this operation."

"I believe in holding on to what you've got," said the man in the bed.

"You certainly did it this time. One of the surgeons on the job told me you're not only holding on to it, you're increasing it. Not enough to have it blocking off a kidney, you now have it extending into the pelvis."

"Go on, Father Matt," said Father Jim with a chuckle, "make it good while you're at it. I suppose the next word is 'inoperable,' is it?"

The chaplain frowned. Father Joe saw that he was nonplused, his face showed incredulity, then some concern. "Do you mean to tell me you don't know, Jim? Didn't they tell you?"

"Nothing like what you've just told me. I can see that my proctologist is not near as happy about this latest operation as he was about the original bit of surgery four years ago, but he has not been very explicit as to the cause of his lack of enthusiasm."

"Well, I'm sorry to have said as much as I have said, then; yet,

since I've gone so far I might as well complete the story, though it
is hardly my place. . . ."

"Let's have it all, Matt. Rather have it from you than from anyone
else."

"But, Jim, I'm chaplain here, not doctor. I'm never supposed to
break any news to a patient without orders or special request from
the medics. But, since I've gone so far, and we are such friends,
not only you and I, but your doctors and all three of us, I guess I
won't be violating any confidences nor medical ethics if I say they
did find it inoperable. They opened you and closed you."

"That's why they've been talking about deep x-ray therapy, then.
I see it all now. Well, I guess you were psychic or something, Joe,
with all your talk today about 'my hour.' . . ."

"Not psychic, Jim," cut in Father Joe, "nor was it mere coin-
cidence. I call it Divine Providence. But, actually, I was not talking
about 'your hour' so much as 'His hour,' and saying that Father Matt
here, myself, and everyone else can look forward to some similar
'hour.' . . ."

"What's this all about? Haven't been giving Jim your distinction
between looking and seeing, have you, Joe? The last time we talked,
you ended with some reference to 'His hour.' Have you been continuing my discussion with Father Jimmie?"

"Not exactly, Matt. I was just telling him of a new find I've made.
Browsing in the library some weeks back I came across a few doc-
toral dissertations on the Gospel according to St. John. They opened
my eyes. I was just telling, Jimmie . . ."

"He was just telling me implicitly what you have just told me
explicitly, Matt. Christ had 'His hour,' we Christians are to have
ours; and mine, I guess, has struck."

"Don't rush things, Jim. I said 'inoperable.' That does not necessarily mean immediately fatal. What do you think we have those
deep therapy machines for down in the cancer clinic? Looking at
you now I'd say you have a lot more work to do for His Excellency
and this diocese. I'm no prophet. But I have seen a lot of cancer
these past five or six years, and I'm willing to bet right now that
you'll be out golfing again before many weeks."

"Optimist! But that reminds me, Matt. . . . There was a nun in here yesterday, a music teacher at that. I must have said something about getting back to work. She looked at me quietly, and then, in one of the most musical voices I've ever heard, said gently: 'Father James, too many of us forget that sickness is as much a part of life as is health. What we consider idleness, because of some illness, is as necessary for our work for God as is our activity.' I must have looked blank, for she immediately went on with: 'Have you never noted that in music there are "rests"? Sometimes we "rest" for only one beat. But at other times we "rest" for as long as six and even eight beats. During those "rests" no note must be heard, else the harmony is marred, and the beauty of the piece ruined. So it is with our lives — especially our lives for God. There are "rests." We call them periods of inactivity. Such, for instance, as the one now forced on you by your illness. But, if we look on these as anything other than "rests" written into the score by the great Composer, God, we are very poor musicians. They are as essential to the beauty and harmony of the piece He has composed as are the notes.' — That is what I heard while she was here, Matt. But it was only after she had left that I understood all she was saying."

"Meaning . . . ?" prompted the chaplain.

"Meaning that I was complaining when I should not have been. Meaning that I'll get back to work — and to golfing — not when I want to, not when His Excellency wants me to, not even when my parishioners want me to, but only when the great Composer and the great Conductor needs me and my work to complete the harmony of His composition. Meaning that I must wait, as do the singers or the orchestra members in a symphony — then come in on the downbeat."

"Were I in my usual corny mood, Father James, I'd call you a 'beatnik' after that long speech. But all I'll say this morning is that that is the greatest bit of common sense I have ever heard come from a music teacher. I don't know what it is, but I have always found them different from us ordinary mortals. It's refreshing to hear of one who sounds so normal."

"More than normal, Matt, and more than common sense," put in Father Joe. "That nun, whoever she was, spoke wisdom. Why is it that we priests of God never learn the lesson taught by God's only

High Priest? Why is it that we always think we must be on the go, always 'producing'?"

The chaplain drew an imaginary bow across imaginary strings with his right hand, while his left hand produced an imaginary arpeggio. "Did you give that downbeat, Jim?" he asked. "Our friend here is off on his aria. Now we'll hear the latest anathematization of activism — from a cloistered religious, of course! But, go on, Joe — hit high C."

"I'll run the whole gamut for you, Matt. But you well know my position on the so-called heresy of action. I believe it has and has had about as much existence in the U. S. A. as had that heresy called 'Americanism.' None! Thank God, for most of us priests and religious, work *is* prayer. How many of us ever went to work as these heresy hunters claim we do — without a single thought about God, grace, or prayer. Our own impotence is too well known to ourselves. But the question before us is sickness. Don't most of us view it wrongly? Aren't we chagrined whenever rendered *hors de combat* by some illness? Yet, how unreasonable of us! We always say we want the will of God. Well, what could be more assuredly His will than our illness? Surely no bishop, archbishop, abbot, or archabbot will ever assign any of us to a sickbed. You know perfectly well that none of us would choose it of our own will. So, when we are assigned there by cancer or anything else, who could question whether it is God's will or not? But I wonder if the question doesn't go even deeper."

"Can we go any deeper than God's will, Joe?" came the quiet question from the bed.

"Of course not, Father Jim, but we can see more deeply into that will. That is precisely what we will do if we think a bit more theologically about sickness."

"You certainly believe in thinking theologically, Joe!"

"It's the only proper way to think, Matt. You two remember well what Trent said about Redemption — that it was effected *principaliter* — that was the word! — principally by what Christ did on the cross. And what did He do? Nothing — but suffer. Yet, it was not His suffering that redeemed mankind, but only His suffering in obedience. In other words: doing His Father's will. How are we going to change that

Redemption into salvation for ourselves and others save by following His example? So when God's will is made manifest to us by an assignment to a hospital bed — all we have to do is — nothing! — That is, nothing but acquiesce."

"Aha!" cried Father Brennan as he turned a chair around and straddled it. "Now I know where Sister James Marion gets her theology. Your repetition of that word *nothing* rang a bell, Joe. I remember now that the good supervisor of First East one day asked me if it were true that we save the world by doing nothing. I've heard of passivism and quietism, even of nihilism. But this 'doing nothing' stopped me. You've just let the cat out of the bag, Joe. Wait until I see her."

At that point an orderly knocked and told Father Joe that he was wanted in the x-ray department. As he was excusing himself, Father Matt wished him good luck with: "Hope the barium sticks, Joe, so that you can do nothing and save the world. If I'm not here when you get back, know that I'm out working. Maybe we chaplains weren't cut out to be saviors, eh?"

Once the monk was out of the room, Father Matt turned his chair about again, lit a cigarette, and while reaching for an ashtray said: "That thought is stimulating, isn't it?"

"And comforting, Matt. I had a refresher course in Sacred Scripture before you showed up. It took me back to what I can now call my happy days at Innsbruck. I didn't call them that when I was there, but that is typical of youth. I'm sorry you didn't make your theology there, Matt. The Austrian Tyrol is simply magnificent."

"Isn't it strange, Jim, that so many of our local clergy know so little of Innsbruck. I've found young priests who claimed they never even heard of it. But when I ask them if they studied Noldin in moral, Hurter in dogma, Grisar in ecclesiastical history, they always say yes. Then when I ask them if they ever heard of von Pastor and his *History of the Popes*, they again say yes. When I tell them those names spell Innsbruck, they frown in puzzlement."

And "Innsbruck is almost four hundred years old," returned Father Jim, "and its theology faculty has always been famous. The only drawback about the place is it charges too much for American cigarettes. Father Joe took me back there today with his talk about

St. John. We had a prof who said John's whole message can be found in that prologue we read as Last Gospel in almost every Mass, but Father Joe improved on that by showing how John was ever conscious of Christ's 'hour.' . . ."

"What I recall of John is life, light, and love."

"Right, Matt. Those are his famous words and his whole theology in a way. But Father Joe says that fundamental to all these is faith. He told me that John does not use the static noun-form to express faith, but the living, dynamic verb-form; not 'belief,' in other words, but 'to believe.' He said it appears about a hundred times; more often in John than in all three synoptics taken together. That's a remarkable fact. It throws special light on that prologue we mentioned, Matt. There we say: 'to those who *believe* in His name He gave the power to become children of God' (Jn. 1:12). That's the 'life' John talks about. This Evangelist is not out to *prove* that Christ is the Son of God, Father Joe claims, but to give us an experience of Jesus as the revelation of God. Whoever knows Christ in this manner possesses life, and even that eternal life John described so well when he said: 'And this is the sum of eternal life — their knowing you, the only true God, and your ambassador, Jesus Christ' (Jn. 17:3). Faith gives us life, Matt, and light and love. This kind of living faith gives us an experience of Christ. You should have been here. Believe me it was an experience! But after actually thrilling me with this concept of faith as alive, breathing, dynamic, and taking me right into God, he began something that was a bit new to me. He says John's one focal point throughout is Christ's 'hour.' "

"That's new to me, too, Jim," said the chaplain as he dusted his cigarette ash into a tray. "How did he prove it?"

"It all seems so obvious to me now. Look, John opens the public life with Cana. There we hear Christ Himself speak of 'His hour.' It's a puzzling passage we all admit. But taking it in conjunction with the other references to 'His hour' we can see that it refers to the hour of His glory by miracles and the hour of His glory in His Resurrection."

"Not so fast, Jim. I've always understood 'His hour' to mean His Passion and Death."

"It does, Matt, but His Passion and Death are never to be taken alone, but only in conjunction with His Resurrection, and even with His Ascension and enthronement. You see, there are seven passages in John that explicitly speak of 'His hour.' Two of these tell how the Jews would like to have taken Him and killed Him, but as John says: 'no one laid his hand on him. His hour had not yet come' (7:30) (8:20). But it is Christ Himself who speaks in the other five passages and clarifies the whole thing beyond all question. Christ calls it 'His hour'; says it is 'come,' and calls it the hour in which He is to be 'glorified.' Palm Sunday's story gives it to us, Matt. Christ enters Jerusalem in triumph. Some Greeks tell Philip they'd like to see Jesus. Philip tells Andrew. The two of them go to Christ. Jesus says: 'Come at last is the hour for the Son of Man to be glorified' (Jn. 12:23). I remember one of my professor's noting how Christ always referred to Himself as 'Son of Man' whenever He was speaking of His Death and Resurrection. It's there in that passage. If you recall, Christ was very shaken as His hour approached. In this same chapter John tells us how He asked: 'What shall I say? "Father, save me from this hour"? No. This is why I came to this hour. Father, glorify thy name' (Jn. 12:27). I believe it is St. Thomas Aquinas who calls this scene a brief anticipation of the Agony in the Garden."

"Sounds like it," put in Father Matt.

"But this was the passage that substantiated the thesis Father Joe was propounding; for it is here that Christ reveals the meaning of 'His hour' in all its profundity. It is not only the hour of His Passion, Death, and Resurrection, but the very purpose for which he came into this world. You can see why some have said every event of His life converges on 'His hour.' Father Joe ran through the Gospel according to St. John in such a way that even I, dumb as I am, could feel the undercurrent in all the events of Christ's life, the steady swell and surge up to the thirteenth, or is it the fourteenth, day of the month Nisan — Holy Thursday night."

"You're beginning to sound like a Scripture Prof."

"Matt, I'm not kidding you, I've been moved by this thing. I want to reread the Gospel according to St. John. I want to keep this idea of 'His hour' before me as I go from that majestic opening: 'When time began, the Word was there . . .' down to 'There are, however,

many other things that Jesus did — ' I feel sure that when I come
to the Last Supper and hear Christ saying again: 'Father the hour
is come! Glorify your Son. . . .' I will have the very experience John
wants everyone to have when they read his Gospel: the experience
of having met, come to know, and to love Jesus Christ as a Friend
and as God. I never knew before how to tie in Cana and Calvary,
nor how to explain that term 'His hour' so completely. If we take
it as glorification we have it cinched. Christ's glorification began with
His miracles — the first at Cana of Galilee. It is consummated, not
on Calvary, nor even on Easter morn, but rather at His Ascension
and enthronement. That is the divine Design, as Father Joe put it.
The Word became Man to redeem mankind and to be glorified in
His humanity as the Son of Man. It makes us look at our own humanity differently, Matt; and especially at our humanity when sick."

"Why do you say that, Jim?"

"Matt, if Father Joe has a point in his thesis about each of us
having 'his hour' . . ."

"But has he?"

"I'm convinced. Tie John in with Paul. Take 'your hour' as that
'filling up of His Passion,' and not only sickness, but death itself
takes on magnificent color."

"What color?"

"The color of God's glory."

"Whew! You're as bad as Joe. What's getting into you men?
Stay on earth. Glory is for heaven."

"But that's just Father Joe's point, Matt. Heaven begins on earth,
he says, or it doesn't begin at all. That's theology, too. Did we not
learn that grace is the seed of glory; that faith is the possession of
God; that our eternity has already begun?"

The chaplain stood up. "There's my page, Jim. I've got to be
going. But I'll be back to give you some realism. If that monk returns
ask him if he's been reading Seeds of Contemplation."

Father Lehmann chuckled as the chaplain went out the door.
But once the door closed he became very sober and entered into deep
meditation on the facts of life — of life in Christ Jesus.

Late that afternoon Father Joe was back. When Father Lehmann
asked him what had been the outcome of his checkup, the monk

said: "As usual, the radiologist raves about the expert surgery that was performed on me. 'Never know you were cut, Father!' It looks as if good Doctor Henry excised all the cancer, Jim. I guess 'my hour' has not yet come."

"That reminds me, Father Joe — have you a few minutes?"

"All afternoon."

"Well, now that I know something of my condition I want to ask you about something that has been bothering me. I believe you've read quite a bit in psychiatry. What do you think about these depth psychologists and their talk about 'unconscious motivations'?"

Father Joe hitched his chair closer to the bed as he smiled and said: "Would you believe it, Jim, that is something that has been on my own mind for months. It was only recently that I came across an article that confirmed me in my own opinion. I've always felt that there was a contradiction in the very term. But let me tell you some of the reasons. . . ." Then the monk began with the fact that Freud was led into his theory on the unconscious in human conduct by a study of some hypnotics. The conduct of these people after they had come out of their trances captured him; for what had been suggested to them, and even commanded them, while in their hypnotic state, they performed when they came out of those states. But they thought the idea of performing those acts originated with themselves. This fact led Freud and others to question whether such actions could be considered free acts.

When Father Lehmann asked if it were true that people did act that way after hypnosis, he was told of an actual case described by a certain Dr. Bernheim, head of a school at Nancy. To a man under hypnosis the doctor had said that at one o'clock that very afternoon this patient would walk up and down a certain street twice. That was at eleven o'clock in the morning. At one that afternoon, Dr. Bernheim looked out his office window, and there was his patient walking up and down the street. He did it just twice. When asked why he had done it, he replied that he just wanted a stroll.

"These men seem to have scientific data, Jim, to back up their claims. The individual thinks himself free and to be performing some act that originated in his own consciousness. Yet, the idea had been planted there by the hypnotist. You can see that if these men are right in the claim, then Spinoza was not wrong when he said that our consciousness of freedom is nothing but our ignorance of the causes that compel us to act. But are they right?"

"That's what I'd like to know."

"Well, Dr. Bernheim claims that such orders given in hypnosis retain their effectiveness hours, days, and even weeks after the trance is over. Yet, others in the very same school at Nancy, testify that they have discovered that not all suggestions made to the patient while hypnotized are carried out after the trance is over. And they give many more examples than does Dr. Bernheim. So let us admit that three points have been established clinically: one, after hypnosis an individual feels an urge to do something; two, he thinks this originates with himself, though in reality it has been planted there by the hypnotist; three — and this is, to me, the most important point — he may or he *may not* follow the urge. I say this is the most important fact, for if one always followed that inclination or urge, which we know to have been planted in him, and of which he is unconscious, we would have a more difficult proposition to face regarding freedom. But, Jim, I wonder if these brilliant analysts have ever analyzed our ordinary behavior."

"What do you mean?"

"Just this: it is not a bit extraordinary for many of our inclinations, urges, needs to arise from our unconscious. Take thirst or hunger. Who ever gives careful consideration to the ultimate depths whence these feelings, urges, inclinations arise? Actually, they lie in the unconscious biological state of our organism. From there they arise. Now I readily grant that the impulses our psychiatrists and psycholgists have been describing arise from a forgotten or unrecognized psychic source, whereas your hunger and thirst rise from the physiological. But the point I stress is the *unconscious* element in both. Don't you agree that many of the drives we feel in the conscious are rooted in our unconscious?"

"I can see the two you mention are. But how about the psychological drives? Or to be more pointed, the moral?"

"Fine, Jim! That's what I thought you were driving at — and ultimately, it is the moral aspect that interests us priests, and should interest all humans. Now my question to these men, and to every man, is this: Who cares about the *source*? It is not the source of these things that make a man free or necessarily determined. It is the actual, lived experience that is his at the time; the *consciousness* of the goodness or the evil in following the urge or of fulfilling the need that is felt at the moment. That is the criterion of the freedom or the nonfreedom of the act performed."

Father Joe sat back a moment and seemed to be searching for some clarification. After a slight pause he shifted in his chair, then leaned forward with, "Perhaps this example will clarify my meaning a bit, Jim. Suppose that you now suggest to me that I read a certain book — say Chardin's *Phenomenon of Man*. Two weeks from today, I am in my library back home. On the table I see a copy of the book. I have forgotten all about your suggestion. I pick the book up casually, leaf through it. My eye is caught by some chapter heading that interests me. I take the book out of the library and read it. Would you, or any other sane man, say that the *only* reason I took that book out was because you had suggested it? or that your suggestion was the *entire* compelling motive?"

"Not the only reason nor the entire motive, but wouldn't it, or couldn't it have contributed?"

"Jim, you're a better analyst than these experts. How right you are when you say your suggestion could have contributed. I'll admit that it could have lain dormant in my 'unconscious' as these men love to say. I'll admit that it could have entered, perhaps, in some way to motivate me; or as you say 'contribute' to my being moved to take it. But what was my *dominant* motive? Was it not my own interest in the matter suggested by that chapter heading? Weren't there many other contributing motives? How about my knowledge of Chadin? How about the reaction to the dust cover, the format, the very title? Jim, we all have many motives for most of our actions. Remember what we learned both in psychology and moral theology about 'mixed motives'?" Father Lehmann nodded. "That's something these experts seem never to have learned. What we want to know, both as psychologists and as moralists, is what was the *dominant* motive. That is the *conscious* motive. And that is the one we are free to follow or to deny. That's where morality really lies. What you and I want in

all our actions is a *pure* motive. When our dominant motive is pure
— that is, for the glory of God — we can forget all the other contributing motives to a great extent."

"Agreed, Father Joe. But what I want to get at specifically is this:
Can it be true that many of the things we have done from what we
considered high and noble motives were actually done from what
these men claim is nothing but 'disguised self-love,' or something even
worse. Take my position as perfect illustration: I have cancer. We
have just learned it is inoperable. That most likely means, ultimately,
it will be fatal. O.K. Now I want to accept this whole thing as you
were saying this morning — as God's will for me. I want to offer it
all back to Him. I want to be His priest through it all, His real
priest. . . ."

"Making your life a 'Mass,' eh? Using this pain as your wheat
and wine?"

"Exactly. Saying to God: 'This is Your body. This, Your blood.' "

"Well, where's the problem?"

"Right there. Have these fellows anything in what they say about
a fellow like me deceiving himself when he thinks he is acting from
a noble motive? Are they right in claiming my offering would be
nothing but disguised self-love?"

"Jim, you know right well that they aren't! That is the kind of
thing that disturbs and even disgusts me with some psychiatrists,
and even some so-called psychiatry. You know Freud claimed just
about everything sprang from our *libido* — our pleasure principle.
And for him that pleasure meant sexual pleasure. Adler broke with
him over that. He thought practically everything springs from our
'inferiority complex' — our need for self-assertion. And he was not
entirely wrong when he said this can lie deep within us, and be
highly disguised in many of our actual motivations. He would say
that you now want to assert yourself, and that your claim to want
to please God by accepting and carrying out His will in your regard,
is nothing but deception. But, Jim, if that be true, then where is
there any possibility of virtue? How could we ever grow spiritually?
How could we ever do what St. Paul says we must do: 'mature,
grow up in Christ Jesus' — and even to the stature of the mature
Christ? Now you have hit on just what angers me with much

psychiatry. It not only wants to rule out sin by making it nothing but a drive, a compulsion, a complex, or a compensation of some sort, but now it seems to want to rule out all virtue by showing us that what we call 'virtuous action' is nothing but self-deception, a failure to recognize our desire for self-assertion. To my way of thinking they not only miss the boat when they make such a claim, they are not even at the wharf."

"That's what I want to think, too, Father Joe. But you know how easily we *do* deceive ourselves. Let me be nakedly honest with you. Look at this. Read it and tell me if I am kidding myself." He took a slip of paper from his breviary and handed it to his friend. Father Joe read: "Most Holy Trinity, I thank You for the pain of the past. I love You for the pain of the present. Please send me such pain in the future as will make You better loved by myself and others. Help me to mean what I say." When Father Joe looked up from the sheet, the man in the bed asked: "Can that be self-deception?"

"About as much as Christ's statement that '. . . I have yet to undergo a baptism, and oh, in what an agony I am till it is accomplished!' (Lk. 12:50.) This psychiatry is causing the very disease it is supposed to cure. If you are really troubled by this talk about 'unconscious motivations,' Jim; troubled enough to question your own sincerity in this magnificent prayer, then you are proof of my contention that psychiatry is causing the sickness it is supposed to cure. It's bothering too many who should never be bothered. I have had parents who got anxious because their children stumbled over the pronunciation of some word, fearing that their children might be neurotic. Stuttering can be a symptom of some neurotic sickness, but every stutter or stumble in pronunciation is not necessarily a symptom. See what I mean? I have had adults, too, who wondered if they were paranoiac because they suspected certain things and certain people — and had very sound reasons for their suspicions. The whole thing is out of hand, Jim. Now let us look at your case. . . ."

"Yes, do."

"Suppose we grant that down in the deepest layer of you there is a drive for self-assertion — and I believe there is one in all of us! Suppose, further, that it is unrecognized by you, and actually does exert some influence in your prayer, and in your present acceptance and offering of this suffering. Is that the *whole* story? Of course not! Nor is it half the story! It is what plays on the surface of your consciousness right now that counts. What you choose to accept and offer up. When you *decide* to be like Christ, despite the cringing of our cowardly human nature, you are not only free, but manifesting wisdom and real manhood. You may have mixed motives — most likely you have — but the dominant motive is conscious, and fully recognized by you. That is the decisive element. Forget all this jargon about the 'unconscious.' When so-called philosophers and psychologists make high sanctity a deception, and nothing but an unrecognized drive from our lower self, it is high time we showed sanity. I still insist that depth psychology, if it can truly be called psychology, is not near deep enough. With Dr. Karl Stern I am adamant in my contention that beyond the psychological is the spiritual. You and I, Jim, are spiritual beings, not mere psychological entities. So again I say: forget all this jargon, accept your cancer as a blessing from God; use it for His glory, your own sanctification, and the good of our generation."

"But you don't deny that they have something."

"No, I don't. But I quickly add that about all they have done is to alert us on ways to make ourselves more free. Far from doing away with free will, they enable us to build it up to greater freedom; for, by waking us up to the fact that we have an 'unconscious' that may influence, they actually caution us to be more alert, to look more diligently into ourselves, and see that our dominant motive is really dominant."

"Then my job is to focus on my desire to please God."

"Precisely. We have mixed motives. Let us unmix them as far as we can, and make our dominant motive pure. It seems to me, Jim, that these supposedly learned men are guilty of the old, old fallacy of *'post hoc, ergo, propter hoc.'* Just because a thing happens *after* something else, it does not follow that it has happened *because* of that something else. The sun comes out after it has rained; but not because it has rained! What is more, I find them doing something no one ever has a right to do. I find them attributing motives to people. And you'll note that they never attribute any noble motive to anyone! They have some sharp insights. But they go altogether too far.

'*Conclusio latius patet quam praemissae.*' They draw conclusions that are altogether too wide. So relax! After your years in Innsbruck, you have sound psychology, true morality, and accurate theology. They have none of these."

"I also have inoperable cancer."

"But don't forget what Father Matt said: that does not mean, necessarily, immediately fatal. You may have many years yet to go before you can utter your '*Consummatum est.*' Never forget, Jim, that there are at least five places in the Gospel which tell how the people of God wanted to put God to death. But 'His hour' had not yet come. We go to God when God wants to take us. Live your prayer. Make your life a 'Mass.' Love Him in the present pain. Is it bad?"

"Just at present, none at all. But, Father Joe, what are those five places you speak about when 'His hour' had not yet come?"

The monk sat back. He was much more relaxed as he began to tell of Christ. So was the patient in the bed. "Jim," he began, "the startling element in all these attempts is that they came just after Jesus had either done some marvelously kind work for them or had just revealed to them some truth that meant their very lives. At Nazareth they wanted to throw Him over the cliff just outside the town because He had given them the grandest news possible; namely, that their Savior was in their midst. At Bethsaida it was just after He had cured the poor cripple who had lain by the pool thirty-eight years in utter helplessness. John says 'the result was that the Jews were all the more eager to kill Him' (Jn. 5:18). In Jerusalem there were three occasions when they would have done Him to death, and all because He had just proclaimed the best of good news, namely, that He was the Christ of God. The striking feature in all these events is the ease with which Jesus escaped, though, humanly speaking, there was absolutely no possibility of escape. Luke tells us that at Nazareth 'he passed through their midst and quietly went his way' (Lk. 29:30). John tells us that in the Holy City 'when they took up stones to throw at him; Jesus was lost to sight and made his way out of the Temple' (Jn. 8:39). Later on he tells us how the Jews 'again were eager to arrest him; but he eluded their grasp' (Jn. 10:39). And always it is simply because 'His hour had not yet come.' So, too, with you. Maybe 'your hour' has not yet come. Maybe the last part of your prayer will yet be granted. But, cheer up, faith will carry you through, the kind of faith John speaks of."

Then the monk got up and walked to the window. "Do you watch the traffic much, Jim?"

"During the day I seldom have time, Father Joe. But at night I often wonder where all the headlights are leading the drivers. There is always a steady stream of traffic going both ways."

"Right now I'm wondering what Christ means to them and how much living faith they have." He turned with that and said, "Has it ever struck you, Jim, that we sometimes make faith too impersonal a thing? Aren't we too prone to take it as an intellectual acceptance of a certain system of thought? It is that, of course. Our definition of faith really defines. It is an intellectual assent into revealed truth, accepted because of the authority of the One revealing — God. But right there, I believe, Newman's distinction between a 'notional' assent and a 'real' assent comes in with shattering force. A 'notional' assent is an assent of the mind — almost detached from the person. A 'real' assent is an assent of the whole being. St. John makes us realize that faith should be just that. As you read him, you realize that faith is a living thing, a personal thing, a dynamic, driving, forceful thing. Actually it is a mode of existence; and very precisely an existence in God, or as St. Paul would say 'in Christ Jesus.' We should never separate faith from the person of Jesus Christ. For it is belief in Christ Jesus that makes us a 'new creature' as St. Paul puts it; 'born of God' according to St. John. That 'birth' and that 'being in Christ' changes all life and all living, Jim. It gives us that *metanoia* you've heard me speak about so often; that total change of mind, will, emotions, and imaginings; that complete change of our whole being, our whole manner of life. That is what I call a 'real' assent, and the kind of assent faith should wring from each of us."

The priest in the bed propped himself up on his pillows, smiled, and said, "If Father Matt were here he'd say you are getting wound up, Father Joe, but do go on. This is just what the doctor didn't order, but what I need."

"Father Matt has a living faith if ever a man had it," said Father Joe as he leaned back on the windowsill. "If he didn't, he'd never be able to go on the way he does with that one eye of his which gives him so little vision, those feet of his which give him constant pain, that sinus trouble which causes almost daily headaches. Matt may fool other people, but he has never fooled me. Christ has a real priest in that man. He is one of my inspirations, and very particularly on this matter of faith. St. John makes one realize that faith is actually a total, unconditional surrender of our personality to God and His Christ, which surrender gives us complete victory. For it is from faith that we get that calm, unconquerable confidence, that surging hope, and a veritable vital experience of God. Thanks to it, Jim, we can 'taste and see how sweet is the Lord.' Once we have done that, all else is easy."

"Are you talking about faith or vision, Father Joe?"

"The faith John inspires is vision, Jim. That is why he is called 'the theologian'; not because he defines or systematizes truth the way our theologians do, but because he *sees* God. After all, isn't that what every real theologian should do? Have you ever closely studied John's First Epistle?"

"Not with the results you're showing."

"I'm no student, Jim. I just fell on some good reading matter. It told me how John considered faith to be a 'union with the Father and his Son, Jesus Christ' (1 Jn. 1:3) an 'abiding in the Son and in the Father' (1 Jn. 2:24). That's more than the 'God-consciousness' I've advocated for years. That makes faith a permanent and most personal union, a new mode of existence as I said before, a completely new way of life and living."

A knock on the door interrupted them, and in came an aide with the patient's tray.

"I'd better be getting back to my room or they'll be paging me. See you later, Jim. Keep the faith."

"I sure will if I can get the kind you've just been talking about."

"You've got it, Jim. Just stir it up and you'll be a 'theologian' like John was; you'll *see* God — as in a dark manner, maybe, as Paul put it, but you'll see Him nonetheless."

That was March, 1956. Father Lehmann had been operated on first in March, 1952. It surprised many to learn that the mass found on his right side had developed so unexpectedly between checkups;

for the zealous pastor had been most faithful in allowing his medical men to check on him every six months. But facts are facts: Father Lehmann's condition was now beyond help from surgery.

During the next two years the medical experts did all in their power to keep the cancer from spreading. Deep x-ray therapy was administered and many searching, and occasionally, very painful examinations were made. Father Lehmann maintained his weight quite well, but every now and then his color told that all was far from well with this always genial priest who went about his many duties as pastor with an ever-ready smile, many amusing stories, and an aura of genuine happiness.

Only his most intimate priest-friends ever got any inkling of what it was costing this brave man to live "his hour" with that Christness he had resolved upon when the verdict "inoperable" had been given him. Yet even these friends had to practically extract it from him.

Few have any idea of the multiplicity of works a pastor of a thriving parish has to perform. They see his church, his school, and some of the various organizations in the parish, but they seldom reflect that while he is responsible for the upkeep of these buildings, and the proper functioning of each separate organization, and that while he has to be something of a financial expert, an authority on education, an able organizer, and a social worker of rare talent and efficiency, yet his fundamental and final concern is the holiness of each and every person in his parish. How can a sick man be all these at one and the same time? How can a man give himself to others with that total giving required of a molder of holiness when he is conscious of something within him that is gnawing away at his own life? Were one to spend a single day in a rectory and share the concerns of a pastor as he answers the incessant ringing of the phone or the doorbell, smooths out the wrinkles caused by clashes of personalities within the conjugal unions, the domestic societies, the parish organizations, and the schoolroom; were one to go with him on visits to the sick and the dying, to observe him as he instructs the inquisitive, directs the youth, the adolescents, and the adults, bends over the parish ledgers, and plans for the future of the parish as an organization and an organism, he would be bewildered by all the demands made on a single human being. If he knew Father Lehmann's physical condition, he would stand aghast at the way the man handled each of the varying situations and different individuals.

"It is beyond human capabilities" might well be his verdict — and that verdict would be just. No mere human can be a true pastor. It requires superhuman aid. Father Lehmann had that aid; for he had taken to a prayerful reading of St. John after his latest operation, and found in the Beloved's writings the directives he needed for superhuman living. The secret of his joy-filled serenity, almost tangible goodness, and warm, ever-surging human sympathy, lay as he confided to his friend, Father Brennan, in his realization that he was "abiding in the Father and the Son thanks to the Spirit" and that they were "abiding in him." Actually his faith was alive, it had gripped his whole person and entire being, and mobilized all his forces for action. That action was exactly what St. John says it should be: it was *love*. Father Lehmann found that St. John's Epistles clarified his Gospel, and he reveled in his work with and for humans since John had placed such stress on the truth that this is the proper way to show our love for God. St. Paul had spoken to his Galatians about faith "which works through charity" (Gal. 5:6) and St. John urges all "not to love in word, neither in tongue, but in deed and in truth" (1 Jn. 3:18) and then goes on to say: ". . . this commandment we have from Him, that he who loves God should love his brother also" (1 Jn. 4:21).

Father Lehmann found himself loving people as he had never loved them before, and learned that secret of all secrets: that love is a power that embraces life in its totality, and that all its inclinations are positive. Consequently he had joy, which is love's inseparable companion. "Abide in my love," Christ had said at the Last Supper, and added, ". . . These things I have spoken to you that my joy may be in you, and that your joy may be full" (Jn. 15:10–11). Love, of course, begets love; and the busy pastor felt his love returned. Hence, his happiness; for the joy of loving and the knowledge that one is loved brings enduring happiness, which not even sickness nor anything else in life, not even the world itself, can take from our poor human hearts. "God is greater than our heart and knows all things"

(1 Jn. 3:20). Father Lehmann felt God in his heart, and knew that peace of which Christ spoke: "Peace I leave with you, my peace I give to you . . ." (Jn. 14:17).

The chapters St. John has devoted to our Lord's discourse at the Last Supper became Father Lehmann's study and steady meditation. Romano Guardini has called the seventeenth chapter of St. John "one of the holiest passages in the New Testament," and insisted that "it should be read with the concentrated powers of the heart and spirit." He readily admits that "more than almost any other part of Scripture, this prayer lies beyond the reach of intellectual dissection," but promises that "God can unveil it to him who asks for understanding." Father Lehmann must have asked for that understanding, for he not only accepted his cancerous condition with humble resignation, but with warm joy, and even a sense of glory. More than likely the truths contained there spurred him on in his labors; for in one passage Christ says to His Father: "I have glorified you on earth by completing the *work* you gave me to do." Father Jim knew the work God had given him to do: to be a suffering pastor of Our Lady's parish. He would glorify Father, Son, and Holy Spirit by staying at his post and helping every human being who came his way to know God better and live a happier, because a holier, life.

It was not easy. Careful observers might have seen his face contort at times when celebrating Mass as pain made some sudden clutch within him. There came a period when organs in the pelvic region swelled to such an extent that walking was almost unbearable. But the pastor walked! He was resolved to stay on his feet and at his work so long as God allowed him a clear mind and a will that could command his ailing body. He now had the secret of a fruitful apostolate as he thought he had never had it in all his years as a priest. "One bears abundant fruit only when he and I are mutually united" said Christ (Jn. 15:5) and followed it with the statement: "This is what glorifies my Father — your bearing abundant fruit and thus proving yourselves my disciples" (Jn. 15:8). The altar became the focal point of his life. Mass was everything to him. And when pain blinded out all horizons, as it did every now and then, he felt that it was then he was seeing God with clearest sight, and being priest in truest truth.

The years 1957 and 1958 saw Father Lehmann performing his duties with geniality and generosity. He celebrated his Silver Jubilee of Ordination with all the grace and graciousness of a very happy and truly grateful priest of God. At every reunion of Innsbruck men Father Jim was his jovial self. And as the various pastors in the diocese invited him to the closing of their Forty Hours they knew Father Jim would appear not only to give glory to God in the Eucharist, but also to give joy to His other Christs in the priesthood.

It was at one of these latter gatherings that Father Brennan teasingly called him "Pharisee." Drawing him to one side Father Matt said: "Why are you always saying you're feeling wonderful, you Pharisee?"

"But I am, Matt. Who wouldn't feel wonderful to know that he is a son of God?"

"Come on, Jim. Open up. Just how are you feeling?" That led to the revelation that St. John had given Father Lehmann a new motto. It was one of three words, borrowed from the opening lines about the Last Supper. John had written: "Jesus knowing that his hour was come . . . having loved his own who were in the world, he loved them *unto the end*" (Jn. 13:1). Father Jimmie confided to his friend that those three words: "unto the end" had come to mean more to him than he could now put in words. "I am going to keep on going 'unto the end,' Matt," he said, "and, please God, I'll go on 'unto the end' loving Him and all He has made."

"You will," said the hospital chaplain. "Never doubt it."

"But I do, Matt. I'm often worried about my ability to take it. Will I be able to measure up when real pain comes?"

Father Matt snuffed out the cigarette he had been smoking and casually said: "Sufficient for the day is the evil thereof."

"Meaning?" questioned Father Lehmann.

"Meaning that we are not supposed to borrow trouble. You've answered your own question, Jim, before you asked it."

"How so?"

"By the past six and a half years. You've taken it as it came along, Jim. You'll do the same in the future — if you have a future."

"What do you mean: if I have a future?"

"Jim, God gives us one moment at a time — only one. Not days;

not hours; just moments. And He gives us grace for the moment at the moment; not grace for the next moment. He gave you the grace you needed for yesterday, yesterday; what you need for today, today; and if you are to have a tomorrow, God will be faithful."

The two friends spent much of that evening discussing this matter of looking ahead. Father Lehmann claimed it was an exercise of the cardinal virtue of prudence to look ahead and plan wisely. Father Brennan listened calmly, then turned and told his friend that he had made it a policy to get all patients to realize that God was their Father and that Divine Providence was a fact. Once he had laid that foundation he went on to build their confidence by stressing the truth that any child who knows his father to be wise, powerful, resourceful, and kind, never has any fear of the immediate future. Now we all know God to be all-wise, all-powerful, ever watchful and always kind. Further, we have Christ's own command to become like little children. "Therefore," concluded Father Brennan, "true prudence is trust in Divine Providence."

That led to a discussion of "spiritual childhood." And they both agreed it was one lesson few mortals learn, and fewer ever live. St. Paul's line about "all things working together for the good of those who love Him" (Rom. 8:28) was quoted and commented upon, with Father Brennan saying that Paul could have used a superlative in place of a positive; that he could have taught that "all things work together for the best . . ." for a Father, such as God is, would never be satisfied with giving His children what was simply good for them; He would give them the best.

As they were preparing to part that evening Father Brennan somewhat surprised his friend by saying: "You know, Jim, I used to feel that it was our business to grow down — and I suspect that that is why so few of us ever take to that doctrine of 'spiritual childhood' with any zest. We don't like to grow down. We all want to grow up. That has been our ambition all our days. But now I know the answer to this puzzling thing. St. Paul told it to us when he told us to grow up. Yes, that is what he said to his Ephesians . . . 'to grow up in every respect . . .'; that they were to 'attain to perfect manhood, to the mature proportions that befit Christ's fullness' (Eph. 4:13–15). That directive is accepted with more relish by each of us."

"But, Matt, how about the 'childhood' we have been talking about all night?"

"There's the secret I've learned, Jim," replied the chaplain with a chuckle. "Christ was God's only Son, He became His perfect child. So we are to become like Christ. A good child is always obedient. Christ was that 'unto the end' as you insist in your motto. A good child is always docile; he waits for his father to plan things. Christ waited for 'His hour' — to quote our friend, Joe. So what have you and I to do but go along from day to day, with the grace of the moment — and have no worry about tomorrow or the next day. It works with patients, Jim. It will work with you. Not thinking of coming to the hospital for a bit of a rest and a good checkup, are you?"

"I'm staying on the job 'unto the end,' Matt. But thanks for the discussion tonight. It means more to me than you know. You really have something tremendous in your talk about 'sufficient for the day is the . . .' I'll change that text to: '. . . the grace thereof.' Pray that it will be 'efficacious grace' every moment, will you?"

" 'Unto the end,' " replied Father Brennan with a smile and a very knowing look.

Father Matt was about the only one who knew what it was costing this brave man to live his resolve; but live it he did. He carried on effectively and most efficiently throughout 1958. Just after Christmas, which he made enjoyable for all his parishioners by giving them the benefit of all the Masses and ceremonies they had come to love, he was forced to admit to Father Brennan that things were getting worse. Father Matt had taken some friends to dinner at Father Lehmann's and noted that the genial pastor took no more than a few spoonsful of soup. When they were alone for a minute, Father Jim said: "Appetite's gone, Matt; weight is falling off; energy is nil. But, please God, I'll go on 'unto the end.' "

"How's the pain?" asked the chaplain. And received as response what he had always received to that question: a smile. Father Matt shook his head as he said: "Neither Mona Lisa nor the Sphinx have anything on you, Jim. What does that smile mean?"

"What it says," replied the pastor with a broader smile. "I'm happy." And that is all Father Brennan could get from him.

New Year's Day came. Father Jim still pushed himself bravely, cheerfully, uncomplainingly. The first month of the new year passed. So did the second. But early in March, 1959, Father Lehmann yielded to Father Brennan's prodding and his urge to use some of that prudence he had one time talked about, and come to St. Joseph Infirmary. He chuckled the day he entered and said: "It was just seven years ago that I consulted my medical man about a cold I could not shake. I thought he would give me a 'shot,' some vitamin pills, and that would be that. Instead he sent me here — and I've been in and out of here ever since. Well, 'seven' is a mystical number, isn't it, Matt?"

When the chaplain did not answer with his usual speed and joking manner Father Jim looked at him and said: "Don't look so funereal. I know what you're thinking. How about giving me the last anointings? That is prudence, isn't it?" When his friend maintained his serious look Father Lehmann said: "Come on, Matt. I'm ready for extreme unction whenever you are. That's the grace of this present moment, isn't it?"

Father Brennan lost no time. As soon as Father Lehmann was settled in his bed the chaplain uncovered his oil stock, prepared the cotton, opened his ritual, and put on his stole. A more serious look came over Father Lehmann's face, but the light in his eyes was that of dancing joy. Father Brennan read the prayers. Father Jim answered with marked gravity, then received each anointing with pronounced gratitude and joy. It was a very warm "Thank you, Matt" that came from his lips after the last prayer had been said and the friend of the long "hour" which had lasted seven years was folding his stole.

Five nights later, the eve of Father Lehmann's 27th anniversary of ordination, Father Brennan received a hurry call from Sister Margaret, supervisor of surgery, and faithful friend to the two priests. She told the chaplain that she doubted that Father Jimmie would last the night. These three close friends spent most of that night in prayer. Father Lehmann was fully conscious. With what little strength he had, he joined in with the prayers of the nun and his fellow-priest, and thus kept his resolve literally to go on loving "unto the end." At eleven that night he breathed his priestly soul into the hands of the God he had served so faithfully and so cheerfully, especially during the years of "his hour."

Many of the parishioners were surprised to hear of his death; for they never realized what a sick man their pastor had been for seven full years. But one of the loveliest tributes paid to him came from one of them who said: "Having loved his own, he loved us 'to the end.'"

It was only after the funeral that Father Matt Brennan received from Father Lehmann's sister what the chaplain called "the shock of my life." Going through Father Jim's papers she came across the slip he had handed to Father Joe the day they had discussed depth psychology. When Father Matt read: "Most Holy Trinity, I thank You for the pain of the past. I love You for the pain of the present. Please send me such pain in the future as will make You better loved by myself and others. Help me to mean what I say" — he looked up and whistled in his customary fashion: "Whew! And I thought I knew Jimmie Lehmann inside out. He was a far greater priest than I ever thought, and I thought him superb!"

VII
"STUMBLING BLOCK—
ABSURDITY—WISDOM"

"What's wrong, Doctor? You look a bit frustrated, to use a very popular word."

"And that is the word to use, Father. It's that patient I saw you visiting yesterday."

"Kitty? — Isn't she a proof of my old contention that 'the patient cures himself'? I know my thesis irritates some in your profession, but what can I do? 'Contra factum non valet argumentum' is one adage I learned in my philosophy. We simply can't deny facts. If a patient does not want to be cured, neither he nor she will be cured. And I'm beginning to believe Kitty does not want to be cured."

"That's what puzzles, Father. There is an intelligent woman, yet . . . well, she simply won't use her intelligence. . . ."

"Easy, Doctor. Easy. It might just be that she is using her intelligence, but not manifesting much wisdom."

The doctor shut the chart he had been writing up, lit a cigarette with too much energy manifest in his snap of his lighter, and too deep an inhale of the first puff, for anyone to miss the fact that he was somewhat angry. He crossed his leg on his knee and took hold of his raised ankle. In this bent-over position he began speaking with an incisiveness the chaplain had seldom heard from this nerve specialist. "Father, that woman was in a very bad accident. Her left arm and left leg have been severely injured. Her spine, too, has been affected. But she can regain much use of both limbs if she will cooperate. I've seen worse cases that have responded to steady therapy. I know we have the correct therapy. But . . ." and he exhaled a very large cloud of smoke.

"But . . . the patient cures himself," said the chaplain as he too lit a cigarette and drew a chair close to the doctor. They were back in the alcove of the nurse's station on the second floor of St. Joseph

144

Infirmary, Louisville, sufficiently deep in the alcove to enjoy some privacy.

"You've given the physical injuries, Doctor," said the priest quietly, "but there is something else in Kitty that was injured in that automobile accident. It happened some months ago, I understand. A former pupil of hers was driving, and escaped without serious hurt. But Kitty was badly messed up. She was taken to some hospital upstate. . . ."

"I know," cut in the doctor. "They did what they could at the time. She has been in five different hospitals – the famous Bellvue Rehabilitation Center in New York being the last. She came here for physical therapy. I was called in for consultation. The x rays show the spine in fair condition, Father. The nerves are not too badly damaged. I believe she can be rehabilitated. But she simply will not give the cooperation necessary."

"That's what I mean about her being injured in something you cannot x-ray. Call it what you will: her spirit, her pride, her psyche, her soul. . . ."

"I deal with nerves, Father."

The chaplain smiled as he dusted ash off his cigarette, then quietly said: "We deal with persons, Doc; both you and I. And it's not easy. Kitty is angry – angry with everyone and everything. She's even angry with God. I'd dare say, especially angry with Him. Physical therapy can't do much with that. . . ."

"But that's the absurdity of the case that irritates me. She's a Catholic. She's a university graduate. She's been a very successful school teacher. She's an extremely intelligent woman. And yet . . ."

"Doc, she's hurt way down inside. Hurt as we men, I suspect, can't be hurt. Women have a pride all their own. It's deep. We sometimes think it is only about their figure or their face. It is about those, of course; but it is deeper, too; much deeper. They know that their appearance is not made up entirely of the physical; that the impact they make on others is not only from their form and features. They know they are persons – and Kitty, whether she knows it or not, is very concerned about her personality and what I call its radiance. If she ever caught the radiance she now emits, she'd die."

"She's an angry person."

"She's more than angry, Doc. She's beaten. An angry person will fight back. . . ."

"She fights back. I tried to let some sunlight into her room just now. You should have heard her. She wants no sunshine. She wants nothing of life or beauty in her room. She does not even want food. She ate next to nothing yesterday. About all she wants is a cigarette, and to be left alone. You used the right word, Father, she's frustrating."

Again that slow smile spread on the chaplain's face as he watched the nerve specialist crush out his cigarette with an angry hand. "You remind me of Doc Law. . . ."

"Law? Who is he?"

"A Chicago surgeon — and a good one. I asked him one day some years ago if he found perfect happiness in his profession. Doc Law is the one-word type of conversationalist at times, almost monosyllabic. His reply was: 'Humiliating.' When I asked how so, he said: 'If the patient is cured, they think you are God Almighty. If they are not cured, then you're simply no damned good.'"

For the first time this morning in late May, 1950, a trace of a smile passed across the nerve specialist's face. It was only a trace, but it showed that the chaplain had relaxed him somewhat.

"Did you have any success with Kitty yesterday, may I ask?"

"Less than you've had, Doc. I guess we priests can echo Doc Law. When we say the right thing, we are 'saints' — 'great men of God.' When we fail to give the right word, we're just 'pious mouths' — if not worse. But I think I dropped a seed yesterday. It may germinate within Kitty in time, and sprout. We have to be patient. Nature — which is, after all, only another way of saying 'God' — works slowly."

"But, Father, there's the difficulty and the danger in this case. Let me show you," and he opened the chart he had so recently slammed shut. Flicking back the pages he found the one holding the history of the case. He glanced at it a moment then turned full on the priest. "Do you know George Colvin?" When the chaplain shook his head in negation, the doctor said, "He was at one time president of the University of Louisville. Before that he was superintendent of public instruction in Kentucky. Quite a renowned educator. But what I want to get at is this: George Colvin was one time head of Ormsby

Village. You certainly know what that is, don't you?"

"Home for Dependent and Delinquent Children — In other words: Orphanage and Reform School."

"You certainly call a spade a spade. O.K. Well the fact that George Colvin hired Kitty Conroy as teacher at Ormsby Village, kept her, and saw her made principal of the school when he went to the U. of L. as president, tells me more about our patient than all these charts, x-rays, or lab tests could ever tell me. George Colvin demanded competency. He just about demanded perfection. So we have no neurotic on our hands who is seeking sympathy as compensation for lack of success. This woman must have been a towering success. When she was injured in the early fall of 1948, she had just begun her eighteenth year teaching at the University School in Lexington. That not only bespeaks stability of character, it tells of a highly successful career. So what is it now that is plaguing her? I can tell you two things: she needs no neuropsychiatrist nor any neurosurgeon. She's stable and sane, and her nerves, while frayed from this accident, call for no radical treatment. You've heard of muscular dystrophy. Well, if Kitty Conroy does not help herself by cooperating with our program, that left leg and left arm of hers . . ." and he shrugged his shoulders.

"The patient cures himself," repeated the chaplain with a smile, and hitched his chair closer. "I've got news for you, Doctor. Marguerite MacLaughlin, who taught journalism at the U. of K., was down last week. I spoke to her about Kitty. Marguerite not only taught journalism, she practiced it. She was on the staff of the Lexington *Herald* for some years. She is still a journalist — has all the facts and figures — and all the news. She filled me in on Kitty Conroy. If I told you all Marguerite told me, your problem would grow. For, according to Marguerite, our patient was just about the most popular person on the campus up in Lexington some twenty-five or twenty-six years ago. She was in just about everything: dramatics, year book, school paper, pep organizations, sororities — and usually at the head of all these things. She graduated with honors, and turned down all job offers to become a schoolteacher — and not an ordinary schoolteacher, but one at that school you named out in Ormsby Village. Does that say anything to you?"

The doctor slapped the page of the chart open before him. "Makes this all the more unintelligible."

"I thought it would," said the chaplain quietly. "You see success written over her whole career, and cannot understand why she is lying down under this accident. For you well know what it takes to achieve the successes that were Kitty Conroy's in any University and at any Reform School. But it is that past which explains the present to me fully. She has had too much success. That has been her failure."

"Getting paradoxical, eh?"

"No. Just practical, Doc. I've seen success cause the failure of many a soul."

"You told me we deal with persons a little while ago. Let's keep Kitty as a person."

"And that is really what I meant, Doctor. Success kills persons. And I want you to look at Kitty as a person — and not as a mass of ganglia. I want you to see her as a person who has failed simply because she has known too much success. A crushed arm, a crushed leg, a crushed spine are nothing in themselves if they do not crush the person. We've got to get the crushed person who is Kitty Conroy out from under, before we can hope for any success on her crushed arm, leg, or spine. Your physical therapy will not work unless you get in some spiritual therapy first, Doc."

"Is that my field? I thought. . . ."

"I know what you're going to say, Doc. Just let's agree that we both treat persons, not separated bodies or isolated souls. I have to keep in mind the state of the patient's body as I make efforts in my field. You must take into consideration the state of the person's mind, emotions, imagination, will — in short, Doc, Kitty's whole soul. She's sick there, as much, if not more than, in her somewhat mangled body. She's got to want to get well before any physical therapy will aid her — and that 'wanting' has to come from her soul, her will. Miss Conroy has to be oriented to wisdom, Doc. Up until now she has only been turned toward knowledge and understanding."

The physician closed the chart again and arose. "You seem to know more about this case than I do, Father. It sounds to me as if it were more your case than mine."

The priest rose with the doctor. "No, Doc. It's a case for both of us."
"Well, I don't know too much about this orientation toward wisdom you've just been talking about. I do know a little about nerves and muscles, and the function of arms and legs. And I'm sure that Miss Conroy must get moving." The chart was back in its proper place by now and the doctor was moving out of the alcove. The priest was right beside him.

They moved out beyond the desk and headed toward the nearby elevator. Obviously the doctor was heading for surgery. The chaplain pressed the button for the car and while waiting for it to descend said, "That's the seed I dropped yesterday, Doc. I told Kitty she had much knowledge but very little wisdom. It may germinate. If it does, we'll have success. If it doesn't, prepare for squalls. This woman not only has an intellect; she has a very stubborn will."

The elevator door opened. "Ride up with me, Father, and tell me the difference between understanding and wisdom."

The Chaplain held the door as he said, "I have to see a patient down the line. We wouldn't have time anyhow. But I'll give you something to think about if I say we all know that Christ went to the cross, but few of us have learned that the cross is the wisdom of God." He let the door close as he smiled at the surgeon and said, "See you later, Doc."

The chaplain was right: Kitty Conroy's spirit had been crushed even more than her body. As she now lay in her bed in the Infirmary staring at the wall, her thoughts were not on the seed the priest had dropped the day before, nor were they on her distant past with its many triumphs. Rather they were centered in angry concentration on what she called her "mangled self." What good was she? What good was all the knowledge she had acquired? What could she now do with all the skills she had gained these past twenty-four years as she worked with children? She would never work again. How could she ever face a class with this paralyzed arm and leg? Her world was in ruins and could not be reshaped. Certainly not by physical therapy. Not by herself. No, not even by God! Why had He allowed this thing to happen? If He is all-powerful, as she had always believed; if He was behind every event in life, as she had been taught; then He could have prevented this.

Or at least He could have allowed her to come out of that smashup as unscathed as had her former pupil. Surely, He could have had the medical men who first worked on her do more than they had done. But, no. Here it was more than seventeen months after the accident, and she was in worse condition, she felt, than when first brought to the hospital in Lexington, bruised, bloody, unconscious. Now she knew her condition. Now she felt this useless arm and that crippled leg. Was there a God? If so, where was His kindness? She gave up this line of thought, reached for a cigarette, lit it angrily, and smoked in what she took to be despair.

A gentle knock came on her door which was quietly opened and a nursing Sister entered. "Good morning, Miss Conroy. Hope you're better today," said the nun as she crossed the room and began to lift the shade.

"Leave that shade down. Please! I want no light in this room."

"But it's a beautiful sunshiny day, Miss Conroy."

"Not for me. It's dark. My whole world is dark. My life is dark. Leave it that way."

Sister Imelda had had difficult patients before, but this woman was proving the most difficult of all. "Let me get you some fresh water," she said, and lifted the pitcher off its stand and left the room. In the corridor she met Sister Philip Maria from the physical therapy department. "She's still in her black mood, Sister. See what you can do."

The therapist entered the patient's room. "Good morning, Kitty," she said. "Had a good night?" And she went over to raise the shade.

"Leave that down!" came the severe command from the bed. Then when she noted the pained expression on Sister's face she softened a trifle. "Sorry, Sister. I know I'm a difficult patient. I'm sure I just hurt Sister Imelda — and she's been so kind, patient, and attentive. But I'm down. Yes, lower than I like to admit. But what can I do? I'm crippled for life, and I know it."

"Don't say that, Kitty. I've seen people in much worse condition than you are regain use of their limbs. Let me massage that arm of yours. This afternoon I'll treat your leg."

"You're wasting your time and energy, Sister. I'll never use this arm and leg again. I'm ruined, I tell you!"

Sister Philip Maria went ahead with her preparations. "No one is ever ruined beyond repair so long as they are alive, Kitty. You'd be surprised at the rebuilding we do with simple physical therapy. Just last month . . ."

"No, no. Don't tell me, Sister. You're good and you're kind. But I know my condition. I know I'll never walk again. I know I'll never teach a class again. Oh, what am I going to do with myself — with my life?" And the woman literally writhed in the bed.

Sister was smiling as she came closer to the bed. "Just now you're going to allow me to stroke some life back into your arm. Then, if you'll do the exercises . . ."

"Stop, Sister. I've never pretended in my life. I'm not going to begin now. I'm through, I tell you. I know." And she reached for another cigarette.

"Oh, what a beautiful crucifix!" exclaimed Sister as she waited for the patient to smoke a bit. "I've never seen one just like it, Kitty. Is it from Europe?" The therapist had gone around the bed to the dresser and lifted the alabaster crucifix from its resting place before the mirror.

"I don't know, Sister. Marguerite MacLaughlin gave it to me the last time she was down. I've hardly looked at it. I see now that it is a beauty." Sister had it in her hands, studying the delicate workmanship on the corpus. "Marguerite said it might help me, and hoped I'd treasure it as a token of real friendship."

Sister held it from her a moment, then said, "Beautiful! *Too* beautiful! Treasure it, Kitty."

"Why do you call it 'too' beautiful, Sister?" asked the patient with some slight show of curiosity.

Sister replaced the crucifix, came around to the left side of the bed, lifted Kitty's hand and began a gentle massage of the left arm before answering. "Have you ever thought of how Christ must have actually appeared on the cross, Kitty?"

The woman in the bed was watching the therapist's fingers stroking her arm, much more intent on the arm than on the question. A frown either of fright or of pain, gathered on her brow. Sister's fingers moved further down the arm. "I doubt that He looked as beautiful as He looks on that cross of yours, Kitty. I doubt that there was as much repose in His body. He was nailed, you know." The massaging went on a bit more rapidly. "Still, I suppose the artists are kind when they do not give us a realistic crucifix. We couldn't stand the sight."

A sharp cry of pain stopped Sister's words as well as her fingers. "Sorry, Kitty! Can you move your fingers?" she asked gently as she held the patient's hand. Kitty made very little noticeable effort.

"They're dead," she replied in a dull tone.

"Try," coaxed the Sister.

"Oh!" snapped Kitty in some disgust, and pulled her hand away from Sister, turned slightly in bed, and buried her head in the pillow.

"Good!" cried the nun. "You moved your whole arm and shoulder just then, Kitty. You're improving rapidly." Actually, Sister Philip Maria felt an inner twinge of impatience with the woman in the bed.

Kitty was silent.

Just then Sister Imelda knocked and entered with the pitcher of fresh water. She took in the scene at a glance, smiled, and said, "A little better every day, isn't she, Sister?"

"Much better every day," came the bright reply from Sister Philip Maria. "She just moved her whole arm and shoulder. It's becoming ever so much more flexible."

"Pfff!" was Kitty's only comment as she let out a cloud of smoke from the cigarette she had just lighted.

"Have you seen her beautiful crucifix, Sister?" asked the therapist as she covered a jar of cream she had used. "See it there on the dresser. It's genuine alabaster."

"Bee-utiful!" said Sister Imelda softly.

"I told her it was too beautiful, Sister; for it does not show just how much Jesus loved us. Real love is not always beautiful to behold. He wasn't beautiful as He died. And He is real love."

Sister Imelda looked at the other nun and caught a knowing look in her eyes. She realized that the physical therapist was giving the patient something not on the chart. She smiled as she said, "It is beautiful, Kitty. It tells us that He is not only love but beauty as well. I hope you will treasure it."

"I've got to be going," said Sister Philip Maria. "Exercise those fingers, Kitty. I'll see you this afternoon. God be with you."

A very unenthusiastic "Thank you, Sisters" followed the nuns out of the room.

Why can't I be more gracious? the patient asked herself. They are doing all they can for me — and doing it with such warmth and cheer. Yet I can't even say a decent "Thank you." She snuffed out her cigarette. A sharp pain in her left leg suddenly set her angrily muttering, "O God! You could have prevented all this. You could have left me whole!" Then as she squirmed, the words *love, beauty* squeezed their way out between her set teeth.

Day after day for the next few weeks the same pattern was followed. Kitty despised herself for being so ungracious, yet realized that the very despising only added fuel to the fire and made her even more ungracious. She would justify her mood and her unmannerliness in tense, angry mutterings at God, then feel more ashamed and more filled with self-detestation. She knew she had a genuine admiration, even some affection for both Sister Imelda, the floor supervisor, and the capable physical therapist, Sister Philip Maria. Yet how niggardly she had been with any manifestations of it. "I'm just an embittered shrew," she admitted to herself. Yet almost immediately added: "But what else can I be?"

Were they to judge from the surface appearances, doctors, nurses, nuns, and even the chaplain might have agreed with her estimate of herself. She *was* a difficult patient. But most of these had seen flashes of the real woman which lay covered by the pain that was in her mind and spirit even more than in her body — and those flashes they found arresting and inspiring. There was character beneath this caricature, they felt certain. They would work, pray, and be patient, hoping that the character would take over before too long.

One morning toward the middle of the fourth week of the hospitalization, Sister Imelda was filled with hope; for she had been told that the principal of one of Louisville's leading schools was to come out that day to offer Kitty a position on the faculty. That will be the therapy she needs, thought Sister, and quietly thanked God for what she considered an answer to her many prayers for this woman who had won her anxious concern despite the fact that she had been so uncooperative a patient.

Before the sun set that same day, however, Sister Imelda was bereft of her hopes, and more nonplused than ever as to what to do for Kitty Conroy. For the principal had come; had been generous with his praise for Miss Conroy's records; and quite obviously anxious to have the woman teaching in his school. Kitty had next to no comment to make either to the praise or to the possibilities opened before her. When the principal tried to score a point by remarking that if Miss Conroy would have to be in a wheelchair for some time in the beginning, this would be a help rather than a hindrance; for the spontaneous sympathy of the children would inspire them to study harder and behave better; he was met after a tense silence with a somewhat withering: "I have too much pride ever to allow children to see me in this condition."

Still the principal persisted. But Kitty Conroy's mind was made up. She finally nodded to the principal somewhat curtly, and said, "You have been most kind to make the offer. I am trying to be as kind in declining it. Thank you for everything."

When he heard of the offer and the refusal, the chaplain's only remark was: "I doubt that Kitty will ever get into a wheelchair. The way things are going she may be bedfast for the rest of her life." He was not alone in this opinion. Some of the doctors on the case shared it with him. But the priest would never let go of his hope that he could drop seeds that would one day germinate. He seldom talked on a personal level with Kitty after his first few visits; for he saw that she resented it. When he talked in general terms, they held some semblance of a conversation. He often managed to suggest to Kitty that there was a difference between knowledge and wisdom. He had a purpose for this insistence, but almost to the very end of her stay in St. Joseph Infirmary Kitty Conroy never rose to his bait.

They talked most frequently on education. On rare occasions Kitty grew enthusiastic on the subject, telling what a thrill it was to see young minds open out, watch them take definite shape, and finally fall into the lines which would mark the character of the man or woman to be. From such bursts of enthusiasm the priest got an insight into the soul of this embittered patient. He saw that her heart had gone out to her fellow humans and strongly suspected that, despite the fact that Kitty was a Catholic, she had unwittingly substituted a cult of humanity for genuine religion. He sympathized with the woman for what he secretly called a "degradation of what is holiest in our Faith." As the days mounted he grew convinced that Kitty's basic difficulty was her lack of a full and proper concept of God. It was nothing new in his experience, and it was this that made it all the sadder for him to see. Many people fail to recognize God's sovereign rights over them; fail dismally to see themselves as creatures — with all the raptures that word connotes. Failing to recognize God as Creator, they can never come to a full realization of their own very nature; for they have already missed the discovery of the origin and the end of their being. Consequently, no matter how active they may be, nor how orderly in their activities, they are like a mariner on an horizonless sea minus a compass. They go on and on; but they really have no ultimate destination.

He had discussed it with his fellow priests, telling how he had found souls more naked to his sight in sickness than even in the sacrament of penance. He claimed that, for many, God was too "distant"; for others, merely "hypothetical" and even "purely imaginary." He saw how these good and earnest people had conceived the notion that their true greatness lay in serving their fellowman, in loving them, helping them, and even forgetting themselves in the process. This was putting man in the place of God; substituting social service for the service of God. "It is extremely attractive to many noble souls," he said, "truly seductive." Then he would add with a sad shake of his head, "But it is truly destructive, also. Genuine personality suffers, and real nobility is lost. What is more, these people not only run the danger of losing eternal life, they are missing out on true temporal living; for there is no real living that is not worship of God. And these people are not worshiping Him." He admitted that such people found some satisfaction in their dedication, but insisted it was not full satisfaction, nor could it ever be; for it was a distortion, of the way God wants us to serve our fellowman. "They are serving man as man, and not as images of God and members of Christ," was his conclusion.

Whenever asked what was the cause of this condition, he inevitably cited education, then made his distinction between knowledge and wisdom. "They get more knowledge these days than formerly," he would say, "but it is not leading to wisdom."

His fellow priests seldom failed to ask him what he meant by wisdom, but Kitty Conroy, though he had tried his thesis more than once, never questioned him as he hoped she would. So in the last week of her stay in Louisville, he one day, lifted the alabaster crucifix off her dresser and after admiring its patent beauty, quoted St. Paul to the effect that "the message that the cross proclaims is nonsense to those who are on the road to destruction, but to us who are on the road to salvation, it is the power of God." When he saw lights kindle in Kitty's eyes he went on: ". . . 'I will destroy the wisdom of the wise, and the cleverness of the clever I will thwart.' . . ." Kitty showed some interest, so the chaplain continued: "Has not God turned to nonsense the 'wisdom' of this world? . . . The Jews demand miracles and the Greeks look for 'wisdom,' but we, for our part, preach a crucified Christ — to the Jews certainly a stumbling block and to the Gentiles an absurdity, but to those who are called, to the Jews and Greeks alike, Christ, the power of God and the wisdom of God. Why, there is more wisdom in the 'absurdity' of God than in all the 'wisdom' of men, and more might in the 'weakness' of God than in all the might of men" (1 Cor. 1:19–25).

"That's magnificent, Father," said Kitty with genuine enthusiasm.

"That's St. Paul, Kitty. He was speaking to the people of his times. He was speaking to the peoples of all times. He was speaking to you and to me. This cross says exactly what He said. It tells of 'absurdity' — 'weakness' and — yes, and especially of wisdom. Don't be surprised if you find a Jew and a Greek in your own Christian self. At times this will look like an 'absurdity.' We are all philosophers as were the Greeks. We reason, and we judge things according to the standards of our own reason. We are ready to accept God as First Cause. But as crucified? That is another question. It appears foolishness. We are also Jews. We are human beings of high sensitivity. The sight of a Man on a cross shocks us. Suffering is still a stumbling block for millions. It makes many of us fall. But if we will only open our eyes and see — and not merely look, we will find in this cross of Christ the wisdom of God. It is the wisdom of *love*."

He laid the crucifix back on the dresser. He had seen the incomprehension in the patient's eyes as he ended on the high note of love. "It's a mystery, Kitty. Don't expect to understand it fully. Faith alone allows us to see the power and the wisdom of God in a Man fastened to a tree. But if you will cultivate that faith, if you will go on looking with love, you will one day get deep insight into this mystery of God which is a mystery of merciful justice, of almighty and eternal love. You will also come to share in the life of this mystery. Then you will live, for then you will really love. Study this crucifix, Kitty. It is the book of all books. It will give you more than knowledge. It will give you real wisdom."

Two days later Kitty Conroy left St. Joseph Infirmary. She was not greatly improved in body or in spirit. She was still bitter about her condition. But seeds had been sown that would one day sprout.

She was moved to a nursing home nearer Lexington. It was less expensive, and closer to her relatives and friends. But Kitty wanted little to do with either friends or relatives for weeks, and even months after the move. The black bitterness was still within her.

Father Brophy, the local pastor, called on her shortly after her arrival. It was but a repetition of her early days at St. Joseph Infirmary. Kitty was not only not really nice to him, she was rather nasty. But Father Brophy was a semi-invalid himself. Polio had left its mark on him. He understood the moods of the shut-ins — and Kitty was very definitely now a shut-in; not only physically because of her body, but even socially and spiritually because of her embittered mind.

Father Brophy came back again and again. Weeks ran into months, and months measured out a year. Slowly Kitty changed. Some would say "the mills of God grind slowly" and the metaphor would not be out of place. But a more apt comparison would be that of the seed and its slow growth. For the many seeds dropped by the nuns at St. Joseph Infirmary and by the cautiously and carefully working chaplain had not fallen by the wayside, nor upon stony ground. Basically, Kitty Conroy was honest, sincere, genuine. It was these very qualities that had caused her, in her emotionally upset condition, to act as she had acted. She would not pretend. She would act only on conviction — and for a long time her conviction was that she had been dealt with harshly. Resentment was honesty. Bitterness was a form of sincerity. Anger showed how genuine she was at the core of her being.

Who could blame her for feeling that her life was ruined? On being graduated from the University of Kentucky with honors — especially in journalism — she had bypassed tempting offers in order to dedicate herself to something she considered more noble: the formation of young minds and the shaping of characters. She gave herself for years to the most difficult segment of the field of education — that of delinquents and orphans. She achieved outstanding success. From Ormsby Village she went to the University School in Lexington, and, for seventeen years filled her days by pouring herself out on others in loving efforts to orient boys to real manhood and girls to true womanhood. Those efforts brought thrilling results. Twenty-four years of life had known harvests that brought peace and joy. Now, in late middle age, all that, she felt, had been taken from her by an automobile smashup. There would be no more opportunity to impart knowledge. Why should she gather any more, if she were to be denied the possibility of giving from all she garnered? No wonder her days seemed "dark and dreary," or that her world appeared black.

The fact was that Kitty, despite all her nobility, had not plumbed the final fathoms of life on earth; had not touched the lowest depths of her being, did not know with absolute clarity what it means to be a creature of God. But, slowly, very slowly, from some reading and much reflection, light crept back into her world. It may have begun with contact with others in the nursing home. These awakened her to the fact that she was not alone in the world of suffering; not the only cripple in existence. It was something of an awakening; for at St. Joseph Infirmary she had paid no attention to other patients — she was totally taken up with Kitty. But now she saw others incapacitated as was she, shut in from the rush of the world. Yet she saw some of these were not only quite content with their position, but even making use of their time and talents. It gave her something to ponder.

Then there were visitors. She gradually awoke to the fact that these showed different reactions to her and her condition. Slowly it dawned on her that those with a sense of God and His dominion, left her with a feeling altogether different from the one that was hers when others whose thoughts seemed entirely taken up with life on earth left her. Gropingly she sought for the reason. Gradually the fingers of her mind touched it – but only touched it. Vaguely she knew it was God. But this realization often stirred some of her earliest resentments.

Kitty was still quite engrossed in Kitty. So she often was demanding. When those whose task it was to serve her manifested signs of impatience with her and her demands, tiny echoes of the ways and the words of the nursing nuns crept into her consciousness. How patient they had been with a much more demanding and uncooperative patient! And what precious words of cheer and encouragement they always left with her. How often she had heard Sister Philip Maria say: "Pray, Kitty, pray. Ask God to help you." How often she now heard in her heart the remark of Sister Imelda: "God will aid you, if you let Him." ". . . if you let Him" – What did Sister mean by that? Kitty did not fully understand. She knew God was almighty. How, then, could a creature keep Him from aiding them?

Had she only analyzed her own thought, concentrating on the one word *creature* until she had distilled its full meaning, she would have saved herself months of anguish. But she had not, as yet, discovered the ultimate depths of her own being. So she suffered – as all will suffer who live on the surface of reality.

But one day there came to her in the mail a little booklet called the "CUSA Newsletter." She opened the first page and read an explanation of that peculiar title CUSA. It is a coinage from the first letters of the name: Catholic Union of the Sick in America, an organization of Catholics whose state of health is an occasion for sacrifice. That came as a completely new idea to Kitty Conroy. Up to now she had not thought of using her condition – but only of relieving it, and even of getting rid of it. But here she was faced with an invitation to join with others – men and women, young and old, lay people and religious, rich and poor – in a union formed by

the common bond of "love and suffering." She had the suffering.
Of that she was sure. But what about the other requirement for
eligibility? She read on and learned the purpose of the organization:
"to help each other and to help other souls." She stopped. "To
help . . ." How could she in her condition help anyone? Her
temptation was to cast the Newsletter aside as "pollyannic pap" —
Kitty would always be honest. Never would she allow herself to
pretend. She had helped others all her life. But now . . . How could
a shut-in help anyone? But curiosity brought her back to the page
and she read that this organization, whose only requirements were
suffering and love, was offered to all and to any who were ill, even
only chronically ill and not bedridden, as "an opportunity to help
themselves both spiritually and materially and to feel that the cross
of sickness, which the good Lord has sent them, can be used for
His greater honor and glory."

She got that far in the letter when her memory played her one
of those tricks memories will play, and she seemed to hear the chaplain at St. Joseph Infirmary quietly saying: "There's a difference
between knowledge and wisdom, Kitty."

She knew she was crippled. She knew that, more than likely,
she would be an invalid for the rest of her days. She knew that,
save for some "miracle" of surgery or medicine, she would be a
shut-in. But had any of this knowledge led her to any scrap of
wisdom? Could it be that the chaplain had meant she was being
unwise not to use the knowledge of her condition as this Letter said
it could be used: for self, for others, for God? She laid the Letter
down, lit a cigarette, and tried to puzzle it out. But always that
thought of her helplessness and physical deformity blocked out any
vision of possible utility. She smoked angrily, for she was thinking
angrily. No, she told herself, she could not help others. She could
not help herself! Here she was bedridden and a burden to everyone —
most especially to herself. What was all this nonsense about helping
self and others? She snuffed out her cigarette and snatched up the
Newsletter once again. She read: "The duties of a member of the
Catholic Union of the Sick in America are very simple: once a month
a group letter comes to each member bringing him news of his group
and a message from their priest-chaplain." "That's simple enough,"

said Kitty aloud. Then read on. "The annual dues are $2, but are not compulsory; and even those who cannot afford stamps for their letters are quite welcome." – Well, thought Kitty, this certainly is not a moneymaking organization. It appears truly altruistic. She turned a few pages and found an article titled "JOY":

"On Judgment Day we will not be questioned concerning our ailments and infirmities," it began, "but concerning our duties. Among those duties, there is one to which we give little thought, and when we do think of it, it is to shut it out of a difficult life: the duty of joy, the duty of seeking and cultivating true joy." Kitty marveled that anyone should think that we had a *duty* to be joyful. Her honest mind questioned the truth of the statement, and led her on further in the article.

She fully agreed with the opening sentence of an early paragraph that said: "There's no cause for rejoicing. . . . My fatigue, my helplessness, my uselessness, are all increasing, this is no source of joy." But then came the refutation. "Joy does not come from us. It comes from God; and in order to find it we must look for it." – Where, thought Kitty, am I to look for it – shut up here in this room in this tiny rest home? Again that temptation to fling his Newsletter aside. But she read on. "If we remind ourselves over and over again, as is absolutely necessary, that despite appearances we are not cast upon the earth by chance, and that even in the most precarious state there is very great security, because God knows all about each of us, even our least annoyances . . ." There it is again, thought Kitty: God! But as she lay there with the Newsletter open on her lap the realization that God had brought her into being; that she had not been "cast upon the earth by chance," deepened. Its truth sobered her. "I am a creature of God," she said half aloud. Then kept repeating as if in some sort of a trance: "Of God . . . of God . . . of God. I am a creature of God. How wonderful! . . . Of God!"

Unknown to herself Kitty was doing what the chaplain at St. Joseph Infirmary had wanted her to do. She was deepening her knowledge, not just broadening it. She was dwelling on a truth. She was drawing the fullness of its meaning into her very being. Knowledge was becoming wisdom.

It was some time before Kitty picked up the Newsletter again, but when she did she realized that her whole attitude had changed. She was no longer angry, no longer resentful, no longer antagonistic toward the writer. She was willing now to consider what was offered by the article. "Joy is in us," she read, "as God is in us, by His grace, but we must discover its source. Once it is found, it gushes forth into our lives and into the lives of all around us, like jets of water from the beautiful fountains that are the joy of so many cities and gardens." Again Kitty set the Letter down and thought. She recalled many beautiful gardens she had seen with fountains whence limpid water was rising in silver splendor, then arching over and falling down with a gracefulness that was well-nigh inimitable. "Oh, to shed joy all about me like that!" she exclaimed softly, and reached for the Newsletter.

"I am not talking of the joy that dissipates, that intoxicates, that takes us out of ourselves — I mean the joy that is love, with which we recognize unmistakably the echo, the trace of God in everything that happens." Kitty let one word only escape her: "Everything?" But read on: "Instead of being buried under the mountains of our difficulties, let us try to find the small window toward the Infinite, and then nobody, nothing will ever be able to imprison us." Where, oh where, is that window? Kitty wondered. But she went on to the end of the article and found the directive "Let us learn to be less superficial; less prone to complain and to see the bad side of things . . . and little by little, this splendid thing will happen: we will be able to say like St. Paul, 'Nothing can separate me from the love of Christ, neither hunger, nor prison, nor death. . . .' But to achieve this state, we must begin by wanting it a little, by emerging from personal preoccupations, in order to discover that there is Someone else continually concerned with us, who will save us despite everything. . . ."

" 'Pie in the sky,' " commented Kitty with a note of disgust and tossed the Newsletter on her table. But all that day and all that night snatches of the article came back to her. Joy, a duty. That little window toward the Infinite. God within her. Someone else continually concerned with her. Then the picture of the graceful fountains and their beautifully arching waters. But it was not until just before Father Brophy arrived some days later that she thought of the reference to St. Paul. He was the one, she remembered, whom the chaplain in Louisville quoted about the Jews and the Greeks, the "absurdity" and the "stumbling block" that was the cross of Christ, which, yet, was the "power and the wisdom of God." There it is again, thought Kitty – wisdom! But she resolved to ask Father about the passage. It might be wisdom on her part to know whence it came.

Father satisfied her request, but was curious about the reason behind the query. Thus he learned of the Cusans for the first time. He was enthusiastic. "What an opportunity, Kitty! You can use your suffering. You have an apostolate. You can help the whole Church. You can help the whole world. You can even help God; for this same Apostle, Paul, teaches that we can 'fill up what is wanting to the Passion of Christ.' This is marvelous!"

Kitty did not agree. She was being her honest self. It would take more thought before she could see her condition as an opportunity. All she could see in it was incapacity. But Father's enthusiasm whetted her curiosity sufficiently to send her back to that Newsletter she had tossed aside in such disgust. She read it from cover to cover, and learned that hundreds, far worse off than she, were actually using their suffering, as the Letter said it could and should be used: for self, for others, for God. Kitty spent a thought-filled night.

The next morning, almost against her will, she picked up the Letter and tried, as well as she could, to read "The Cusan's Morning Offering" – and make of her reading a prayer. "Dear Lord," it began, "here is a new day Thou hast given me in which to love Thee and help others to love Thee as well." It went on to ask "above all things, help me to love and accept Thy holy will." Kitty had never prayed that with full heart before. This morning she felt there was some sincerity in her request. The night had done something to her. She went on to pray: "Lord Jesus, in giving me this cross of my present condition, it is Thy desire to bring me nearer to Thy divine Heart, and especially didst Thou want me to offer my cross, united with Thine own, for the salvation of souls.

"Help me today not to waste a single one of the trials – both large and small – which are the lot of the invalid and which, if borne with patience, can obtain so many graces. I offer them to Thee with all my heart. . . . Bless my brothers and sisters in CUSA and may we all glorify Thee and give proof of our love for Thee by bearing courageously and even joyously the cross which is ours."

Just what it was, Kitty could not say, but somehow or other that day was different. Things did not seem so burdensome. She found herself more pleasant to her fellow sufferers. That night she wondered if this was what Sister Imelda had meant by her oft-repeated "if you will let God help you." Maybe it was God who had helped her through this day. The thought of Sister Imelda awoke Kitty to the fact that she had not written to Sister in weeks — or was it months? She must write and beg her to come to see her if possible.

The next day, and those following, Kitty made the same Morning Offering. She went on for weeks doing the same and was more and more impressed by the words: ". . . in giving me this cross of my present condition" — and those others about "Help me today not to waste one of the trials. . . ." Could she really believe that God had allowed that accident for her good? It was difficult to accept such a belief. But she had no difficulty at all in realizing that if trials could be utilized, she certainly had wasted months and months of them! But *how* in the world could they be used? was one question Kitty asked again and again.

An answer came one sleepless night when her eyes fell on the alabaster crucifix Marguerite MacLaughlin had given her, and which had been such an object of admiration for most of her visitors. As she looked at it this particular night she suddenly recalled Sister Philip Maria's words: "Too beautiful." She looked at the crucifix thoughtfully. Why had Sister called it "too beautiful," she asked herself — and remembered two snatches from Sister's explanation: "He was nailed" . . . and "Love is not always beautiful to behold." Kitty Conroy meditated that night. She thought long on the fact that this was a representation of reality. That this was a symbol of that Sacrifice which was the heart of the religion she professed and was supposed to practice. This was God's only Son. This was God Himself — nailed. The thought seemed to stop there — and yet it grew and grew. God — nailed! Soon she felt that thought go beyond her mind and enter into her heart. What were these emotions of hers? Sympathy? She never before sympathized with Christ on the cross. But now . . . yes, she was filled with a sympathy that hurt! She knew what it was to have a pain-filled body – to lie in one position, yet be alive with ache to change that position. She always managed somehow. But He . . . The thinking went on, but always to the throb of that major thought: God – nailed! Now her heart was not pulsing with sympathy, but with shame! He – God – had become Man – and we men had nailed Him . . . His own people! His chosen people! Deeper and deeper went the thought. Kitty was ashamed of men, of mankind! Then came the realization that she had had part in this reality – she, Kitty Conroy, had helped nail God! Now she wanted to stop thinking. She could feel the blush rise to her cheeks. But she could not take her eyes from that crucifix. Now she understood Sister's remark: "Too beautiful!" Indeed! Altogether too beautiful! How could crucifixion – the nailing . . . and the very word seemed to screech in the silence of this throbbing night . . . how could nailing a Man ever be beautiful? And this Man was *God!* "Oh, Jesus!" was all she said, but with those words her whole womanly heart seemed to burst forth in sympathetic love.

Whether she wept salt human tears from her eyes, she could never say. But that her heart wept tears of blood she felt certain. It was a long meditation. How long, Kitty never knew. But from that night on she knew how to pray with all her being, and she knew the difference between knowledge and wisdom. She groped for a definition to bring out the difference. She tried qualifying knowledge to see if she could bring it out. Wisdom, she thought, might be defined as "loving knowledge." But no. That did not satisfy. "A love that knows" seemed better to Kitty; but she feared it would be meaningful only for Kitty. So she went on groping. When Father Brophy next visited he found a different woman awaiting him. When she asked him the difference between knowledge and wisdom, he was nonplused. So she told him something of her experience of the sleepless night. She ended with the words: "Now I *see!*" Father seized upon them and asked if that might not be the difference between knowledge and wisdom. The knowing man looks; the wise man sees. But Kitty refused it as both too subtle and too superficial. Suddenly she brought her good right hand down on her bedside table and exclaimed: "I've got it, Father! Wisdom is knowledge that leads to God. Any knowledge that stops short of Him is not real knowledge. It is not wise with true wisdom." When the priest seemed hesitant to accept this, she went on: "Look, Father, I thought I knew myself all these years. I had quite a knowledge of what makes me me. But I will never know my real being, my real self, all that I am, and how little I am, until I see myself in relation to God. If all my knowledge about myself does not finally lead me to the realization that I am His creature — His creation! — I know nothing about myself!"

That precipitated a discussion that lasted longer than Father had intended to stay, but as he made his way home he realized he had just come from a woman who had been singularly graced by God by an insight into her creaturehood which seemed destined to change her whole outlook on life. It had already changed her attitude toward her suffering. She had asked him if the saying: "Is not the potter master of the clay" had not come from the Bible. He had assured her it had. "Does not that explain me and my condition? God is the Potter. I am His clay. He shapes me as He likes. That accident was part of His shaping." As the priest walked along recalling such words from the woman he had gone to console, he had to admit that he was the one who had been consoled, and even instructed, this morning. This insight into God's dominion and the docility that should mark us, His creatures, would have been ample reward for all the months he had spent on Kitty Conroy. But when Kitty had gone a step farther and shown that as Creator God could do as He willed with us, but as Father He would do only what we willed — provided our wills were right, Father Brophy felt he was listening to one who had gone beyond mere meditation, and had been blessed with something bordering on the mystical. But the climax of the visit had come for the priest when he heard this patient who had been so complaining for over a year quietly say: "Suffering is not only *from* God, it is *for* God as well."

"Where . . . where did you learn all this, Kitty?" he had been forced to exclaim.

She smiled at the exclamation, pointed to the alabaster crucifix, and said: "From this 'too beautiful' a thing." Then came the full revelation of her night of meditation. Father Brophy felt that he would have no more problems from Miss Conroy, and from his heart thanked God for such nuns as Sister Philip Maria.

By one of those arrangements of Providence which humans so often name "accidents," Sister Imelda had an opportunity to pass near the town where Kitty was living, and had obtained an exceptional permission to call on the woman. The first thing Sister noticed on entering the room was the shade on the window. It was down. She had heard from Kitty on and off through the two years and more that had passed since Kitty was a patient at Louisville, and had thought her whole attitude had changed. But the sight of that lowered shade made her wonder. She walked across and lifted it saying: "Look at God's beautiful sunshine, Kitty."

The woman in the bed smiled. "Leave it up, Sister," and she smiled more broadly. "I know what you're thinking, Sister. I, too, remember those days at St. Joe's. Actually, this is about the first and only time that shade has been up. But it has not been because I was afraid to see God and His beauty outside, but only because I wanted to see more of Him and His beauty inside. I've changed, Sister. I've learned how to pray. Not merely say prayers, but pray! You were so right to tell me to pray, Sister. Sit here and I'll tell you of a surprising answer I had to a prayer that was a bit importunate."

Sister took a chair and moved it close to the bed. Kitty told the nun much about Father Brophy and his many visits. "That man is a living saint, Sister. And I'm sure I've helped make him one. I was terrible to him for the longest time. As bad as I was to you. . . ."

"You were never bad to me, Kitty," said the nun softly.

"If a little girl may contradict her elders . . . and I'm trying to be a little girl, God's little girl. . . . So, if I may contradict one who may be my elder. . . . Hard to guess your age, Sister! But, at any rate, I know I was nasty to you. But let me tell you about the TV. . . ."

Father Brophy had found it difficult to hold real conversation with Kitty until she acquired a TV. Then he discussed programs with her. He told about Bishop Sheen's program and won a ready audience; for Kitty had always admired Fulton Sheen ever since he first broke in on radio. The priest told her that the Bishop was going to be televised in a Midnight Mass on Christmas. She grew excited as Christmas neared. But then, on Christmas Eve, her TV went dead. She telephoned every repair man in town, and in nearby towns. None could come. All were too busy that afternoon. Kitty grew aroused, then angry. She wanted to view this Mass more than she wanted anything in a long, long time. She called friends. She called acquaintances. She even called people she had never met. No one could suggest anything. Kitty stared at her dead TV and was near tears. Then she thought of the Mother of Christ, and said the *Memorare* with more intensity than she could ever recall having felt. Hours went by. Nothing happened. The lights sprang up in the town. Homes had their windows and doorways gaily lit. On some lawns trees were sparkling with green, red, and golden lights. Greetings that were gay came to Kitty from within the Rest Home and from outside on the street. But Kitty was not one bit cheerful. Again she turned to Mary Immaculate. "Please, Mother of God!" she whispered earnestly. Then at six o'clock a knock came on her door. She did not want to answer. The knock was repeated. "Come" was all Kitty managed. The door opened, and there stood a man with his TV repair equipment by his side.

"What is it, Miss Conroy — a burnt-out tube?"

Kitty could not answer. She simply pointed to the machine.

"I saw Bishop Sheen that night, Sister. I loved it all — and I prayed for you who so often told me to pray."

They had a most enjoyable visit that afternoon, and Sister Imelda saw the way God works with souls. She realized how fittingly St. Paul had described the process when he had told about his planting, Apollo watering, and God giving the increase. She saw that what had been dropped as seed in Louisville, had been watered here in Mt. Sterling by Father Brophy, friends, and that Newsletter from the Cusans. But it was God — and Kitty's cooperation — that brought the harvest. And harvest it was! It was a bit of heaven for this hard-working nun to hear how this woman, who once was so resentful toward God, could not get enough of Him these days. Communion had been brought once a week. The crystal rosary on the bedside table was fingered every day, some days many times. The prayer book, beside it, was well worn. But what Sister Imelda never expected to hear came to her when Kitty said: "Oh, how I love the Mass, now. I never knew what it was before. But now . . . ! Last Easter some friends — at Father Brophy's suggestion I strongly suspect — hired an ambulance and had me taken to church for High Mass. I dare say,

Sister, that Mary Magdalen, in the Garden that first Easter, knew
no greater joy than I did last Easter. I dared to call Him 'Rabboni,'
even as had she. And, I felt in my whole being, that He returned
that greeting, and called me 'Kitty.' Could it have been?"

"What else would He call you, Kitty? You are His child."

"I'm trying to be, Sister. But it is hard. We mature wrongly. I
want to be a wise child. Oh, you can tell the chaplain at St. Joe's
that I've found out the difference between knowledge and wisdom.
Only children are truly wise, Sister, only children of God. I'm trying
to be one of those, and I'm trying to teach my pupils the same."

"Pupils?"

"Yes, Sister, I'm teaching again. Some of the children from nearby,
who have had difficulty with their classes, were recommended to me.
It has not always been easy. I love to teach; but children do not
always love to learn. They can be trying – and you know my temper."

Then Kitty again introduced the subject of the Mass and lamented
her inability to assist physically. Sister told her that she was "in"
every Mass being offered the world over. Then went on to explain
how she could make her room, there in the Rest Home, a veritable
"sanctuary" – her bed, an altar; her crippled arm and leg, her "wheat
and wine." God will "transubstantiate," promised the nun. "Write to
the chaplain, Kitty. He will be delighted to hear from you."

A fortnight later the chaplain was reading a letter from her about
her discovery of the difference between knowledge and wisdom, but
she added that she was still, at times, both a Jew and a Greek. She
confessed that her "cross" was a "stumbling block" certain days – and
an "absurdity" other days – but most of the time she found it what
he had said it to be. She asked him to pray for her.

Kitty's "hour" still goes on. It has already been twelve years in
duration. She falls over her "stumbling block" now and then, but
quickly picks herself up.

She knows now that Christ is Truth – and that all His words are
truth-filled; but none more personally so than the one that says:
"Your sorrow shall be changed into joy" (Jn. 16:20). She is living
"her hour" in joy! Bitterness has gone. Now all is beauty; for all is
Christ! The sown seeds have blossomed into flower. She prays the
flowers will yet turn into fruit.

VIII

SHE COULD NOT AWAIT HER HOUR

Father Joe and Father Matt had been discussing many matters in the chaplain's quarters at St. Joseph Infirmary one snowy afternoon in February, 1960. Father Lehmann's "hour" had been one of their topics. When Father Brennan disclosed that their mutual friend had actually been anxious, toward the end of his illness, to go to God, the monk told how he had read of an abbot who appeared after his death to announce that he had been assigned to purgatory for forty years simply because he had not desired, with sufficiently ardent desire, to get to heaven.

"Private revelation," was Father Matt's first comment. "Pious story," was his next. Then came his final one: "And, if you ask me, a pious exaggeration."

"I didn't ask you, Matt," said Father Joe with a quiet chuckle. "But I will now ask you how many of us ever really *long* to get home? I believe there is a point to the story — pious as that story may be, and as exaggerated as you find it. If we really believed what we claim to believe, why wouldn't we all be filled with longing for heaven?"

That generated a heated discussion. The hospital chaplain insisted on what he termed Christian realism, maintaining that we were placed on earth by God to *do* something as well as to *become* someone, and that we will never become what we are supposed to become unless we do the thing we are put here to do. He attacked what he called a pseudomysticism that was becoming something of a fashion, but what was actually only a fad. Without roots there can never be solid growth, was his contention; and many who talked about religious living and true spirituality were without roots. Their piety did not seem to be based on dogma, the chaplain claimed; and while he would not accuse them of posing, he did suspect that their reach exceeded their grasp by far. "They have missed the paradoxes of Christ and Christianity," he said with some warmth.

170

"They have not understood that genuine Christian detachment from creatures demands a very real engagement with all creation. They think a lot, and talk a lot about 'losing their lives' — but they never complete Christ's own statement about 'finding' them. They've got some warped idea that they could never love God aright if they felt any love for anyone or anything else. What they are seeking is something that has been given only to a few great saints. They want an experiential knowledge of God. They want to 'feel' Him. I tell you, Joe, it's unsound." Then he climaxed his attack by saying, "Let them *work* their way to heaven. That will convince me they have a genuine *longing.*"

"You're a workingman, Matt," said the visiting priest just as the conversation was interrupted by a phone call for the chaplain. It was from the emergency room. He was wanted down there immediately. Twenty minutes later he was back looking somewhat grim. "That was for a fellow who wanted to get out of this world, but I doubt that it was a case of longing for heaven. Slashed his wrists in an attempt at suicide. I believe he'll live."

Father Joe waited for the chaplain to light a cigarette and smoke off some of his tension before he quietly asked, "Have you ever considered the possibility that suicide could be heroic, Matt?"

"Heroic? I think suicides are all cowards."

"I was reading an article by Sigrid Undset a while back, and she saw just such a possibility. Of course you have to grant her suppositions before you can ever accept her conclusions."

"They would have to be some suppositions before I would ever accept her conclusions," said the chaplain with some disgust.

"Well, look Matt, suppose a man had never heard anything about religion, God, Christ, or original sin. Suppose he had heard something vague about human nature being innately good, as I think Rousseau claimed. And suppose he believed in the perfectibility of his own human nature, and made some efforts to bring it to that. Of course he would slip; he would fall. Human nature does that, you know! Suppose he picked himself up a few times, only to fall again and again. Don't you think he might possibly get the idea that he was one of those freaks of nature, a real mistake, a hopeless case. Don't you see that he might just possibly come to the conclusion that he was not fit to live? and that the only decent, honorable, and courageous thing he could do would be to take himself off the face of the earth. Would that be cowardice if he carried it out?"

As Father Matt began to answer, Father Joe held up his hand. "Now get the suppositions, Matt. This man has never seen Christ crucified. He may have looked at a crucifix, but he has never seen it; never realized what it represents. Paul's words about 'filling up what is wanting' would be utterly meaningless to him. He has no idea of God's grace. He thinks merely in human terms."

"Ever hear of the natural law, Joe? Ever hear of the primal instinct for self-preservation? I still say every suicide is a coward if he is not actually crazy."

"Going against that primal instinct for some misconceived noble motive might just possibly be an heroic thing. That's the case Sigrid Undset made out for this utter pagan. In fact she pointed to what we have come to call the 'heroes' of ancient literature as proof. Didn't we admire Hannibal and Mithradates — men who could not survive the defeat of their nation? And how about that Gaul who killed his wife and who is represented holding her dead body in one hand while with the other he aims his dagger at his own breast — rather than allow his wife to be taken into slavery or go there himself? With no concept of Christ ruling from His cross, nor any idea of how one can ennoble the state of slavery, did he not act according to his principles and perform a brave, and even an heroic deed?"

"Now you're making murder, as well as suicide, heroic. . . ."

"You're denying my very suppositions, Matt. You're thinking only with a Catholic and Christian mind."

"I'm thinking with a man's mind, the human mind. Who was it said *Anima humana naturaliter Christiana* — meaning every human, by his very nature, tends toward Christian thinking? What are you driving at, anyhow?"

"I'm going to tell you a story I heard from the lips of the Father General of the Trappists. It illustrates the two topics we have discussed most today. But I want to preface the story with the admission that you and I know suicide to be a sin, a grievous sin, a sin, which, if committed knowingly and willingly, leaves us with no hope for the guilty party; for there seems no way to forgiveness. But, thank God, we can distinguish between material mortal sin and formal mortal sin; thank God, too, that most of us are convinced that the drive for life is such that practically anyone who takes his life must be deranged mentally. I'll go further and agree with you that most suicides are cowards. But now to the case of one who was anything but cowardly. . . . Let me tell it the way it was told to me. . . .

"You may not know it, Matt, but there are five Trappist monasteries in Japan; four of women, and one of men. What I have to tell took place at one of the monasteries for women. Don't ask me at which one, for I do not remember. But that it happened, I have the word of no less an authority than the Father General. He was on a Visitation over there a year or so ago. At the entrance to the church of one of the Trappistine monasteries he found a grave surmounted by a cross such as the nuns use in their own cemetery. Naturally he asked for an explanation. He got it from the chaplain of the monastery — a Frenchman, a Trappist priest who had been sent from France to be confessor, spiritual director, and so forth, for the nuns.

"The general prefaced the story by telling me how much he admires the Japanese people. He was loud in his praise for any and all who come into the Church; for, according to him, they have to give up just about everything we humans hold dear: not only father, mother, and family, but even their country."

Father Joe then recounted what little he knew about Shintoism. It wasn't too much, but it was enough to show how near and dear the family was to every Japanese who accepted Shintoism as their religion. It was enough, too, for Father Matt to see how they would regard their emperor as sacred, and patriotism as a religious virtue. The story he told was about a Japanese girl who had come to the Trappistine convent chapel and attended one of the choral services — some "hour" of the canonical office. There was nothing remarkable about this; for many of the Japanese from surrounding towns often came to the chapel. But this girl returned again and again. Soon the portress, the sacristan, and even the Mother Abbess, all of whom were Japanese, noticed that this young girl would remain after the Office and kneel as reverently and recollectedly as the most devout

of the nuns. This continued for weeks. Then one day after leaving
the chapel, the girl appeared at the door of the monastery and requested an interview with the Reverend Mother Abbess.

"Reverend Mother," she said after a few polite formalities, "I
would like to become like you are. I would like to become one who
worships God all the day long as do you and your nuns."

The Abbess had recognized the name the child had given as
that of the family of the leading man of the village — and she knew
that family to be Shintoists who also cultivated something of
Buddhism. After making the young girl feel at ease in her presence,
the Abbess finally asked her if she had spoken of this desire to her
father or family. She had not. The Abbess then told her that only
Catholics could become nuns, and that she would never receive
anyone into the convent without some sort of parental permission.
The young girl was somewhat dismayed by these facts, but soon she
was voicing her determination to speak to her father about it, saying
that the more she came to the chapel the greater became her longing
to stay there praising God as did the nuns.

The Abbess encouraged her to pray daily, assuring her it was very
pleasing to God, and invited her to come to the chapel more often.
But she dismissed the girl thinking that this first interview might
very likely be the last; for Japanese parents do not lightly grant anyone
in the family permission to forego the religion of their ancestors —
and of the land.

Weeks did pass — and the girl did not even appear in chapel,
let alone seek out the Abbess; and most dismissed the matter from
their minds. But then came a day when the girl came running to
the monastery and almost breathlessly asked for Reverend Mother.
The youngster was in a state of elation. "I may come, Reverend
Mother. I may come!" she told the Abbess as soon as the latter entered
the room. Then came her story how hard it had been to convince her
father. "I told him I could never be happy anywhere else on earth.
He did not believe me at first. He told me of many other ways of
life and assured me that I would find great happiness in any one
of them. But I told him they were not for me. Finally, he consented.
I know it was his great love for me that won that consent. I also know
it hurt him to give it; for he knew what you told me: that I would

have to become a Catholic before I could become a nun!"

Father Joe stopped his narrative here to tell Father Matt how the General of the Trappists had insisted that very few in the Western world would ever understand all it cost that father to give that consent; for few in the West have any keen appreciation of the oriental mind and heart, and their dedication to the cult of their ancestors. The man had to love his daughter dearly to grant such a permission — and the daughter had to be specially graced by God to seek it with such ardor.

"The Abbess," said Father Joe, "handed the case over to the chaplain. It is from him the General got the rest of the story. The child came to him for instructions in the Faith. This is the way the General recounts the events. . . ."

The chaplain claims that while he has instructed many in the Faith during his years as priest, never had he a neophyte who was more eager to learn, or more easy to teach. He began with the articles in the Creed. "I believe in God . . . ," the first article, caused no difficulty once he had shown the girl that, even in Shintoism, this is a basic belief. For the mythology of Shintoism tells of the "three gods who created heaven and earth — Ame-no-minakanushi." The girl readily accepted the priest's explanation of the Triune God who is no myth, and who did create heaven and earth and all things. In fact her eyes glistened with enthusiasm as the chaplain explained to her just who God is. "I believe in God, the Father . . ." was an article that brought forth little exclamations of joy from this young girl who had possessed almost a religious reverence for her own father. "Creator of heaven and earth . . ." took up more time than any of the preceding articles, not because of any difficulty inherent in the truth, but because of this girl's keen appreciation of the wonder and beauty in each smallest part of God's handiwork. This came not only from her highly developed aesthetic sense, but also from her religious verve; for Shintoism is an admixture of nature worship as well as of ancestors. She had always looked on rivers, trees, roads, stars, clouds, flowers, and all else, as holy things. To learn that she now could love every flower, star, wind, rain, and the sunshine with a love quickened not only by appreciation of God's artistry, but with a love resplendent with joy because of God's paternal immanence in each and every creature whose existence is an act of obedience to His creative *Fiat,* set her agog.

"And in Jesus Christ . . ." brought out the stories of the Annunciation, the Visitation, and of Christmas, and filled this young Japanese with a love she never dreamed possible of containment in a human heart.

The nuns noted that the girl's absorption in prayer became ever more profound. There were days when she spent all the daylight hours in the chapel, never once getting off her knees. The Abbess saw that she would be receiving a child who had all the marks of a true contemplative, once this girl was baptized and had entered the postulancy. She grew almost restive for that happy day. But the wise chaplain was not to be hurried. He knew, as only priests of long experience know, that a strong, unshakable intellectual grasp on the truths revealed by God is essential for perseverance in the Faith.

The article dealing with the Passion and Death of Jesus Christ was presented to the girl with true French fervor. The chaplain had to stop early in the explanation, for the girl, by a very sincere question, asked him the reason for this tragedy called Redemption. He had to explain sin to her. For quite some time he had difficulty getting this girl to realize that men and women did, and yet do, offend the good God. He pointed out to her that we will never recognize sin for what it is in reality until we look long and lovingly at God Incarnate, as Representative of mankind, writhing in Gethsemani's garden, then drooping from that felon's cross on Calvary — a corpse. God — a corpse! That is what sin does — and, in a way, what sin is. As the chaplain told about those trials of Christ before Annas, Caiphas, Pilate, and Herod, then climaxed them by a description of the Roman Governor washing his hands as he let the Jews have their way, the girl wept.

Those tears did several things to that French chaplain. They showed the impact gospel truth has on a thoughtful soul when presented for the first time. They made him somewhat envious — for here he was a "cradle Catholic," born in a country that has been called "the eldest daughter of the Church," schooled in what St. Benedict has named the "School of the Divine Service," and in what is recognized as the most exacting class in that "School" — the Trappists; here he was a priest of the Most High God, a cloistered contemplative — yet when had he wept over the Passion and Death of his Lord as this young neophyte was doing? Those tears gave this man a newer realization of the essence of sin, and of God's loving mercy. They also gave him a rebirth of fervor as they dug a new depth to his compassion for Christ.

His explanation of the "descent into hell . . ." really Limbo . . . was long; for he gave a rapid review of the Old Testament as he told of all those who were waiting there for the coming of Christ. He thus introduced his neophyte to the patriarchs: Abraham, Isaac, and Jacob, told her the touching story of Joseph, then went on to David. She was entranced by it all. He showed her the prophets, giving special attention to Isaias because of his references to the Incarnation from the birth from a Virgin to the death in dereliction. When he told of St. Joseph, the foster father of Jesus, being there, he endeavored to conjure up the tenderness that must have marked the meeting between the Man-God and the one who had saved Him from Herod's sword by the flight into Egypt.

As the chaplain paused, the girl asked him a timid question: "Do you think that, possibly, some of my ancestors were waiting for Him?"

"Not possibly; not probably; but most assuredly, my child," had been the chaplain's reply. Then he explained to her that everyone who worships God with sincerity, even though their concept of Him be, through no fault of theirs, erroneous, would be rewarded by the one and only God, who is the God of love.

The chaplain could give this reply and explanation with sincerity; for the Japanese had fascinated him from the very beginning of his stay among them. He had studied their way of life and looked into their religion. He was convinced that most of them were in what is called "good faith." The girl went home from that instruction in a state very close to rapture.

It was with a touch of regret that the chaplain began his instructions on the Resurrection; for it was wintertime in Japan when he came to talk of what is the springtime of Christianity. But his course had to be consecutive. It was snowing the day he began to tell about Christ rising from the dead. The dark eyes of the little Japanese girl glowed as the chaplain told of this victory of victories for Christ, and of all it promised for the Christian. She tried to imagine herself with a body possessed of all the properties of Christ's risen body. She felt as light as any falling snowflake — and she smiled her warm, winning smile as the chaplain dismisssed her for the day.

It was snowing again the day she came for the chaplain's explanation of Christ's ascent into heaven. After having heard so much about the qualities of His glorified body, and of the many apparitions He had made following His Resurrection, His ascent into heaven caused her no difficulty whatsoever. She rather expected it. But what she now eagerly awaited was the chaplain's description of heaven whither Christ had gone "to prepare a place for you . . ." as He had said.

The chaplain was almost as eager as the girl; for thought of heaven was familiar to this contemplative, and he had a genuine longing to share his thought with others. So after a rapid résumé of the Creed from the eternality of God, down through Creation, the Fall, the Incarnation, and Redemption, he plunged with real feeling into his delineation of that home which is our home. At one point he stole a page from the Curé of Ars, most likely all unwittingly, for he leveled his finger at the Japanese before him and kept on repeating: "You — shall see God! You — shall see *God! You* — shall see God!"

The chaplain knew enough about the oriental mind to realize that those four monosyllabic words were enough to occupy this girl's whole being for days on end. Yet he felt an urge to go on and dare what even the great St. Paul, while under divine inspiration, had not dared. This fervent French priest endeavored to particularize for his neophyte what St. Paul had generalized for his Corinthians when he wrote: "What no eye has ever seen, what no ear has ever heard, what no human heart has ever thought of, namely, the great blessings God holds ready for those who love him" (1 Cor. 2:9).

He did not borrow from the Apocalypse. He said nothing about the river or the tree of life; nothing about the city of gold, or the gates of pearl; nothing about the walls of jasper or foundation stones of sapphire. He did not even describe the throne with its rainbow of emerald around it, and before it that sea of glass resembling crystal. He told her nothing of the harpers or those voices like many waters. What he dwelt on could be called the social joys of heaven, the personal and intellectual bliss that awaits us. He began by trying to tell the girl what it would be like to see God face to face, to see Him whom we call "Father" with such filial familiarity, to meet the Second Person with the human nature He had assumed, to greet the Holy Spirit who had overshadowed Mary, led Christ into the desert to be tempted, and, as St. Paul says, led Him on to His Passion and Death.

It was a brave effort on the chaplain's part, yet it left the girl straining her imagination to formulate the Substance of that vision. But when he set about the description of the thrill it would be to meet Christ, both he and his listener were more at ease. It was not difficult for them to form their own imaginative picture of this "most beautiful of the sons of men." The chaplain had taken the girl through the gospel narrative, so she already had her own concept of this Man among men, who was so gentle yet so strong; so tender yet so vigorously virile; so loving, merciful, and ever kind yet who could grow fierce with indignation and wither His opponents with fiery "woes." Only recently the chaplain has shown Him to her in His glorified body as he told her about those many apparitions that marked the forty days between His Resurrection and Ascension.

Undoubtedly the young Japanese would have begged him to go on talking about Jesus, for whom she had conceived a glowing love, had not this fervent French priest let the full flood of his love for Mary flow forth as he attempted to tell what it would be like to meet this Mother of ours face to face for the first time. The child before him sat entranced.

The chaplain knew it was growing late but the theme was too dear to his heart to drop with any suddenness, so on he went with what can only be called an open declaration of a strong man's tender affection for Our Lady of Fair Love. But he checked himself finally with St. Bernard's own words on the subject: "Numquam satis de Maria — We can never say enough about Mary." He gave the girl a broad smile as he said it, then went on with, "But there are others in our family whom we shall meet in heaven." Then he rapidly coursed down through SS. Peter, Paul, John, James, Andrew, Thomas, and the rest of the Apostles. With a wide gesture he terminated this part of his instruction with the phrase from the Apocalypse so often heard during the Feast of All Saints: "a multitude which no man can number." Then he turned to angels and tarried over the nine choirs, telling the joy it would be to meet these exalted spirits.

He paused a moment to remark on the chill that had entered the room. "It is not only snowing hard, it is getting colder and colder," he said. But the girl only smiled. He took it as a plea to go on. Since his was a very special devotion to the angels he welcomed the invitation. He had found these special servants of God and His trusted messengers on almost every page of the Old Testament, and had often spent long hours prayerfully pondering their works for God. He had watched the angels of the Passover — marking doorposts in mercy, then slaying Egypt's firstborn as a curse. He had seen the angels at Sodom and Gomorrha — saving Lot and his kindred, but allowing the cities to be destroyed. But, for the most part, he knew them as guardians, companions, and friends. When he told the young Japanese that she would see her own guardian angel when she went to heaven, he learned that he had missed something in his course of instructions; for she asked him with breathless wonder: "Have I an angel all of my own?" Her slanted eyes widened as he assured her she had, and told her how God had appointed one to watch over her from the moment she had been conceived, and that he would return with her through the cold and heavily falling snow as she went home after this session.

It was at this point that the chaplain arose, took another look out the window, rubbed his slightly chilled hands, and said: "And I think you and your guardian angel had better get started, for this storm is increasing and will most likely last through the night. Don't you let him or yourself get frozen as you make your way home."

But she was loathe to leave. She could not repress the queries: "How soon will I go to heaven?" and "Will any of my ancestors be there?"

The priest chuckled. "You are truly greedy for God, my child," he said in a warm, kindly tone. "But none of us can see God until we have first seen death. We must die first — Such is God's decree since man first sinned. But never doubt that you will find many of your ancestors up there with God. But come now, the hour is getting late — we have been long on this beautiful subject — and this storm is getting fierce. Will you be warm enough in those clothes? I feel chilled." She did not answer him directly. She simply arose, wrapped her coat about her, and kept on saying softly: "I must die first. I must die first." The chaplain made out the words, and smiled as he led her to the door. His "good-bye" took the form of "Greedy little one, God must love you greatly."

The priest was right: the storm did continue all that night and on into the early morning. It was a clean white world, but a bitterly cold one, that greeted him as he stepped from his quarters prepared to hurry across to the Sisters' chapel for morning Mass. He breathed the clean air deep into his lungs. The temptation to saunter and enjoy this wonderland of white was strong; but he knew he must not keep the nuns waiting a single moment. Their day was so ordered and orderly that the slightest tardiness in beginning any function in the day not only upset the entire schedule of the day, but seemed somehow to mar the perfection of their offering of that day to God. He was silently thanking his guardian angel for having helped him to be so punctual through the years of his chaplaincy when the Portress opened the sacristy door with an unusual abruptness. She excitedly pointed to the front of the convent and made the Trappist sign which means "Reverend Mother." When the chaplain did not move with the alacrity the Portress hoped for, she made another Trappist sign which meant: "Wants to see you immediately." The chaplain smiled as he nodded that he had understood the signs. But the Portress did not smile back. She looked frightened. The chaplain sobered as he realized that something extraordinary must have happened. Orientals, especially oriental nuns, do not externalize their feelings this way. He quickened his pace.

The parlor door opened as he neared it. Reverend Mother seemed to tower and fill that door with command and majesty. When she saw the chaplain, she bowed gravely and stepped aside. On the threshold he, too, stopped and stared. For there on the floor lay his neophyte. The posture was most peculiar: hands outstretched — legs drawn up. He could not fail to grasp it. She was dead.

He stared for what seemed a long time. Then he turned questioning eyes to the Abbess. Finally he managed the one word: "Frozen?"

"Sister Portress found her in the snow when she opened the door this morning," said the Abbess softly. "The child's hands were outstretched toward the front of the chapel. She was on her knees. She was covered with snow. She must have been there most of the night."

The chaplain looked at the frozen body and he heard again the child's parting words: "Before I see God, I must die. I must die."

Father Joe stopped his narrative there and looked at Father Matt. "Suppose that girl had deliberately exposed herself to that snow and cold, Matt," he said quietly, "would you call her act cowardice — or would you conclude as did the chaplain and the Father General: that it was an Act of Love for God, an Act of Longing for heaven?"

"Was it deliberate?" asked Father Matt.

"All the evidence points that way. The oriental mind. The last remarks she made to the chaplain. The amount of snow on the body when found. You see, the chaplain had not explained any of the Commandments to the girl. He concluded that she was so alive with longing to go to heaven that she took advantage of the storm and the cold to enable her to go there. He told the General he considered it a veritable Baptism of Desire. I'd almost be ready to call it a Baptism of Blood. How about you?"

Father Matt snubbed out the cigarette he had been smoking. "Whew!" he whistled. "If we go by definition she committed suicide; for she took her own life. But that was one suicide that most certainly was not sin. What did the General do about it?"

"He agreed with the chaplain. He left the grave where it was and the cross atop it. He was deeply moved by the whole thing — even when he was telling it to me. He saw it as an Act of Love. He seemed to envy this little girl her ignorance — or rather it was her longing and her love that he envied. He followed his account with this. . . .

While on that Visitation he received an invitation from the father of the girl to dine with him in his home. The General said he has made it a rule never to accept such invitations, but on this occasion he felt he had to make an exception. He said he dined in oriental fashion. At the end of the meal all rose and turned toward the end of the room where an image of Buddha rested. The family then offered what we Christians would call 'Grace after meals.' As the men in the company were withdrawing for what we would call 'cigars and coffee,' the wife of the man of the house motioned to the General to stay behind. When all had departed she nodded to one of the servants. He approached the statue of Buddha and wheeled it to one side. There, behind where the Buddha had been, stood a magnificent shrine of the Immaculate Conception with a life-sized picture of the little girl, who could not wait for 'her hour,' to one side of the shrine — posed as if she were visiting our Lady.

Once the shock of surprise passed, the General could not restrain himself. The anomaly of the whole situation — a Catholic shrine in an oriental's house; the Immaculate Conception supplanting, as it were, the statue of Buddha; and a memorial to this young girl who had given up the religion of her family and the usual commitment of Japanese to their country and their emperor — was too much for him to remain silent. He turned to the woman and asked: "Your husband — he does not object?" The reply he received I think is tremendous, Matt. That woman simply said: "He loved our daughter."

Father Matt sat in thought for some time. Finally he said. "I wonder if we preach enough about heaven. I've instructed many a convert. I never had any react like that."

"Well," said his friend with a little laugh, "we wouldn't want all of them to freeze to death."

"No, Joe, we wouldn't. But I wonder how many of them we warm to life — that kind of life which is a real longing to see God. It could be that we priests of God are guilty of some sins of omission — and they could be very serious sins. That little Japanese acted wrongly, but her heart was right. She believed, as you so often put it, what we profess to believe. She was more anxious to go to God than was our friend Father Jim. He waited for 'his hour' to end. She seems to have anticipated hers. The story has done something to me, Joe. I'll not only be more gentle with attempted suicides, and less censorious of successful suicides, but I'll think more of heaven myself, and talk about it more — shall I say 'sociably' — to others. That French chaplain had a humanistic approach."

Father Joe put on his coat. As he buttoned it preparatory to departure he smiled waggishly as he looked at Father Matt and said: "That little Japanese would never get forty years in purgatory, would she, Matt?"

The hospital chaplain chuckled appreciatively, but maintained his stand by saying, "Pious stories are for pious ears. I haven't got any. But the story you've just told is a holy story — and that kind is for every human heart, especially the hard of heart such as myself."

IX

THE LONG, LONG HOUR OF THE "LUCKY STIFF"

Things that "could not be done" have been done. Mary Ellen Kelly did them. It was said that a girl paralyzed from head to foot "could not travel." Mary Ellen left the tiny town of Marcus, Iowa, her birthplace, on trips to Chicago, New York, Hollywood, and Canada. She even crossed the Atlantic, visited France, Italy, and Portugal. It was said that a shut-in "could have no real social life." Mary Ellen Kelly socialized with friends and acquaintances from coast to coast, most frequently being "the life of the party." It was said that one totally crippled and held fast to her bed for more than twenty years "could not possibly have a career." Yet, at her death, May 9, 1961, even the New York *Times* carried a two-column story about her, while her hometown of Marcus shut down its business, had all flags at half-mast, and gave a police escort to her funeral procession. It was said that a girl who could move her right hand only about one inch — just far enough to form seven letters — "could never be a writer." Yet Mary Ellen Kelly wrote a daily column for her home newspaper, founded, edited, and contributed to a magazine called *Seconds Sanctified,* a bimonthly whose three thousand copies reached readers in every state of our Union and thirty-six foreign countries, and then went on to write her classic autobiography *But With The Dawn, Rejoicing.* It was said that a total invalid "could never be a leader of any sort." Yet Mary Ellen Kelly, from her bed in Marcus, Iowa, founded the *League of Shut-in Sodalists* whose rolls, before her death, held more than two thousand five hundred names of members. It was said that a girl as sick as Mary Ellen was, and for so long a time, "could never be anything but filled with self-pity, and never know genuine cheerfulness." Yet Mary Ellen was the one who coined the phrase "Lucky Stiff" as properly descriptive of herself, and after twenty-two years, brilliant with utterly unaffected cheerfulness, she dictated from her deathbed, amid excruciating suffering, this last bit of wit and wisdom, which not only speaks for itself, but speaks for Mary Ellen, her Captain Christ, and reveals the best

185

possible manner for any Christian to end "his hour."

"We'll entitle it: It Finally Happened To Me," she said, then went on with this dictation:

It was a bright, sunny Saturday morning. At our house this day gets off to any early start because it is one of the two days each week on which our pastor, bless him, brings me Holy Communion. As usual, for the previous two months or so, I was extremely drowsy — an unpleasant sensation which caused both my mother and me to fear that I might accidentally fall asleep, or start nodding before Father left.

"Here's Father, now," Mother warned me. "Are you awake, Mary Ellen?"

At that precise moment I was wide awake; sixty seconds later I was in another world. After this had continued for several hours, it was agreed that we call the doctor when mother could no longer rouse me. That evening my supper was served to me in the old familiar habitat: St. Joseph Mercy Hospital, in Sioux City.

Awakening Sunday to a pleasant greeting that announced, "Father Kelm is here," wasn't much unlike the way mother greets me at home on Communion days. But the series of bells, the loud voice of the paging system, and the rattling of carts that later joined the morning chorus, left me vividly aware of my new whereabouts.

Multiple tests followed, some of them — especially those involved with needles — sharpened my half-forgotten memory of my own numerous human frailties. When things are going well, it is so easy to be brave and filled with courageous thoughts. Funny how quickly my bravery begins to wobble when a hypodermic needle enters the picture. The drowsiness which had been interfering with my work for several weeks seemed a trifle less bothersome, but x rays showed areas of congestion, the condition caused largely by the inability of my lungs to expand normally. It was what my doctor termed "pulmonary insufficiency." Oxygen was ordered, in a complicated contraption referred to in medical circles as a "positive pressure machine." With just two more doohickeys on it and maybe one more tube, it could have easily passed for a new style missile, soon to be launched at Cape Canaveral.

I can't help respecting this machine, since it helped my lungs to expand and "decongest." Beatniks, with their love of the "offbeat," should positively adore it.

Monday offered no new distractions, so the oxygen tube in my nose provided a continued feeling that I was about to sneeze, while fifteen minutes of every four hours were spent playing a modified version of "Masquerade Party" as I wore my positive pressure machine.

Then came the question, "Do you wish to receive Extreme Unction, Mary Ellen?"

Even now I cannot truthfully say whether or not the question jolted me. Perhaps it did, though, because I recall thinking that I must be sure to be very calm about this. After all, being anointed doesn't necessarily mean that a person is going to die. As the nurse explained, "There is an element of danger."

She received her answer very shortly: "I shall be happy and honored to receive it."

The hospital chaplain then proceeded to administer what we have come to call "the Last Sacraments."

I was appalled to see how seldom I had given serious thought to this merciful bonus from God. As the priest interceded for my salvation, nothing was missed; the crucified Christ had overlooked nothing.

As the grace was being sought to forgive the evil into which my five senses had led me, I thanked God for the opportunity to be forgiven the sins I had forgotten, pushed aside, denied existed, and referred to as the fault of another.

The simple application of the holy oils brought the magnitude of the sacrament more closely home than ever. The priest's words begged forgiveness for every step I had taken that had led me temporarily away from the arms of our Lady.

A sweet sense of peace came over me as the chaplain continued our three-way communication with Christ.*

That phrase: *"the arms of our Lady"* explains what otherwise is inexplicable in the girl's life.

This "doing the impossible" had begun here in St. Joseph Mercy Hospital in 1939 when, Mary Ellen, then seventeen, admitted to herself that she was a helpless invalid. Up to then she had had hopes. At the age of twelve, it is true, she had had to give up roller-skating, bicycle riding, dancing, and most other forms of activity girls of that age delight in; for what were first taken as "growing pains," then as "rheumatism," were now recognized as some form of arthritis. For five years, despite all sorts of medicines, those pains kept on growing, and her ability to move became less and less. By 1939 both knees had so stiffened that she could not walk, let alone run or dance. During the day about all she could do was sit. And even then she would have to be lifted every two hours and her position changed.

* Reprinted by permission from *Queen of All Hearts*, Bay Shore, N. Y., July–August, 1961.

At night it was the same. But she and her family went on hoping. They even managed a trip for her to the Mayo Clinic in Rochester. The verdict given there was: "Rheumatoid arthritis, and secondary anemia. All advisable treatment and medicines have been tried. Can suggest no further course." Even then hope did not die. Again and again she would look at her brother, John Robert, who shifted her position every two hours during the day, and ask: "You do think this will let up soon, don't you?" Of course he did! So did her mother and father. On the very day she was taken to St. Joseph Mercy Hospital her mother had sent her off with the words: "Don't worry, dear. You'll be home in a few weeks."

Five years later Mary Ellen was still in the hospital, alive — but with hope for a cure very dead. She looked at herself and, as she wrote in her autobiography, saw that her "jaws were locked; spine, hips, knees, and ankles were rigid; elbows, wrists, fingers were poker-stiff; and shoulders about two per cent less unyielding." She might as well face the fact: she was a cripple, her body totally immobilized. Medicine could not help. But she was alive. What was she to do with her life? Up to now she had been concerned mostly with days — frequently, only with hours. But now . . . ? She lay there as if listening. She knew God existed. She knew God was good. She was sure He had some purpose in this. But what could it be? Was it at all possible that a young girl like herself could have a call, a veritable vocation, to a life of suffering? a career as a bedfast invalid? No answer came to those questions. But as she lay there as if listening, down deep in her being she heard dimly, very dimly, something similar to what Peter, James, John, and the rest heard that first Holy Thursday night as they sat in the Upper Room with the Master at the head of the table. "Her hour" had struck.

When the Apostles saw Christ take bread that Thursday night, watched Him bless it, break it, then hand it to them, saying: "Take ye and eat — This is My Body," they did not know that He was hearing hammer blows and feeling nails that bit and burned their way through His hands and feet. Then when He lifted the cup and over it said: "This is My Blood," they did not see what He was seeing: leaded lashes, piercing thorns, blood-thirsting, heart-seeking lance. So when Mary Ellen Kelly, on this winter night in late 1939,

looked at her limbs and found them all locked tight in the grip of
arthritis, she did not say: "This is Your body, Jesus — This, Your
Blood," but she did sense vaguely, very vaguely that her Christ-career
had begun.

It was not any clear-cut plan she formulated that night, just some
general determination to "go along with God." Two more operations,
long weeks and even months led her into the secret of more intimate
prayer, real converse with God, and taught her, as she herself put it,
that she was sharing "in some great and powerful mystery." Her
mistake then, as it would be her mistake for some time to come, was
that she thought that "mystery" was some thing.

She had been baptized when a baby. But even as she neared her
twentieth birthday, she had yet to learn all that "being born again
of water and the Holy Spirit" really meant. Actually, it would be
years yet before she came to the complete realization that just as He
had taken wheat and wine into His hands in the Cenacle that they
might yield their substance to Him, so that He might live on earth
in sacramental mystery, yet fullest reality, so, through rheumatoid
arthritis, He was taking her into His hands, taking her flesh, her
blood, her bone, that He might again say: "This is My Body. This,
My Blood," and live again on earth mystically, yet in fullest reality.
But, He would never pronounce those words, with their consequent
wonder, without her consent. And, as yet, she did not know, with
clearest knowledge, that what had sounded for Him in the Upper
Room nineteen centuries earlier, was sounding for her in that hospital
room now. There "His hour" had come. He knew it — and rejoiced!
Mary Ellen would yet come to know the same thing and tell all the
world that, like Him, she, too, was *rejoicing*. But learning God's plan
for any individual's life is like all true learning — a very slow process
not always free from many gropings and fumbling mistakes.

At first, like many another sufferer, she considered the possibility
that her affliction might be a punishment. That is an Old Testament
idea, but one that is deeply rooted; and, like all deeply rooted things,
dies slowly. Of course there is some theological truth in the idea; for
man was not made originally to suffer, far less to die. Therefore, in
one sense, every suffering is punishment — and, very definitely, punishment for sin. But not every suffering visited upon a person is for

his own personal sins. The Man of Suffering and the Mother of
Sorrows knew no sin. Yet what person, be he human or divine, ever
experienced similar sufferings? Still, theologically, sin was at the root
of all Their woes, and all Their sufferings were punishment for sin.
But, thanks to the sufferings of these Two, pain now, far from being
punishment for the individual visited by it, can be, and ultimately is
meant to be, a *privilege*. For all suffering can now be sublimated into
sacrifice — and Christians can complete the completed Passion of
Christ. But Mary Ellen had just learned to pray a bit. She had not
as yet been introduced into the realm of real meditation. So, while
she knew she was an invalid, as yet, she did not know exactly why.
She was proud to be a Christian, but did not, as yet, realize fully
that that meant she must be *Christ*.

At this juncture in her life she openly confessed that while she
was convinced that God had chosen her for the role of suffering,
she was far from clear as to just why He had done so. Was it for her
own salvation, or for the salvation of others? She was not sure. But
of this she was positive: her life as invalid was not a punishment,
nor was it to be a wasted life. The reason for her positiveness was
this: "she had dedicated her life to our Lady, and she knew our
Mother takes better care of her gifts than to allow them to be wasted."

That bit of reasoning was not "whistling in the dark," even though,
owing to its indefiniteness, there was still much darkness connected
with it. But it was not long before even that darkness was made more
bright. For a visiting priest put the question to her: "What do you
know about meditation, Mary Ellen?" The girl laughed. She thought
Father must be kidding; for she was sure that meditation was only
for religious, for nuns and others like them. And she was sure she
was anything but a nun. The priest was sharp enough to see that
Mary Ellen had not caught the seriousness nor the depth in his
question, so very quickly, but quite clearly, told the girl a few things
about mental prayer. Mary Ellen admitted later that up to then she
had been "only a kid in the realm of the spirit and in the art of
contact with God."

So well had this priest done his work that afternoon that the
invalid awoke to the fact that into a part of her, which she had
not known existed, a door had been opened. What lay behind that

door was still a mystery to her, but she there and then resolved that "some day, with God's help, everything within there would be flooded with His light."

Who can appreciate all that she meant by "everything within there"? Perhaps only another completely paralyzed person, or some other shut-in can even surmise what Mary Ellen meant. But that our Lady, Seat of Wisdom and Mother of Fair Love, knew, becomes quite evident as one reads on in the story this brave girl told of herself. Anyone acquainted with real mental prayer will know what happened, for if sickness can awaken one to his creaturehood, his utter dependence on God, mental prayer will show him the reality of that creaturehood and let him see that in its depths it is Christhood. Christ, the Anointed One, was a Creature. The human nature He assumed was as dependent on God for its coming into being and its remaining in being as is any other human nature. Mary Ellen came to know all that that means as she meditated; for all genuine meditation finds its center in Jesus Christ. If one begins with meditation on Mary, he soon finds himself meditating on Mary's Son; for every prerogative of this superlative human being came to her because she was Mother of Jesus Christ. So Mary Ellen's love for Mary brought her to a dynamic love for Christ; for meditation on His life showed her how she was to live. He was "like to us in all things — save sin." From Him, then, we can learn all that we are to be. Mary Ellen did; but it was a gradual process.

Everyone who knows the ways of mental prayer will be amused by Mary Ellen's confession concerning her resolution one afternoon soon after she had learned to pray with her mind, will, imagination, and emotions. She admitted that, more than likely, she had set the whole court of heaven smiling at her as, in the elation of the moment, in the half-light of her hospital room, she very earnestly declared aloud: "I'm going to become a saint!" She was wrong in her conclusion that she had set all heaven smiling in amusement at her because of that declaration; for that is a declaration of any and every man's ultimate purpose on earth, and the only real goal of life. But what this girl meant was that anyone, with any clear ideas of what it costs to be what we are supposed to be, would have to smile at Mary Ellen if she thought that her mere declaration would bring about achievement. She herself learned the only way most humans learn — the hard way of bitter, personal experience. It was this way that Mary Ellen learned how to meditate; for it was not long after this brave declaration that she was "going to become a saint," that she was confessing ruefully that she "found meditation difficult."

Who hasn't? It is an art; and, like all arts, requires schooling — and schooling takes time. But that Mary Ellen was putting in that time, and learning the hard way, cannot be missed when one reads, so soon after her thrilling lines about the joys of mental prayer and the way it leads one on to the resolve to be a saint, that "spiritually, I feel neither progress nor recession; only the tastelessness and the dryness of inertia. Honestly, I can call it a lethargic, despairing lassitude."

What Mary Ellen was learning was that the life of the spirit is very like being on a seesaw. Now one is up; now one is down. But what perseverance in mental prayer taught her was that God was doing the tilting. It was He who lifted her high, and He who let her sink low. Once she realized that, then she knew that even in His "absences" He was present; that desolation of spirit and dryness in prayer could be as beneficial to her soul as rapture and ecstasy.

The "door" which had been opened into that part of her which she had not known existed, was letting in light, and even floods of light, and what had been "mystery" to her before became luminously clear: creaturehood meant Christhood. She would have to use everything she found "behind that door" the way Christ had used it.

First there was the lesson on pain — both physical and mental. Kelly, as most came to call her, knew pain. It ran through her at times like a wild and savage thing. It had been her constant companion, both day and night, from the age of twelve. It beat in her blood. It was deep in her bone. Medicines helped at times, and nature itself developed a certain tolerance. Yet she always knew it was there. But worse than physical pain is the mental affliction so often accompanying bodily pain: the hopelessness. Anyone can be brave for a day or two, possibly even for weeks, especially when there is hope for alleviation, if not surcease. But when one has to face the fact that he will be in pain just about always, one experiences a surge of fierce rebellion, followed quickly by a veritable whirlpool of self-pity which drags one down to the dark, deep center where lies black depression. Mary Ellen had to face that fact. Mary Ellen experienced the rebellion, the self-pity, the depression — until she meditated. Then she learned what Mary and Jesus had done with the selfsame things. Jesus had cried out in Gethsemani and on Golgotha. Mary had cried out when she found Him in the Temple after her three days of agony. It is not wrong for any sufferer to cry out — provided they cry as did Jesus and Mary; provided they cry out to God — and their cry is one for assistance plus a petition that "His will be done" *in* them and *by* them.

That was the deepest lesson Mary Ellen learned from meditation: Christ *used* His physical and mental sufferings; used them for others! Mary Ellen, and every other Christian can do the same. There was redemptive value in every pain Christ knew in body and in soul. There can be saving value in every pain any Christian suffers in mind or flesh. All he has to do is offer them up "in Christ Jesus" and, thanks to the reality which is the Mystical Body of Christ, offer them up as Jesus Christ.

Of course Mary Ellen did not learn all that in one single meditation. But that was the ultimate lesson she learned by being realist enough to look at her condition with wide-open eyes and see it for what it actually was. Hers would be a lonely life no matter how many visitors she had, friends she made, or acquaintances came her way. The life of every shut-in is lonely. It can be brightened temporarily. But that brightness passes with the departure of visitors, and only intensifies the darkness of their inescapable loneliness. In her very real loneliness she had, because of her utter dependence, absolutely no privacy; for there was nothing, literally nothing, she could do for herself. Mary Ellen was intensely independent by nature and temperament. This lack of privacy and this complete dependence on others was most humiliating to a girl of her innate tendencies. What a future stretched before her! Black indeed it would be had she not Faith. Bleak enough even with Faith, had she not learned how to meditate. But pondering prayerfully, pondering with mind, heart, will, and all her womanly feelings on the lives of Jesus and Mary, she saw that They had all she had, and had it all intensified to almost an infinite degree. They had been lonely. They had been dependent. They had lacked real privacy — even in what is called the hidden life. As for depression — Jesus sounded very depressed as He wept over Jerusalem. A careful reading of St. John's Gospel shows it to be a long narrative of disappointment, sadness, sorrow. "He came unto His own, and His own . . ." why, His own sent Him to death on a cross! Thus it was that meditation let the full light of God's own glory shine upon all that "lay behind that door" which first opened when she learned to pray with her whole being; and she saw that what she took, at first, to be "mystery," was actually the reality of her relation to God: she was His creature, who was to become His helper. She was to take all that He sent her and use it as had His Christ. Her pain would serve Him as reparation and be a petition for mercy on mankind. Her loneliness would be filled with Him as the object of her adoring love and her loving adoration. Her dependence on others would remind her always of her utter dependence on Him, and make her ever more an obedient child of His. There was nothing that she could not use for her Father's glory. Her world, painful as it was, was filled with light — and that light was really The Light of the World — Jesus Christ.

While still in St. Joseph Mercy Hospital, and while still groping her way toward greater and greater intimacy with Christ and His Mother, Mary Ellen grew more and more conscious of a craving to be able to write. One day she asked her doctor if there was any possibility whatsoever of getting enough freedom at elbow and shoulder to enable her to "put characters down on paper, spell out my own name," to be able to write and, as she rather coyly put it: "to be able to tell the world what a wonder you are." The doctor smiled then, but a few days later came back with the answer that if Miss Kelly would submit to another operation there was an outside possibility that she might gain enough motion in hand, arm, and shoulder to be enabled to write. Mary Ellen said she would gladly undergo that bit of surgery he talked about. And it was successful! To the joy of all about her, that operation gave her such freedom that for months after it Mary Ellen — the "Lucky Stiff" as she would later call herself — was in her glory as she answered all her mail, wrote notes to other patients, and just could not find time enough to do all the writing she desired.

But if Mary Ellen forgot, in the thrill of the new freedom, that she was on a seesaw, and that God was doing the tilting, she soon learned that He had had her high up. For one day she awoke to find her elbow almost as stiff as ever. A few days later she noted that her shoulder was as immobile as before the operation. Then at the end of the week, with her heart in her throat, she asked the nurse to place the pencil into her hand. Slowly she moved it across the paper. She labored to force it further, but there was no "give" to her shoulder or elbow. She had formed exactly seven letters. She could spell out her last name. But that was all. God had left her with the ability to move her hand only a few inches. "It wasn't much," wrote Mary Ellen, "but with my left hand and the point of my pen I moved the paper over — and formed seven more letters."

That was the way this girl wrote in 1943. That was the way she kept on writing until 1961. Yet she managed to write at least six hours every day, and eight hours many a day. Thanks to that tiny movement of her right hand this nation, and the world, gained the League of Shut-in Sodalists, that bimonthly *Seconds Sanctified,* and that challenging, comforting, heart-warming autobiography: *But With the Dawn, Rejoicing.* Thanks to the same tiny movement, what should have been an orderly, quiet, hospital-clean room in her mother's home at Marcus, Iowa, became very like the messy workshop of a very busy, and somewhat harried job printer; for it was there that Mary Ellen did her writing, and from there sent out her letters, magazines, and newspaper articles, even as in there she kept her papers, books, files, carbons, and mimeograph. Thanks to that tiny movement, Mary Ellen became one shut-in who would never be idle.

The same year of this operation another question from another priest brought something new into Mary Kelly's life. Father McShane, S.J., on a visit to Kelly happened to ask: "Do you belong to the Sodality of Our Lady, Mary Ellen?" What a question, thought Kelly. How could she, fast to this hospital bed, belong to Our Lady's Sodality? She could not join the Nurses' Sodality; for she was a patient. She could not join any college Sodality; for she did not go to college. She could not join the Married Ladies Sodality; for she was not married. And there was no other Sodality that she could join.

She wanted to belong, she told the Jesuit. In fact, there was little else in life that she wanted as much as to be a Sodalist. But what could she do? Father McShane quietly asked: "Why don't you start a Sodality of your own?"

That did it. That question set Kelly in action. Sixteen months later she had done just what the priest had suggested that she do. With the permission of the National Sodality Headquarters and the permission of the Most Reverend Edmund Heelan, Bishop of Sioux City, Mary Ellen Kelly founded the League of Shut-in Sodalists. It was so novel an idea, and so daring an undertaking, that neither permission was very readily granted. But Mary Ellen was on the move, and when she got in motion, even bishops bowed. Fifteen years after those permissions had been granted, that League, started by this physically helpless girl, had enrolled over two thousand, five hundred sick and disabled men and women. What Mary Ellen had started, she kept going!

Her aims for this League were set out with precision:

> To unite the sick, aged, and disabled in prayer and suffering for the glory of God, and the sanctification of their own souls.
> To foster in the members an ardent devotion to the Blessed Mother, and to attain, through the help of her Sodality, a more intimate union with Christ crucified.
> To show our members the value, need, and power of illness and deformity; to bring the sick encouragement and comfort; and to acquaint the afflicted with each other.

What a program for helpless people! The first and second objectives hold appeal enough; for every Catholic who has received even ordinary instruction in the Faith knows he is on earth for God's glory and his own sanctification, and that the surest way to these two goals, which are really one, is through Mary and Christ crucified. But that third objective . . . One has to look long at illness and deformity before one can see their "value, need, and power."

Reading her autobiography, one is led to liken Mary Ellen herself to that blind man Christ cured by spitting upon the ground, making a lump of clay, spreading it over his eyes, then telling him to "Go, wash in the pool of Siloe" (Jn. 9:6, 7). That Christ had treated Mary Ellen's spiritual eyes no one can doubt. But one can question if she were not like this one or that other blind man whom Christ cured gradually. At first this man saw "men like trees" (Mk. 8:24). But then Jesus placed His hands on the man's eyes a second time, and he saw clearly. Both stories tell the analogous truth. If you select the first, then the Shrine of St. Anne de Beaupré, in Canada, will be your "Pool of Siloe." If you prefer the second, then it will be there that Christ placed His hands over the eyes of Mary Ellen's soul for the second time. For it was there that she came to see, with the clarity of real vision, that her illness was meant by God to hold value, serve a need, and generate power.

A graduate from Notre Dame University dreamed a dream one night that officials in commercial travel circles thought was a nightmare. This man would organize a "Pilgrimage of Invalids." Such a thing had never been dreamed of before. But Patrick O'Grady made his dream come true. Under the leadership of Francis J. Beckman, Archbishop of Dubuque, Canada's three major shrines: Brother André's at St. Joseph, in Montreal — Our Lady of the Rosary at Cap-de-la-Madeleine, near Three Rivers — and the famous St. Anne de Beaupré's — were to be visited by a group made up entirely of invalids.

Mary Ellen had reason to call herself the "Lucky Stiff" as far as this pilgrimage was concerned, for an unnamed benefactor wanted to send some invalid on this pilgrimage and left the selection of the one to go to Father McShane, S.J. — the very man who had set Miss Kelly at that work of founding the League of Shut-in Sodalists. He named Mary Ellen. She could hardly believe her ears when it was told her. But a few days later she could not trust her heart — for she learned that her benefactor, a Chicago newspaper publisher, hearing that Miss Kelly was to make the pilgrimage, ordered his secretary to make out a check to cover not only Mary Ellen's expenses but her mother's as well.

She knew she was lucky. She could not forget that she was stiff. Though she was going to the shrines of Christ's foster father and His Virgin Mother before she went to that of His grandmother, it was only of this last she thought whenever she dwelt on the possibility of a cure. She dwelt on it! She even, in some dim way, expected it. "How will I look in a dress?" she found herself thinking long before she left Marcus. Then she was feminine enough to wonder: "Will the scars on my shoulders, elbow, and leg show?" She went even further and began to think about "What kind of a job will I get?"

Obviously, then, Mary Ellen had looked at that third objective of the League of Shut-in Sodalists, but had yet to see it. But the Lady in whose arms she had placed herself would take her to the "Pool of Siloe" — or, if you prefer, have her Son pass His hands a second time over Mary Ellen's spiritual eyes.

On the feast day of St. Anne, Mary Ellen lay at the foot of her statue in the mighty basilica hoping, hoping that she would not have to return to Marcus, Iowa, on this cot of hers; hoping that there would be no more pain, no more surgery, no more utter helplessness and this complete dependence on others; hoping that she would rise an agile, able, graceful woman; hoping — all the day long. The day died. The night was lit by thousands of candles as devotees formed in procession and marched to the basilica singing their hymns. Mary Ellen still lay there — hoping. As the song swelled and the lights grew nearer and brighter, Mary Ellen's hopes rose. The feast was not yet over. The age of miracles had not passed. St. Anne, Christ's grandmother, and Mary Ellen's very own, would not be unmindful. . . . But soon the crowd began to move away. The singing grew more distant. Finally, all the lights in the basilica were switched off. Then — there in the darkness — Mary Ellen Kelly *saw*. She saw clearly! This was her "Pool of Siloe." Christ had just passed His hand over the eyes of her soul for the second time! She now saw that God wanted her to help His Son by being an invalid. She heard as clearly as she saw. She heard distinctly this night what she had heard only dimly that other night five years earlier in the hospital room at Sioux City; she heard the striking of "her hour."

But in what a mood! Nothing like the exalted mood so evident in Christ's words Holy Thursday night in the Cenacle when He addressed His Father and said: "The hour is come!" Mary Ellen's mood was much more like Christ's as He walked toward the Garden of Gethsemani. She was not only weary, heartsick, and sorely disappointed. She was actually depressed. "It is clear now that God wants me to remain an invalid" was all she was able to say to herself. But she repeated the sentence. Then she listened to it as she said it aloud. Hearing it, she knew a strange feeling of surprise; for she found that this sentence, which was really a life's sentence, and represented so stark and staggering a reality, held no bitterness whatsoever. This discovery more than surprised her. Actually, it gave her a feeling of strange happiness, and with that feeling all fears of the future seemed to disappear. It would seem that what happened to Christ in Gethsemani after He had prayed so earnestly thrice that "the chalice might pass," happened to Mary Ellen Kelly in the dark of the Basilica of St. Anne de Beaupré: some "Angel of Consolation" had come to strengthen this girl for the years and years of stonelike immobility that stretched ahead. This "Angel" enabled her to say more than she had said at St. Joseph Mercy Hospital. If her mood and mind there can be called "Resignation" and summed up in the meaningful word "Amen," her mind and mood here, in Canada, can be called "Acceptance," and signified with the more meaningful word "Fiat."

But, though Mary Ellen had come far spiritually, she had not yet arrived at maturity or full growth. She had not yet found her truest self. There was still a further depth she was to fathom. Origen's well-worn phrase: *anima humana naturaliter Christiana*, meaning that every man's soul, by its very nature, is Christian, yields treasure to those who will mine its depths. It destroys that erroneous concept, entertained by too many, that a Christian is someone imposed upon man. Just the opposite is true. The Christian lies deep, as deep as nature itself, in every man. Faith and baptism bring him to the surface, and let every thinking man see that his creaturehood spells Christhood; that he will be himself only when he yields himself to this Other in him, so that it can be said with truth that he lives *"per Ipsum, cum Ipso, et in Ipso"* — In other words, man is living as man should live only when he can say with St. Paul: "Christ is my life" (Phil. 1:21). Mary Ellen had come close to this but, as yet, was not quite there.

That Mary Ellen had come far is evident from the "Ten Don't's for Invalids" which she drew up and included in her autobiography. Perhaps she was thinking of the Ten Commandments when she limited herself to that exact number, but that she was far from "playing God" is clear from the tenth of her "Don't's." She had written: "Don't delude yourself into thinking that God has abandoned you, or that your illness is necessarily a punishment. He permits these things to happen for a good reason which, in His own time, will be revealed." That tells how well Kelly had listened at St. Anne de Beaupré, and how much she had learned. But that she actually had to fight her way to this truth about God's will, God's plan, and God's providence is patent when one reads what she has to say about "a misunderstood and much maligned word: *Resignation.*"

Sincerity shines through every sentence. Some might say: "So, also, does asperity." For, quite obviously, Mary Ellen had been aroused by the topic, and toward the end of her observations, she pulled out the diapason. She got into her subject quickly enough by saying that to be resigned does not mean that one has gone into a stupor, or is enjoying some sort of a rest. Far from it. For resignation does not call for any cessation of activity. In point of fact, she insisted, that before one can reach the height of real resignation, one must climb like some "determined Alpine climber," realizing all the while that the height he would reach is "a pinpoint peak." And, once there, he must be continually on his guard lest he lose his balance and fall from the peak he has conquered at such a cost.

Then the honest Kelly comes to the fore as she confesses: "Even after years of practice," she had to put herself through a "third degree" every now and then so as to maintain her balance. That "third degree" is most revealing. She would ask herself: "To what must I resign myself? What does it involve? What will be gained by it?" Then she would answer her own questions by saying: "I must resign myself (with our Lady's help) to God's will. It involves the admission that He knows more than I do; the suppression of my own desires in deference to God's; and the constant effort to channel everything to my soul's sanctification and the spread of God's honor and glory. Finally, I will gain God's blessing, give Him pleasure; I will know peace of mind and soul, and possibly give inspiration to some other soul in dire need of it; I will know the joy that my life is useful to God, that I am performing an important job — that of reparation; and that, if I keep at it, I'll win heaven." She concludes with the tremendous understatement: "No bad exchange, eh?"

Mary Ellen was most right to let herself go on this "much maligned word," but she had one further lesson to learn about herself and true Christian living. It does not lie in "resignation" so much as in "acceptance," or, better still, in real, trust-filled, joyous "abandon." Neither Christ nor His Mother showed mere "resignation" in their lives for God and man. Mary was not "resigned" when she whispered "Fiat" to Gabriel. Christ was not "resigned" when He took up His cross and laid down His life. In what we call His Passion there was much more activity of soul than there was passivity even of the body. He had come, as St. Paul has Him telling the Father: ". . . to *do* your will, O God, as is written in the roll of the book" (Hebr. 10:7).

When an individual comes to regard every visitation, be it of sickness, misfortune, or even deformity, the way a woman looks upon the coming of her own child to birth, and recognizes this "child" as Christ — then that individual has arrived at Christian maturity. No real mother merely "resigns" herself to having her child; she is eager for it to come. When it does come, she is not simply "resigned" to having it; she is exultantly happy to have it. Yet, look at the changes that child will bring to that mother's life: it will change her entire day and entire night — every day and every night for years on years. The mother will have to change even her tone of voice — modulating it always for the sake of her child. Her very words will have to be carefully chosen, and practically her every movement altered, all regulated just to suit the needs of this tiny bundle of humanity that has just arrived on the scene. Rooms will have to be rearranged for the sake of the child — even the very temperature of the house will be regulated to suit the child, not the parents. Restraint will be the order of the day and the night. That child will change the entire world of that mother. But the mother will look upon such changes as avenues, new avenues opened for her day after day, down which she can run to that child with newer love. So with the real Christian and every visitation from God. They open avenues down which he can speed to His Father with newer abandon — the "wild abandon" of genuine love.

Mary Ellen Kelly came to this kind of life and this kind of love at Fatima, Portugal. She went there on another Pilgrimage of Invalids. And if her description of that first such pilgrimage will do things to any man's heart, her description of this one to the Shrines of Our Lady at Lourdes and Fatima will do things to any man's soul.

At Lourdes the drama of St. Anne de Beaupré was re-enacted. Mary Ellen hoped. Mary Ellen did not see her hopes fulfilled. Yet, despite the disappointment, there was no bitterness. She accepted it gracefully. But it remained for Fatima to bring "acceptance" to real, whole-souled "abandon." For there, after long indecision, she finally determined to ask Mother Mary for, at least, a partial cure. With growing excitement she watched the Bishop of Kansas City, U. S. A., near her as she lay on her cot among the invalids. He was lifting the monstranced Christ over each of the sick. What would she say when Christ was lifted over her? The Bishop was only a step away. Mary Ellen writes: "suddenly I felt a pulling sensation that withdrew me from the present and dissolved the crowd at either side. I was back in Galilee, and coming toward me was the Son of God. . . ." A desperate longing, that started from deep within her, pushed its way up into her aching throat, and through her lips, into the pleading cry: "O, dear God, if it is Your holy will, make me well again! Let me walk again! Dear God, please!"

She admits that for one time-suspended moment she waited — waited for God to answer that soul-deep plea. She knew He could grant it. Down in her deepest depths she knew that He *would* — if it were for His greater honor and glory and Mary Ellen Kelly's everlasting good. The moment passed. The answer came. "Regret ripped through me like a fiery sword, leaving a path of scalding tears." The answer was: "No!"

In that afflicted girl's soul-deep cry: "Let me walk again!" one can hear the echo of Christ's own plea as He knelt in Gethsemani: "Let this chalice pass!" The answer Christ heard then was identical with the one Mary Ellen heard in Portugal. So, too, was the immediate sequence. For, to Mary Ellen Kelly there came a "sweet, indescribable peace, and clarity that left no room for confusion." She now knew, beyond all doubt, that God wanted her to remain a *complete invalid*. "This was God's will," she wrote, "and all of me accepted the decision." That "all of me" tells the story. Mary Ellen Kelly had arrived. Now she would live with complete "abandon" as she let Christ live in her, and she went on living in and as Christ.

That God was pleased with her Act of Abandon was made clear to Mary Ellen a few days later when she, with the pilgrims, was outside Castel Gondolfo, and Pius XII suddenly appeared on the balcony. He spoke in English and told how happy he was to welcome the invalids. "In particular," he said, "it is a great joy to Us to greet those of you who have endured great sacrifice, and even pain, to come from your homes thousands of miles away. . . . We know that you are members of the League of Shut-in Sodalists, which was formed largely through the persevering efforts of one of you, our beloved daughter, Mary Ellen Kelly. . . ."

Mary Ellen could not believe her ears. But then came the question from His Holiness: "Which is she?" A man behind Mary Ellen's cot pointed her out. The Pontiff leaned over, looked directly at her, and the Vicar of Christ broke into one of his most radiant smiles. Mary Ellen's spirits soared higher than they ever had in all her life and, she writes, "I could feel my soul smiling back."

But neither God nor Christ's Vicar were through with Kelly as yet. The Pope went on to say: "You are specially dear to the heart of our Divine Master, to His Blessed Mother, and also to Us, for with St. Paul, we may say to you: 'The grace that has been granted to you is that of suffering for Christ's sake, not merely believing in Him.' Treasure this suffering that is yours through God's Will; bear it always in union with our Suffering Lord, offering it to Him for the increase and sanctification of the members of His Body. Thus you will help to 'fill up the sufferings of Christ . . . for His Body, which is the Church.' In the words of St. Peter, the first Vicar of Christ, We exhort you: 'Do not be surprised, beloved, that this fiery ordeal should have befallen you, to test your quality; there is nothing strange in what is happening to you. Rather rejoice when you share in some measure in the sufferings of Christ; so joy will be yours, and triumph, when His glory is revealed.' Carry this message of Ours back to all the other members of your Sodality and League of Shut-in Sodalists. . . ."

With good reason she could call herself the "Lucky Stiff." Small wonder that she, then and there, echoed old Simeon when he first beheld Christ: "Nunc dimittis — Now You can dismiss Your servant, O Lord . . . in peace!"

But the good Lord did not dismiss Mary Ellen then and there.

"Her hour" went on. But now she saw it as a "career for Christ." In it she knew that "just as in any other career, I can be successful, mediocre, or a flop. I want the first — not for the usual reasons — but because, in this case, success means my will being one with God's, and the more it is, the more He can work through me." How far she had come since that first night in Sioux City! Now she saw. Now she knew. "God had indeed chosen me for Himself," she wrote, "wanting me to reach Him through the vocation of suffering. With my bed as my cloister, my improvised blouses and assorted sheets as my habit, and my stiff joints as my binding vows, I have been called to serve Him. . . . Our willingness to suffer should be motivated not by the thought of eternal reward and temporal compensation, but by the clear truth that suffering is a golden opportunity and, for us, a basic duty."

What, at first, she saw as something to be resigned to, then went on to view as something to be gratefully accepted, she now recognized as a veritable gift from God, a "golden opportunity" and even as a "basic duty." Indeed Kelly had arrived. *"Amen"* of resignation, and *"Fiat"* of acceptance, was now the *"Alleluia"* of abandon. She was now a mature Christian who saw life — and very especially a life of suffering — as a glorious duty to be given to God as a Sacrifice worthy of Him. That could only mean making her life a "Mass" and offering it "in Christ Jesus" and as Jesus Christ. That is why she could answer the nurse at Sioux City who had asked her if she were ready for extreme unction — which really meant: "Are you ready to meet God face to face? Are you ready to die?" with the joy-filled words: "I shall be happy and honored to do so."

The ninth day in Mary's month marked the ending of Mary Ellen's "hour." Twenty-two years makes a long, long "hour." But Mary Ellen Kelly would laugh at anyone who told her so now; for she knows with utter clarity how wise Paul was when he wrote to his Romans: "Why, I count the sufferings of the present time as not worthy to be compared with the glory to come that will be revealed shining upon us" (Rom. 8:18). The longest "hour" is very brief when we see it in the Light. Kelly is in that Light now and she knows that she was indeed a "lucky stiff." Dawn broke for her May 9, 1961, and she will go on rejoicing in it *forever.*